FEDERALIST DELAWARE
1775–1815

Federalist
DELAWARE
1775-1815

John A. Munroe

Rutgers University Press

NEW BRUNSWICK · NEW JERSEY

1954

Copyright 1954 by the University of Delaware

Library of Congress Catalog Card Number: 54-11929

MANUFACTURED IN THE UNITED STATES OF AMERICA
BY VAIL-BALLOU PRESS, INC., BINGHAMTON, NEW YORK

This study, Number 6 in the University of Delaware Monograph Series, is published by the Rutgers University Press in cooperation with the University of Delaware.

Other monographs in the series, published by the University of Delaware, are:

1. A. J. DeArmond, *Andrew Bradford, Colonial Journalist*
2. W. O. Penrose, *Freedom Is Ourselves*
3. W. Kirchner, *The Rise of the Baltic Question*
4. E. J. Moyne (translator and editor), Alexandra Gripenberg's *A Half Year in the New World*
5. D. Bushnell, *The Santander Regime in Gran Colombia*

Preface

THIS is a study of the infancy, or rather of the youth of an American state. In the four decades between 1775 and 1815 an obscure English colony lacking a simple name, a colony of three counties lying down the river from Pennsylvania, cut its ties with the motherland, experimented with independence, and finally emerged from these trials as the State of Delaware. The narrative that follows examines first the various topical strands which composed the fabric of Delaware life in the two earlier decades; then, after 1795, the chronological mid-point of this study, it attempts to interweave these strands so as to synthesize the story around political developments.

For it is politics, of course, that gives to this period its peculiar importance. In the concepts of the average Delawarean about the history of his state, he recognizes this fact, for the two incidents of this period which he recalls pre-eminently, however vague he may be about their details, are both political: the one, Caesar Rodney's Ride, and the other, the ratification of the Federal Constitution that gave Delaware her title as First State. Rodney rode to Philadelphia to cast Delaware's vote for independence, to place Delaware with her sister states in the decisive roll call of July 2, 1776. Eleven years later a Delaware convention unanimously ratified a Federal Constitution that completed the union which independence had nurtured. In both of these events, in 1776 and in 1787, Delawareans were clinging to the promise and the protection of a unified action, a federal association.

The federal spirit that led Delaware into the adventure of independence and of national government helps also to explain her political alignment within the new government. For in the early period of party strife, Delaware was the Federalist state paramount—a fact as little known in Delaware or elsewhere as the concepts of "Rodney's Ride" and "the First State" are famous. Under the Constitution, the Atlantic highway and the community and interdependence of the Delaware River basin were powerful factors in attaching a state that was a coastal niche to the Federalist party. To it Delaware was pledged for decades to come, longer than Connecticut, Massachusetts, or any other state, beyond the time when Federalists elsewhere despaired of their party or their nation. In 1822 Judge John Fisher declared to Caesar A. Rodney (nephew of the rider): "You are the first democratic Senator, ever elected into the Senate of the U. States from Delaware. The circumstance is notable, as the government has now been organized nearly about one third of a century."

Obviously the year 1815, the limit of this study, is no end-date for Delaware Federalism. Nor is 1822, the year of Rodney's election, significant in this regard, for the Federalists were soon able to choose Rodney's successor. Indeed, even when the party name died with the appearance of new national parties, the Delaware Federalists were by no means vanquished. The bulk of them became Whigs, and for two decades these Whigs ruled Delaware, deriving their strength essentially from the habits and desires and prejudices that had supported the old Federalist party. By 1815, however, the patterns of life in Delaware had become reasonably clear, and among them the political pattern of a Federalist control which had outlasted the early Jeffersonian challenge, survived a war without taint of treason, and bolstered its strength for the years ahead.

Acknowledgment of aid is due and gladly extended to many persons: to Dr. Roy F. Nichols, in particular, and to Dr. Richard H. Shryock, Dr. Arthur C. Bining, and Dr. H. Clay Reed, for encouraging my interest in the history of my native state; to Mr. Henry B. du Pont, the late Mrs. Florence Bayard Hilles, Miss Gertrude Brincklé, Mr. Leon de Valinger, Jr., the late Dr. George H. Ryden, Dr. Arthur R. Dunlap, Judge Richard S. Rodney, Mr. Charles Gilpin Dorman, who have helped me in various ways; and to the staffs of the Historical Society of Delaware, the Public Archives Commission of Delaware, the Wilmington Institute Free Library, the Memorial Library of the University of Delaware, the Historical Society of Pennsylvania, the University of Pennsylvania Library, the Philadelphia Society of Promoting Agriculture, the Presbyterian Historical Society, the Manuscripts Division of the

Library of Congress, the New York Public Library, and the Maryland Historical Society, whose patience has seemed unending. I am grateful to the committees on research and on faculty publications of the University of Delaware for their aid in the completion and publication of this study. My greatest debt is due to my wife for her encouragement and for her assumption of the most tiresome of the historian's chores (a euphemism for typing). Had it not been for the sympathetic understanding of my parents, to whom this book is dedicated, I could never have begun it.

JOHN A. MUNROE

University of Delaware
Newark, Delaware

Contents

FEDERALIST DELAWARE
1775–1815

Prologue

OLD though it is, in the Anglo-American measurement of age, the State of Delaware is little known. Nor is its history, complicated by Swedish and Dutch interludes, and by annexation to New York, quarrels with Maryland, and partial union with Pennsylvania, long remembered. Yet anyone who traverses the middle eastern seaboard of the United States passes through Delaware, little as he may learn of the land through which he goes or of the people among whom he does not tarry.

Proud as the Delawarean may be of his small area and its long tradition, he cannot avoid an unusual consciousness of the larger and more populous states about him. He can hardly stir abroad for a Sunday drive without crossing a state line. He can travel from one end of his state to another for dinner and then come home to sleep. No matter where he lives, his capital town of Dover cannot be much more than an hour distant; his governor and legislators can and do commute from their homes to their offices. If he goes to the North, he finds himself called a Southerner; to the South, he is a Yankee. What he is, of course, is an Easterner, a denizen of the coastal plain and of the first and lowest of the Piedmont hills. His is a border state, the last home of slavery and yet the one slave state where statistics evidence that slavery was, without war or other cataclysm, coming certainly and shortly to an end.

In a double sense, geographic and cultural, Delaware is the Middle Atlantic state. In its position lies its fortune. Set in the center of the most densely populated part of America, midway between Baltimore and Philadelphia, between Washington and New York, Delaware profited as these cities grew. Its farms became their country gardens; its mills produced merchandise for their markets. The ships and rails and roads that linked them brought Delaware ever closer to their destinies and their dollars.

Eventually the corn and wheat that Delaware grew and milled for the Philadelphia merchants were rivalled by the fruits it shipped to the cities and the truck crops it loaded on the cars of the Dela-

3

ware Road. Today great refrigerated tank trucks from Philadelphia dairies call at Kent farms for their milk; still other trucks rumble up the state highway with their poultry burden that enriches Sussex. The Wilmington factories which succeeded the water-powered mills of the Brandywine produce a great variety of goods—ships and leather and vulcanized fiber, for example. On upper Market Street appeared the white collar of Delaware, the administrative offices of great industrial enterprises. In the green fields beyond arose the test tube of the state and nation, busily experimental research stations.

This growth meant opportunities for livelihood that lured migrants from other states, from other nations. To join the colonial stocks—the Swedes, Finns, and Dutch, Africans, Englishmen, Welsh, and Scotch—came Frenchmen, Irishmen and Germans, Italians, Poles, and Ukrainians. The small population grew steadily, if not remarkably; in the decade prior to the 1950 census Delaware grew more rapidly than any coastal state to the north.

Compared with the nation, the numbers remained small, and as the country expanded, the area of Delaware came to seem still smaller. But there was still room here for a division, a bifurcation into an upstate and a downstate. Upstate is hilly; downstate is flat. Upstate is urban; downstate is rural. Upstate is industrial; downstate agricultural. The people upstate come from more diverse national backgrounds and represent a greater variety of religious groups. Downstaters are more frequently natives who are the sons and grandsons of Delaware natives. Downstate has greater political prestige and power through a constitutional arrangement by which legislative seats are distributed according to a fixed geographic pattern. Upstate Delaware bears a close similarity to southeastern Pennsylvania; the life of downstate Delaware more closely approximates that of the Maryland Eastern Shore.

Still, the geographic schism in Delaware is not as divisive as it might at first glance seem. There is a continual migration toward Wilmington from downstate, and many of the migrants bring with them old Delaware names and connections that assure them a leading place in upstate life. There exists also a slighter countermigration from Wilmington southward. Further, the small size of

Delaware encourages close personal relationships that serve to diminish urban-agrarian friction. And the small size of the state encourages the development of common aims and attitudes and endeavors.

Delaware, as it is, is the product of over three centuries of growth and change. European knowledge of the Delaware began with the exploratory voyage of Henry Hudson in 1609. Dutch mariners followed Hudson to the New World and traded with the Indians along the banks of what they called the North (Hudson) and South (Delaware) rivers. The first Dutch settlements were planted on the Hudson, but they settled on the Delaware too. The first settlement in the area now the State of Delaware was near Lewes, not far from the mouth of Delaware Bay, in 1631. This first settlement was destroyed by Indians, but it served later to prevent the absorption of Delaware into the Maryland grant of Lord Baltimore.

Dutchmen dissatisfied with the monopolistic Dutch West India Company, which planted the Dutch settlements in America, sought foreign sponsorship and found it in the Swedish crown. A New Sweden Company, partly Dutch in the beginning but later purged of Dutch influence and made practically an adjunct of the Swedish government, sent an expedition to America in 1638. A Swedish fort was built at Wilmington and for seventeen years the tiny colony of New Sweden clung to both shores of the river in northern Delaware, southeastern Pennsylvania, and West Jersey opposite.

But the Dutch retained one West Jersey settlement which they moved in 1651 to New Castle; four years later, Dutch Governor Stuyvesant, provoked by Swedish attack, conquered all New Sweden. Swedish customs and individual property rights continued to be respected, and the Swedish settlers remained, and with them many Finns who had accompanied them to the New World. New Sweden became a part of the New Netherland, and New Castle (then New Amstel) became a subsidiary capital to New Amsterdam. As settlement of the land proceeded, more Dutchmen came to live beside the Swedes and Finns.

But just as the Dutch had resented Swedish colonization, so now the English resented the Dutch. When in 1664 an English fleet, without declaration of war, came to North America and seized all the New Netherland, the Delaware settlements, like those on the Hudson, became the property of James, Duke of York, heir to the English throne. The duke speedily gave away New Jersey, but retained control of the west bank of the Delaware in spite of the fact that his grant from the king did not cover this land.

The river settlements in Pennsylvania and Delaware thus became part of the New York colony, though, because of the distance from Manhattan, New Castle remained a subsidiary capital. English colonists joined the earlier European settlers and the African slaves whom the Dutch had brought. As the land filled, courts were established and, around the courts, counties. In 1681 the bounds of Delaware at last appeared, for when in that year King Charles made his grant to William Penn, it was ordered that the new province, Pennsylvania, should not come closer than twelve miles to New Castle and thus New Castle and the two southern counties were retained by the Duke of York.

But only for a short time did he retain them. In 1682 Penn, fearing his new province might be cut off from the ocean, obtained from the duke a grant of these three counties lower down the river than Pennsylvania. Arriving in America in that year, Penn established representative government through an assembly comprising an equal number of elected delegates from each of his six counties, three upper counties in Pennsylvania and three lower counties in Delaware. By his successive frames of government, he established a tradition of written constitutions in his colonies.

Delaware was now united to Pennsylvania both in the person of the proprietor and governor and in a common legislative body. Delaware was not part of Pennsylvania; the latter was Penn's province, and the Delaware counties were territories appendant thereto. The union, however, proved to be but a temporary one. By 1701 quarrels in the assembly caused the Delaware delegates to refuse thereafter to meet in a joint body. Delawareans, it seems, desiring to remain masters of their own bailiwick, feared domination by a colossus arising to the north which soon might upset the balance in the assembly by securing a majority of delegates. Penn agreed to Delaware's request for a separate legislature and in 1704 a general assembly of the counties of New Castle, Kent, and Sussex upon Delaware met in New Castle. Delaware and Pennsylvania continued to share a governor, but the brief legislative union was ended; a new colony, Delaware, had been born and its political status established in the form which it bore at the beginning of the year 1776.

Part I

The Three Lower Counties
Become the Delaware State

I. The Evolution

THE history of Delaware from 1775 to 1815 is not a story of violent change. While the United States fought two wars, while France was in revolution, while agricultural, commercial and industrial changes spread throughout the world, changing events in Delaware followed a comparatively placid course. Here the Anglican gentry continued to dominate society; Reads, Ridgelys, and Rodneys were elected and reelected to high political posts; Quaker millers ground their grain along the Brandywine; free and indentured whites and free and enslaved blacks tilled their farms; and shallopmen carried their produce to the markets of Philadelphia.

Yet in this period of the founding of a nation changes occurred in Delaware that were consequential if not convulsive. The three counties established their independence from the Penns and the British Crown, and then, as the Delaware State, joined first a weak confederacy and later a strong national union. Two state constitutions were written, and the franchise was democratized on the basis of taxpayer voting. Organized political parties appeared, developed their local machines, and established ties with national parties.

Cotton, paper, and powder mills grew on the Brandywine above the grist mills, thus laying the foundation for the industrialization of New Castle County and the growth of Wilmington. Agriculture and husbandry were improved by the draining of swamps and the introduction of new techniques and new species. Streams were dredged and canalized, wharves constructed, ferries regulated, bridges built, and turnpike companies incorporated to improve the roads. Stage coaches and packet ships ran on fixed schedules. At least two banks were opened in each county. Printing presses multiplied, and the first newspapers appeared. Libraries were opened, and in Wilmington a lyceum was organized. Throughout the state the physicians associated in one of the first state medical societies in America. Steps were taken to improve the jails, to construct poorhouses, to provide care for the insane.

The population grew as immigration continued, especially from

11

neighboring states, and from England, Ulster, and, for a time, Haiti. The traffic in slaves, except within the state, was banned, and the cause of abolition was pressed.

After the Revolution old academies reopened, and new academies and subscription schools were begun in most of the towns. A public school system was foreshadowed by the establishment of a school fund. The foundation of a college was proposed and a "College of Wilmington" was actually incorporated, though it never was worthy of the title it bore.

The transition from an Anglican to an American Episcopalian church was accomplished with the loss of little prestige but of many members. In the wake of Asbury, Coke, and Garrettson, a Methodist church was formed that soon grew to be the most popular sect in the counties of Kent and Sussex, which, with the Eastern Shore, formed the cradle of Methodism in America.

In other words, the years between 1775 and 1815 saw the evolution of the three lower counties into a state with the basic cultural pattern of modern Delaware. Through the interplay of static and dynamic forces the framework was constructed for the civilization of this small area through the next century, a framework which foreshadowed the future development of Delaware.

II. The Separation

ON July 1, 1776, the Continental Congress, meeting in Philadelphia, resumed consideration of the resolution of Richard Henry Lee, originally presented on June 7, "that the United Colonies are and of right ought to be free and independent states and that the political connection between them and Great Britain is and ought to be totally dissolved." Nine states favored the resolution, two opposed it, and two were undecided. Because there was some reason to hope that delay would bring unanimity, final decision of the question was postponed one day.

Delaware was one of the undecided states, for it had but two delegates present and they disagreed. Favoring the resolution was Thomas McKean, an austere, vain, ambitious, able lawyer, born in Chester County, Pennsylvania, of Scotch-Irish descent, who had come to Delaware to read law with his cousin David Finney in New Castle and remained to win political preferment. Although in 1774 he returned to his native Pennsylvania, where greater opportunities offered, he retained and even augmented his political position in Delaware.[1] In every year of the Revolution with one exception he represented Delaware in Congress. At the same time he began a service of more than two decades as chief justice of Pennsylvania, the state which he later served as governor.[2]

Opposing the resolution was George Read, a Philadelphia-trained New Castle lawyer, who had been born in Cecil County, Maryland, but had moved to Delaware at an early age. Of high ability and integrity, Read rose to the forefront of the Delaware bar and eventually became chief justice. He also possessed great political acumen and might have filled any office he chose in the state. He was especially influential in the state legislature and regardless of whether or not he happened to be a member of it, he came nearer to dominating it than any other man.[3]

McKean related, years later, that when the decision on independence was postponed for one day, he dispatched an express at his own expense to the third Delaware delegate, Caesar Rodney, bidding him come to Philadelphia at once and break the tie. Rodney, speaker of the Assembly, was probably on his estates east of Dover, in Jones's Neck, when the message reached him. Though suffering from asthma and from cancer, this tall, thin, country gentleman started immediately to ride to Philadelphia, about seventy-five miles away. "Tho detained by thunder and Rain," [4] he arrived on

---

[1] And his economic position, as well. As late as 1810 he owned three plantations, totalling 940 acres in southern New Castle and northern Kent counties. *American Watchman; and Delaware Republican* (Wilmington), Sept. 8, 1810.

[2] *Delaware Register and Farmers' Magazine* (Dover, 1838), I, 108–110; *DAB*, XII, 79–81; William T. Read, *Life and Correspondence of George Read* (Philadelphia, 1870), 332–344. For longer treatments, see Roberdeau Buchanan, *Life of the Hon. Thomas McKean* (Lancaster, 1890), and James H. Peeling, The Public Life of Thomas McKean, 1734–1817 (Ph.D. thesis, University of Chicago, 1929).

[3] *Delaware Register*, I, 95–108; *DAB*, XV, 422–424. William T. Read, *op. cit.*, is an interesting biography, including much source material.

[4] C. Rodney to T. Rodney, Philadelphia, July 4, 1776, George H. Ryden, ed., *Letters to and from Caesar Rodney, 1756–1784* (Philadelphia, 1933), 94; Edmund

July 2, coming up to "the State-house door in his boots and spurs as the members were assembling." McKean led him into the hall and, as he recalled the incident thirty-eight years later, when Delaware's vote on Lee's resolution was called, Rodney "arose and said: 'As I believe the voice of my constituents and of all sensible and honest men is in favor of Independence and my own judgment concurs with them, I vote for Independence' or in words to the same effect." [5] With two of the three Delaware delegates favoring independence, the state's vote made unanimous the acceptance of Lee's resolution by the twelve states voting. Two days later, on July 4, the formal Declaration prepared by Jefferson was accepted. Later still, when the Declaration was being signed, George Read threw his full support to the Revolutionary cause by adding his name to the document. [6]

The action of July 2 and of July 4 was not, however, so decisive for Delaware as it might at first seem. On May 10 of the same year Congress had recommended to the states "where no government sufficient to the exigencies of their affairs have hitherto been established, to adopt such government as shall . . . best conduce to happiness and safety of their constituents in particular; and America in general." [7] A preamble, adopted May 15, explained the necessity of suppressing "the exercise of every kind of authority under the . . . crown"; hereafter government should be "under the au-

---

C. Burnett, ed., *Letters of Members of the Continental Congress* (Washington, 1921–1936), I, 528.

[5] T. McKean to C. A. Rodney, Philadelphia, August [Sept.] 22, 1813, Burnett, *Letters,* I, 534. One may, of course, doubt whether McKean so many years later remembered details correctly. See the discussion of Rodney's ride in William B. Hamilton, *Anglo-American Law on the Frontier* (Durham, 1953), 21–22.

[6] Read, *Read,* 165–166, 229. For further material on the signing of the Declaration, see Burnett, *Letters,* I, 528–532, and Charles Warren, "Fourth of July Myths," *William and Mary Quarterly,* third series, II, No. 3 (July, 1945), pp. 242–248. George Read, editor of the two volumes of the *Laws of the State of Delaware* (New Castle, 1797), includes a note in Vol. I, addenda, p. 3, on the late signing of the Declaration which is not cited by recent studies on the subject. Only twelve states voted on independence because the New York delegates were forbidden by their instructions to support it but agreed to refrain from casting any vote at all. Edmund C. Burnett, *The Continental Congress* (New York, 1941), 182, 184. A recent discussion of the signing is in Julian Boyd, ed., *The Papers of Thomas Jefferson* (Princeton, 1950–   ), I, 299–308.

[7] *The Journals of the Continental Congress, 1774–1789* (Washington, 1904–1937), IV, 342; H. Clay Reed, "The Delaware Constitution of 1776," *Delaware Notes,* sixth series (Newark, 1930), 8.

thority of the people of the colonies." [8] After an acrimonious controversy within the state as to whether a change in its government was desirable, the colonial assembly met on June 11. On June 14 McKean, having hurried to New Castle, personally presented the resolution of Congress and urged compliance with it. That day the assembly approved the resolution, and on the next day it suspended government under the crown and directed all officers "to continue in their duties in the name of the three counties." [9] Consequently June 15, 1776, is the real birth date of an independent Delaware. The action taken that day to divorce the three counties from Great Britain was supplemented by the joint action taken in Congress on July 2, 1776, birth date of the nation.

These facts beg an inquiry into the conditions which lay behind them. Did the same causative factors operate in Delaware as in the other colonies, and, if so, to what degree? What peculiar local conditions could have influenced Delaware's action? To answer these questions, it is necessary to have a clear view of life in Delaware during the last year of dependence, and some understanding of the important social and economic trends of the 1770s before and after the Declaration.

III. The People

THE population of Delaware in 1774 on the eve of the Revolution numbered approximately thirty-seven thousand, and was fairly evenly divided among the three counties of New Castle, Kent, and Sussex, which lie beside the Delaware River, the Delaware Bay, and the Atlantic Ocean, respectively.[10] As a whole this area is

---

[8] *Journals of Congress,* IV, 357–358.

[9] Peter Force, comp., *American Archives . . .* (Washington, 1837–1853), 4th series, VI, 883–884; John H. Hazelton, *The Declaration of Independence; Its History* (New York, 1906), 125; Peeling, Life of McKean, 47; Read, *Read,* 245–246; Rodney, *Letters,* 91–92.

[10] Stella H. Sutherland, *Population Distribution in Colonial America* (New York, 1936), 124, 135. *Cf.* E. B. Greene and V. D. Harrington, *American Population before the Census of 1790* (New York, 1932), 121; Read, *Read,* 291; Henry C. Conrad, *History of the State of Delaware* (Wilmington, 1908), I, 149.

shaped like a shoe with the heel to the south, the toe to the north, and the tongue lying along Delaware Bay. Maryland bounds this area to the south and west, Pennsylvania to the north, with the three waterways on the east.

The northern third of New Castle County consists of hilly, rolling country, reaching the highest elevation, about 440 feet, at Centerville near the Pennsylvania line. The rest of the state below Newark and Wilmington is a flat expanse stretching down to Cape Charles at the tip of the Delmarva Peninsula on which Delaware lies. On the west, separating the waters which flow into the Delaware from those flowing to the Chesapeake, is a sandy tableland running from north to south along the Delaware–Maryland boundary until it approaches Sussex County where it veers southeastward away from the line.

The southern boundary goes through the Cypress Swamp (known locally as the Burnt Swamp), northernmost habitat of the cypress tree. Along the Atlantic the coast of Sussex County is a sand bar, separating shallow bays from the ocean. On the Delaware bay and river the shore line is low and marshy, higher and firmer land appearing in New Castle County.

The northern boundary is circular, being part of a twelve-mile circle based at New Castle. The southern boundary is a straight line running directly westward from Fenwick Island on the Atlantic to a point halfway across the peninsula.[11] From this southwestern corner, the boundary runs northward in a straight line to form a tangent with the twelve-mile circle.[12]

The exact location of the southern and western boundaries was long disputed. Maryland had claimed and actually governed a sec-

---

[11] Fenwick Island was originally named Cape Henlopen, since it appeared like a cape when seen from the sea. When the Penn-Calvert boundary controversy was finally settled, Cape Henlopen was named the southern boundary, but an old map was used on which Fenwick Island was marked as the Cape. Edward B. Mathews, "History of the Boundary Dispute between the Baltimores and Penns resulting in the Original Mason and Dixon Line," *Report on the Resurvey of the Maryland–Pennsylvania Boundary, Part of the Mason and Dixon Line* (1908), 165–166. On the boundaries in general, see Dudley Lunt, *The Bounds of Delaware* (Wilmington [1947]).

[12] Since the tangent point was some miles south of the Maryland–Pennsylvania boundary, a wedge-shaped piece of land between the circular line, the Maryland–Delaware line, and the latitudinal Maryland–Pennsylvania line remained in dispute for years.

tion of western Kent and a much larger section of western and southern Sussex, but this area finally became part of the Delaware counties in 1775 as a result of the settlement of the boundary on the basis of the then most recent survey.[13] The western boundary was drawn by Mason and Dixon as part of their task of delimiting the Penn and Calvert claims.[14]

The people who lived in the three counties in 1774 were predominantly of British blood. The great majority were descendants of Englishmen who had come to Delaware after 1664, when the Dutch colony on the Delaware had been conquered. Another large segment of the population was the Scotch-Irish. In the eighteenth century they invaded the valley of the Delaware River in great numbers, having been impelled to leave Ireland by the denial to them of the benefits of the Navigation Act, by the closing of English markets to Irish cattle, and by religious disabilities applied to all who were not members of the established Church of Ireland. They migrated in such numbers after 1700 that the Presbyterian population of Ireland was estimated to have declined by one-half in this century.

New Castle, usually the first port entered on the Delaware River, became their favorite port of entry; as early as 1729 forty-five hundred of them arrived in the Delaware counties.[15] Later they came directly to Wilmington, small boats towing the ships and brigs up the Christina. Ropes were thrown to the crowds waiting on shore who gladly pulled the vessels to the wharves. There on a midsummer's day the immigrants would land, good health shining from their cheerful faces, bonnetless, often wrapped in red or blue cloth cloaks. Averse to the restrictions of English government, many of them started off to the Pennsylvania frontier in a few days, drifting

[13] *Laws,* I, 567–571, for an act of Sept. 2, 1775, to ascertain and fix the boundaries of counties and to remedy inconveniences arising from the recent boundary settlement with Maryland.

[14] Thomas D. Cope, "The Stargazers' Stone," *Pennsylvania History,* VI, No. 4 (Oct., 1939), 206. The recent acquisition in the South became known as "New Sussex," Conrad, *History of Delaware,* 683–684. Professor Cope is engaged in a comprehensive study of the work of Mason and Dixon. On the boundaries with Maryland, see William H. Bayliff, *Boundary Monuments on the Maryland–Pennsylvania and the Maryland–Delaware Boundaries* (Annapolis, 1951).

[15] Sutherland, *Population Distribution,* 138, 141, 150; Ambrose Serle, *The American Journal of Ambrose Serle, Secretary to Lord Howe, 1776–1778,* E. H. Tatum, Jr., ed. (San Marino, Calif., 1940), 259.

later down the great valley to the backlands of the South. Others remained along the river, the poorest among them hiring out as redemptioners, or indentured servants, for three to seven years.[16] One "young gentleman passenger" arriving on the brig *Brothers*, which brought 170 passengers, celebrated his safe journey in verse:

> *In Wilmington we landed; for a tavern*
> *did enquire,*
> *To toast our noble captain, by all the*
> *crew's desire;*
> *The natives they came crowding in, our*
> *merry men to see,*
> *To welcome us as Irishmen, just landed*
> *from the sea.*[17]

The reaction of the old English stock of the lower counties to the new immigrants was not always as favorable as it seemed to this riming Ulsterman. The Irish were educated, ambitious, and industrious. They seldom sought charity and showed a remarkable "spirit of Independence." [18] Their dislike for the English government and its laws, their Presbyterianism, their restless striving for position made them a challenge to the established order of affairs.[19] They were the bulwark of the patriotic cause in the Revolution and the main strength of the Democratic–Republican party at the end of the century. From them came the first printer of Delaware, the first chancellor, the first president, and the founder of the state university.[20]

A Welsh settlement had also existed in Delaware since 1703, when a group originally from Pembrokeshire migrated from Pennsylvania to the large grant below Newark which is still called the Welsh Tract.[21] Descendants of the early Swedish and Dutch settlers were still living in their former colony, but long years of proximity and of intermarriage had nearly merged them with the larger

---

[16] Elizabeth Montgomery, *Reminiscences of Wilmington* (Philadelphia, 1851), 163.

[17] *The Delaware Gazette, or the Friendly Centinel* (Wilmington), July 4, 1789.

[18] Montgomery, *op. cit.*, 163.

[19] J. D. Schoepf, *Travels in the Confederation, 1783–1784*, A. J. Morrison, ed. (Philadelphia, 1911), I, 339.

[20] James Adams, William Killen, John McKinly, and Francis Alison, respectively.

[21] Richard B. Cook, *The Early and Later Delaware Baptists* (Philadelphia, c. 1880), 14; A. H. Newman, *A History of the Baptist Churches in the United States* (New York, 1894), 208.

English stock.[22] The largest group in the colony after the British was, however, the African. It is estimated that two thousand of the thirty-seven thousand people in Delaware in 1774 were blacks.[23] The majority of these people were slaves [24] and were employed on the farms.

Nathaniel Luff wrote that in the 1760s his parents, who lived in Jones's Neck, Kent County, saw no harm in keeping slaves, "the emancipation of negroes not then being introduced, at least in those parts." Yet his father "would hire in and out those who had contracted marriages, and often put himself to great disadvantage to accommodate them on that account. They were well clothed, and had no scarcity of food, and were not severely worked—the family generally making use of the principal part of the product of the farm. . . ." [25] Since Luff became an abolitionist, he may be suspected of trying to justify his father's slaveholding.

Thomas Rodney, also of Jones's Neck, argued that Negroes are naturally disposed to be "Hughers of Wood & drawers of Water; . . . it is Impossible for them to rise above it—Their Conduct in D[elaware or Dover?] seems very much to confirm this Reasoning for they appear so much delighted in drawing water that they are never happy but when they are at it." To attempt to upset this natural order was "vain folly," he argued. "You may ask perhaps Why the Negroes were born Slaves . . . more than others? And may you not as well ask why the Buzzards are obliged to eat nothing but Carrion, & the Tumble Bugs to work continually among Excrements? Nature answers by saying It was Nec[e]ssary & therefore she has fitted them for it & made it their delight." [26]

[22] For the Swedes, see Nelson W. Rightmyer, "Swedish–English Relations in Northern Delaware," *Church History*, XV, No. 2 (June, 1946); American Council of Learned Societies, "Report of the Committee on Linguistic and National Stocks in the Population of the United States," *Annual Report of the American Historical Association for the Year 1931*, I (Washington, 1932), 121–122, 393.

[23] Conrad, *History of Delaware*, I, 149; Sutherland, *Population Distribution*, 135.

[24] This is assumed from the 1790 census.

[25] Nathaniel Luff, *Journal of the Life of Nathaniel Luff, M.D. of the State of Delaware* (New York, 1848), 9–10.

[26] Thomas Rodney, essay on Negroes, undated MS., Brown Collection, HSD. Note the comment of Nicholas Ridgely to his son Charles, Dover, Sept. 29, 1752: "My man Robin, your Mother's Mare, and my Dog Lyon all Dy'd this summer, w[hi]ch are losses." Leon de Valinger, Jr., and Virginia E. Shaw, eds., *A Calendar of Ridgely Family Letters, 1742–1899, in the Delaware State Archives* (Dover, 1948–), I, 72.

Not all Delawareans agreed with Thomas Rodney. Indeed his own county, Kent, was the center of the early abolition movement in the lower counties. In October, 1767, to a bill for regulating slaves there was proposed an amendment forbidding their importation. It was strongly supported by the Kent County members, including Caesar Rodney, Charles Ridgely, and Thomas Collins, but was defeated, seven to nine.[27] In 1775 the Assembly passed a bill to prohibit the importation of slaves, but Governor John Penn vetoed it.[28] Finally in 1776, when the first state constitution was written, the importation of slaves was forbidden.[29]

This legislative activity seems to represent truly a mounting disapproval of slavery. Manumissions were occurring, both in wills and while the slaveowner was alive.[30] Francis Asbury, coming to Delaware in 1778, declared that "the more pious part of the people called Quakers are exerting themselves for the liberation of the slaves." [31] The most active Delaware abolitionist of any faith was Warner Mifflin, a wealthy Quaker farmer, who was born on the Eastern Shore of Virginia but resided at Camden, in Kent County, where he owned more than 1,950 acres.[32] He freed all the slaves

[27] *Minutes of the House of Representatives of the Government of the Counties of New Castle, Kent, and Sussex upon Delaware at Sessions Held at New Castle in the Years 1765–1766–1767–1768–1769–1770* ([Dover] 1931), pp. 127–128; Reed, "Delaware Constitution of 1776," 30.

[28] Dr. Ridgely was especially active in supporting this measure. Reed, *op. cit.,* 30–31.

[29] Article 26. Francis N. Thorpe, *Federal and State Constitutions, Colonial Charters, and Other Organic Laws* (Washington, 1909), I, 567; Reed, *op. cit.,* 30. Dr. Reed points out that this was the first state constitution with such a provision, and that this provision was declared in Article 30 to be one which "ought never to be violated on any Pretence whatever."

[30] Will of Joshua Clayton, of Little Creek Hundred, Sept. 2, 1760, copy, Corbit, Higgins, Spruance Papers, *HSD;* Luff, *Journal,* 34–35. Luff freed slaves worth £ 900. Yet manumissions were not altogether popular. An act of 1767 declared that anyone freeing a slave must give security worth sixty pounds against the freed Negro's becoming a charge on the state. The preamble to the act declared, "it is found by experience, that free Negroes and Mulattoes are idle and slothful, and often prove burthensome to the neighbourhood wherein they live, and are of evil example to slaves." *Laws,* I, 435–437. C. S. Shorter, Slavery in Delaware (unpublished M.A. thesis, Howard University, 1934), is a well-conceived but incomplete study. Helen Black Stewart, The Negro in Delaware to 1829 (unpublished M.A. thesis, University of Delaware, 1940) is less pretentious but is based on original sources.

[31] Francis Asbury, *Journal of Rev. Francis Asbury* (New York, 1852), I, 280. In 1779 Asbury heard a freedman preach in Delaware. *Ibid.,* 307.

[32] MS. petition of heirs of Warner Mifflin, *c.* 1809, Legislative Papers, DSA.

whom he inherited and did his utmost, individually and through societies organized for that purpose, to persuade others to emancipate their Negroes. When he died in 1798, this second Woolman was carried to the grave by faithful blacks.[33]

In spite of these signs of an awakened public conscience, the slave was still subject to much ill-treatment. Cuff Dix, a slave of Mark Bird, escaped from the New Castle County jail in 1776 with "an iron ring in one of his ears." [34] Many slaves were kidnapped, probably to be carried south where the demand was greater. The stealing of slaves—and of horses—having "greatly increased of late years in this state," resulted in a law of 1779 providing that the convicted thief should thereafter receive thirty-nine lashes, stand for one hour in the pillory, have the soft part of one ear cut off, restore the stolen property or four times its value in money, and pay the costs. If he could not pay, he was to be sold into service for a period of not more than seven years.[35]

IV. The Towns

THE towns of Delaware in the 1770s were of less importance than the countryside. To an extent this was true of the united colonies as a whole—and especially when contrasted with the same area today. The countryside has dwindled in importance as the city has grown. In the mid-1770s, for example, Delaware had about thirty-seven thousand people and the city of Philadelphia only thirty thousand. Today Delaware has less than four hundred thousand people and Philadelphia has over two million. Within Delaware, Wilmington

[33] Luff, *Journal*, 91–92. See also *Delaware Register*, II, 145–148. Much interesting material on the early abolition movement is to be found as compiled by Hilda Justice in *Life and Ancestry of Warner Mifflin, Friend-Philanthropist-Patriot* (Philadelphia, 1905). In this work, see particularly the "Biographical Note" by Sarah Mifflin Gay, 38–40, "The Defense of Warner Mifflin against Aspersions," 77–101, and "Manumissions of Slaves," 111–121.

[34] *Pennsylvania Gazette* (Philadelphia), Oct. 16, 1776.

[35] *Laws*, II, 667–668.

has grown from a village of less than two thousand to a city of more than a hundred thousand people in the same time.

In 1775 an English traveller, however, considered Wilmington "a large place," well built, "the houses being all of Brick, & very neat," giving "all the appearance of one of the English county towns" with "all trades carried on." [36] "A pretty town on the River," Nicholas Cresswell called it the next year.[37] And in 1777 a British officer stated it had 335 houses and 1,229 inhabitants, including fifty-seven Negroes and slightly more men than women.[38] "There are two Places for markets," wrote another British visitor, Lord Howe's secretary, "but no Buildings public or private of much account. It is certainly in a good position for trade, and inhabited principally by Quakers. . . ." [39]

Just north of Wilmington was a village it would one day encompass, Brandywine, where there were eight mills "in a quarter of a mile, so convenient that they can take the grain out of the Vessels [directly] into the Mills." [40] Just south of Wilmington was a town it was already overshadowing, the Dutch-founded colonial capital New Castle, nurturing its pride and its grudges beside the river. With "no Wharf or Dock where Ships [can] ride out of the strong Current," Serle remarked, "it does not seem probable that this Town will ever grow (at least not grow rapidly) into Consequence." [41] Almost a century earlier it had been forced to sit by and watch the proprietor-favored Philadelphia usurp its place as the river metropolis. Some consolation came in 1704, when the Pennsylvania connection was largely cast off and New Castle became the

[36] Robert Honyman, *Colonial Panorama, 1775; Dr. Robert Honyman's Journal for March and April*, Philip Padelford, ed. (San Marino, Calif. 1939), 11. Ten years earlier a French traveller said Wilmington was a "very well situated little town," but was "so near the City [Philadelphia] that there is but little trade Caryed on. Tavern keeping is the best business that is Caryed on in all those small towns, therefore they are well stocked with taverns." "Journal of a French Traveller in the Colonies, 1765," *American Historical Review*, XXVII, 77.

[37] *The Journal of Nicholas Cresswell* (New York, 1924), 160.

[38] Anna T. Lincoln, *Wilmington, Delaware; Three Centuries under Four Flags, 1609-1937* (Rutland, Vt., c. 1937), 86. The source of this statement is not identified. The same population estimate is found in Greene and Harrington, *Population before 1790*, 123.

[39] Serle, *Journal*, 256.

[40] Cresswell, *Journal*, 160.

[41] Serle, *Journal*, 257.

seat of government of the Lower Counties. But a half century later even this diminished position was being challenged. The local Anglican missionary wrote that "the town of Newcastle . . . waxes poorer & poorer, And falls into Contempt more and more, every year, haveing Several houses without inhabitants, & Some not fit for habitation. . . . This dying condition is partly owing to an upstart village on a Neighboring creek [Wilmington], which yields a convenient port to the adjacent Country. . . ." [42] As late as 1765, a traveller described New Castle as "a prety town . . . , looked upon as next to philadelphia In the province," [43] but Wilmington's sheltered, though shallow harbor and its greater proximity to the trade of the interior, especially of Chester and Lancaster counties, doomed New Castle to second place in its own county. The Assembly deserted New Castle for Dover in 1777,[44] and pressure was soon begun to move the county courts to a more central location, although such action was postponed for a century. A combination of river packets and stage coaches connecting Philadelphia and Baltimore via New Castle and the Elk River gave the town a measure of prosperity at the end of the century, but available water power for manufacturing and the development of land routes of travel, and eventually the railroad, finally established Wilmington's position of primacy. Still the environs of New Castle were pleasant and fertile and though, with "scarcely more than a hundred houses" [45] it was "inferior in Size & every other Respect to Wilmington," New Castle remained, in an administrative sense, "the principal Town of the County, where Courts of Justice [were] held," and where there was "a Parish Church, a Presbyterian Meeting House, a Court House, a Goal, a Pillory, a Pair of Stocks, one old Cannon for Signals or rejoicing Days and a Pound for Hogs." [46]

Up the Christina from Wilmington lay Newport, a trading and milling center, "a pretty little town, about as large as Newcastle

[42] Rev. George Ross to the Society for the Propagation of the Gospel, New Castle, March 27, 1750, S.P.G. MSS. as quoted in Nelson W. Rightmyer, *The Anglican Church in Delaware* (Philadelphia [1947]), 21.

[43] "Journal of a French Traveller, 1765," 77.

[44] *Laws*, II, 619–620.

[45] Andrew Burnaby, *Burnaby's Travels through North America* (New York, 1904), 87; Greene and Harrington, *Population before 1790*, 123.

[46] Serle, *Journal*, 257.

well built & has 3 or 4 stores & as many taverns in it." [47] Farther up-stream "Christiana or Christeen as they call it, lies in a Bottom at the head of Christeen creek over which there is a Bridge here & to which the Tide flows, bringing up sloops & such like vessels," which loaded much flour here, "there being several large mills in the neighborhood." [48] It was about the size of Newport, and "on account of the convenient communication to be had here between the Delaware and the Chesapeake Bay" was expected, by at least one traveller, to grow in importance.[49]

Dover, in Kent County, was neither a shipping point nor a manufacturing center. It owed its development to its central location and to its choice as seat of the county courts, but its growth in the eighteenth century was very slow.[50] Camden was still Mifflin's Cross Roads and Smyrna had not yet replaced Duck Creek Cross Roads.[51]

Lewes, the oldest town of Sussex County, was faced by a threat similar to that facing New Castle, a loss of its pre-eminent position. For as the interior of Sussex County was settled, the farmers there protested that Lewes was too far away to be a proper county seat—especially since the only polling place for assemblymen was the courthouse. "Lewes Town," a resident protested, "is the most Suitable place I apprehend in this county for the Publick buildings; we have opportunitys almost every Week for nine months of the year to send for necessaries to Philadelphia. There are many able farmers near Lewes, who can Supply the Town with other necessaries; beside the advantage of the fishery. . . . Lewes is pleasantly Situated and Esteemed a very healthy place, & the Land is good in and about the Town for five miles round." [52] Much of the rest of Sussex County was sparsely settled, though with a large number of mulattoes on a subsistence economy.[53]

---

[47] Honyman, *Colonial Panorama*, 11; Greene and Harrington, *Population before 1790*, 123. It is unlikely that Newport was as large as New Castle. Cresswell called the former "a trifling place." *Journal*, 160.

[48] Honyman, *op. cit.*, 11.

[49] Schoepf, *Travels*, I, 376; Greene and Harrington, *Population before 1790*, 121.

[50] J. Thomas Scharf *et al.*, *History of Delaware, 1609–1888* (Philadelphia, 1888), II, 1050; *Calendar of Ridgely Family Letters*, I, 19–22.

[51] "A Morning's Walk in the State of Delaware," *Analectic Magazine*, X (1817), 378; Scharf, *History of Delaware*, II, 1099.

[52] John Rodney to Caesar Rodney, Lewes, March 3, 1779, Rodney, *Letters*, 33.

[53] Sutherland, *Population Distribution*, 137–138.

V. The Farms

IN 1776 Delaware was, as it has always been, essentially a rural, agricultural area. The soil is on the whole fertile, consisting of a strong clay in New Castle, a sandy loam in Kent, and a loamy sand in Sussex County. The chief crops were wheat and Indian corn, along with other grains, garden vegetables, and orchard crops. The wheat and barley, and rye, too, were sown in the early fall and grown over the winter, which lasted three months. The temperature during the year varied from ninety-six degrees Fahrenheit to five degrees, moderate on the whole, but liable to sudden changes.[54]

The size of farms varied, apparently being smaller in the first-settled regions and larger in the areas where men were slowest to migrate, as western Kent and southern Sussex. The average farm in New Castle County probably contained between one and two hundred acres,[55] though we hear of many larger plantations. Waitman Sipple, for example, owned more than six hundred acres in what is now West Dover Hundred, Kent, John Marim about eighteen hundred acres in southern Kent, Levin Crapper of Milford "many thousand acres" in Sussex, and twenty thousand acres, called Dagworthy's Conquest, were warranted to General John Dagworthy in

[54] "James Tilton's Notes on the Agriculture of Delaware in 1788," R. O. Bausman and J. A. Munroe, eds., *Agricultural History*, XX (1946), 179–180. It has been said that cotton was grown in Sussex County at the beginning of the Revolution. J. Leander Bishop, *A History of American Manufactures from 1608 to 1860* (Philadelphia, 1864–1868), I, 353. *Cf.* three studies by R. O. Bausman, *An Economic Study of Land Utilization in Kent County, Delaware,* and similar works on New Castle and Sussex, published as *Bulletin* 224 (April, 1940), 228 (Feb., 1941), and 233 (Oct., 1941), of the University of Delaware Agricultural Experiment Station, Newark.

[55] This is an estimate based on figures for York and Lancaster counties given in Sutherland, *Population Distribution*, 159. Since Delaware did not use the plot system of recording conveyances, farm size averages cannot be compiled for Delaware as for Pennsylvania. Farms of 540, 315, and 250 acres were advertised for rent or sale in 1776–1777. *Pennsylvania Gazette*, Sept. 11, 1776; *Pennsylvania Journal*, April 9, 1777; *Pennsylvania Packet*, March 25, 1777. Delaware farms today average about one hundred acres in size.

southern Sussex County in 1776.[56] The tendency was for the great
original grants from the proprietors to be divided and redivided
into ever smaller tracts through inheritance and sale. With the
acquisition in 1775 of the disputed areas on the Maryland line,
much vacant land was acquired which was almost immediately
taken up, although often forming farms too large for their owners to
cultivate.[57] What vacant land remained was poor and of little value,
for the state had no great interior frontier as its neighbors had.[58]

Practically no quitrents had been paid in Delaware since 1713.[59]
Land rents before the Revolution are said to have been paid in
money, but in 1769 John Bell let his plantation in Murderkill Hundred, Kent, with one Negro, one white servant, three "plough
creatures," 2 oxen, and 3 cows to Henry and John Lambert, who
were to receive a share of the produce, one-fourth of all "Grain,
Seed, flax &c." and one-third of the "Sider and Tobacco." [60]

In spite of the existence of slave labor, no evidence has appeared
of really large slaveholdings in Delaware. Much agricultural labor
seems to have been accomplished by hired field hands, often
Negroes, free or slave. In Kent in 1775 they were paid about three
shillings, nine pence, apiece for each day's work, though the stipend
varied with the nature of the task.[61]

The land was so cheap downstate that little care was taken to
improve it. "So soon as one field was worn out, another was cleared,
and the first left to grow up again in woods." The result was that the
land was worn out, "until at last that which is fresh cleared, is even
at first of an inferior quality, and in a few years not worth farming."
Better treatment was given the land in New Castle County, where
it was more expensive.[62]

[56] Conrad, *History of Delaware*, II, 645, 663, 676, 743. See also typed copy of
will of John Dagworthy, June 18, 1781, and of will of John Dickinson, January 31,
1803, HSD. Dickinson also owned several thousand acres, but his holdings, like
those of Warner Mifflin, already referred to, were divided into very many tracts.
On Dagworthy's immense holdings see MS. memoir of John Dagworthy in HSD,
and petition of residents of Sussex County, c. 1794, Legislative Papers.
[57] Conrad, *History of Delaware*, II, 698–699.
[58] Richard S. Rodney, "The End of the Penns' Claims to Delaware, 1789–1814;
Some Forgotten Lawsuits," *Pennsylvania Magazine of History and Biography*, LXI
(1937), 203.
[59] *Ibid.*, 188.
[60] Indenture, January 16, 1769, Brown Collection.
[61] T. Rodney, An Acct. of Harvest Wages, 1775, Brown Collection.
[62] *Delaware Register*, I, 43–44.

Agricultural enterprise in the state was encouraged by the fact that almost every farm was within twelve miles of navigable water. Consequently every farmer could fairly easily send his produce to Philadelphia, Wilmington, or the markets on the Chesapeake. The Christina River was navigable for ships of three to four hundred tons and for sloops and schooners as far as the village of Christiana, and most of the creeks opening on Delaware Bay admitted vessels of 50 to 150 tons. The Nanticoke and its tributaries, Broad Creek and Deep Creek, were navigable to vessels in the Chesapeake trade.[63]

The wheat of the peninsula was of an especially soft, fine quality, favorable to the manufacture of superfine flour which often commanded an enhanced price. It was said that the hard, flinty wheat of the highlands of Pennsylvania and New York could scarcely be ground into superfine without an admixture of the peninsula wheat.[64] As a result, an extensive milling industry was developed in the three Delaware counties.

VI. The Mills

THE earliest mills in Delaware were built in the pre-English period.[65] Throughout the eighteenth century new mills arose along the creeks of the three counties. Most of these were probably custom mills, grinding flour for the farmers for a fee, and as such they were rather a by-product of an agricultural economy than an evidence of an imminent development of manufacturing. An immediate usefulness to agriculture and the fact that milling needed few workers allowed this type of manufacturing to develop amid an agrarian culture and a shortage of cheap labor. Indeed early milling was generally a family industry.

From these humble beginnings, however, a great industry was to

---

[63] *Ibid.*, I, 112.
[64] "Tilton's Notes on Agriculture," 184.
[65] Bishop, *History of Manufactures*, I, 140.

develop. The rocky Brandywine, coursing through the hills of Chester County and northern New Castle County to join the Christina at Wilmington, offered innumerable excellent mill sites. Upon these the flour millers seized, and after them the makers of paper, textiles, and powder. The result was a development as important to the history of Delaware as the Revolution of 1776.

Not the first mill on the Brandywine but the real beginning of the cluster known as the Brandywine mills was founded in the 1740s by Oliver Canby, a Quaker, on the right or south bank near the road to Philadelphia. Other mills were soon built on this side of the stream, but its full possibilities were not realized until shortly before the Revolution. It was then that Joseph Tatnall, another Quaker, the son of a carpenter, constructed a millrace and overshot mills on the rocky north bank of the Brandywine.

The situation of these mills was especially well chosen. Close to the rich farms of Chester and Lancaster counties and of northern New Castle, the products of which required only a short overland haul by Conestoga wagons to the Brandywine, the mills also easily obtained wheat from downstate Delaware via shallops which were loaded at landings on the Appoquinimink, the Duck, and the St. Jones. Then out the creeks they sailed, up the Delaware into the Christina and the Brandywine, and unloaded right beside the mills. When the grain was turned into flour it was marketed just as easily. Philadelphia, with its large West Indies trade, was the leading flour market of the colonies. And Philadelphia was as convenient to the mills as were the wheat fields of Lancaster or Kent.[66]

No wonder then that this industry developed rapidly at Brandywine. Twelve mills were erected in the immediate neighborhood within two or three decades. These were merchant mills, in contradistinction to the earlier custom mills, for the Brandywine millers bought the grain and marketed their flour. Tatnall was the first important industrialist of Delaware and entered many other business activities, becoming the first president both of the Bank of

[66] "The most notable concentration of mill industries in the colonies was at Wilmington, where an ample and reliable water-power in the chief grain-growing district of America was united with river and ocean navigation." Victor S. Clark, *History of Manufactures in the United States*, I (New York, 1929), 185. *Cf.* Henry S. Canby, *Family History* (Cambridge, 1945), 20, 23; Canby, *The Brandywine* (New York [1941]), 82–85.

Delaware and of the Chesapeake and Delaware Canal Company. His son-in-law Thomas Lea, Thomas Shipley, William Canby, George Evans, John Morton, John Welsh, John Buckley, and Cheney Broom were other Brandywine millers.[67]

With the coming of the Revolution, the mills became an important source of supply for the continental troops. But when Howe landed his troops at the head of the Elk River, Maryland, in the late summer of 1777 and prepared to march overland to Philadelphia, Washington ordered the mills dismantled so they would not be of use to the British. The grindstones were marked and hidden, a wise precaution, for the Americans were unable to prevent a British crossing of the Brandywine, which was accomplished just over the state line, at Chadds Ford, Pennsylvania. The British sent a raiding party to Wilmington after the battle, but soon sent them on to Philadelphia, whereupon the mills were repaired and put back to work.[68]

Another local industry that was closely allied to farming was shipbuilding, for the vessel was necessary, in a day of poor roads, to transport the agricultural surplus to market. One scholar suggests that shipbuilding and its allied industries "must have ranked next to agriculture in importance," for ships were built on almost every stream flowing into the Delaware River and Delaware Bay.[69] Most of the vessels built in the lower counties were small, however, for the Delaware creeks were generally shallow.[70]

Ironmaking was another colonial industry of Delaware. It, too, was necessary to the dominant agrarian culture, which required such products as horseshoes, tools, and nails. Three ironworks were established in New Castle County in the 1720s, but "a scarcity of

[67] Bishop, *History of Manufactures,* I, 143–145; Conrad, *History of Delaware,* II, 418; Lincoln, *Wilmington,* 264; Scharf, *History of Delaware,* II, 734–735, 760, 786–787; typescript from MS. book of Benjamin Ferris, in Garrett Family Collection, HSD.

[68] Conrad, *History of Delaware,* II, 418; Lincoln,*Wilmington,* 264; Scharf, *History of Delaware,* II, 787; Sutherland, *Population Distribution,* 137. For references to mills in other parts of the state, see advertisements in the *Pennsylvania Gazette* for January 11 and 18, 1775, and for a subsidiary business, *ibid.,* August 30, 1775. Assistance was given by the state to would-be millers by allowing the condemnation of necessary lands. *Laws,* I, appendix, 53–54, 72–74.

[69] Sutherland, *Population Distribution,* 165.

[70] Bishop, *History of Manufactures,* I, 77–78; Lincoln, *Wilmington,* 253; Montgomery, *Reminiscences,* 171–172.

good ores and difficulties in financing" led to their failure.[71] Others
were opened in Sussex County, along the Nanticoke River, before
the Revolution. In 1764 the Deep Creek Furnace and Nanticoke
Forge was established in this area, and a stone wharf was built on
the Nanticoke to permit the transportation of the iron by water.
For about ten years this enterprise, the largest industry in Sussex
County at the time, was successful, but the Revolution interfered,
as British ships made the Chesapeake unsafe for commerce.[72] One
of the promoters, Joseph Vaughan, received a commission as a
captain in the Delaware Regiment, January 21, 1776, and, after
rising to the rank of lieutenant colonel, was captured at Camden,
South Carolina. In the 1780s he moved to Maryland, where he
died.[73] Another early Sussex ironworks was the Pine Grove Furnace, erected by a group of Philadelphia and New York merchants.
It lay at the site of the town of Concord and was abandoned in
the Revolution.[74]

The tanning of leather, still a prosperous Delaware industry,
also dates back to colonial times. The proximity of clear water, of
black-oak bark, and of grazing grounds for cattle helped to establish the industry here. Imported as well as local hides were used in
this business where they were the chief item of investment and
where a rapid turnover of funds gave the proprietor an especially
solvent status and therefore unusual investment opportunities.
The Delaware tanneries were founded in the pre-English period
and existed, in the 1770s, in Wilmington, Middletown, Cantwell's
Bridge, New Castle, and farther downstate.[75]

Sawmills operated throughout the state, but the most extensive
lumber business was carried on in Kent and, especially, Sussex.
The white oak forests near present-day Milford were early ex-

[71] Arthur C. Bining, *Pennsylvania Iron Manufacture in the Eighteenth Century,
Publications of Pennsylvania Historical Commission,* IV (Harrisburg, 1938), 53, 187;
Bishop, *History of Manufactures,* I, 552, 583.

[72] Conrad, *History of Delaware,* II, 702.

[73] Henry H. Bellas, *A History of the Delaware State Society of the Cincinnati,
Papers of the HSD,* XIII (Wilmington, 1895), 71.

[74] Conrad, *op. cit.,* II, 737.

[75] Bishop, *History of Manufactures,* I, 443, 461; Conrad, *History of Delaware,*
II, 680–681; Lincoln, *Wilmington,* 78, 265; *Pennsylvania Gazette,* April 5, 1775;
Corbit, Higgins, Spruance Papers and John Ferris Papers, HSD. "My father an
ambitious, industrious man Carried on his business the tanning of leather with such
success that he even thought as he has often told me that he could not possible
ever stand in the need of money." Autobiography of William F. Corbit, HSD.

ploited, while the Cypress Swamp and abundant pine and cedar forests in Sussex occasioned a considerable traffic on Indian River.[76] In a codicil to his will, July 27, 1782, John Dagworthy specifically empowered his executors "to cut trees and timber for lumber for sale . . . in the Swamps at the mill or elsewhere." [77]

Other smaller industries developed in the state. Salt was manufactured along the coast.[78] Matthew Crips, of Wilmington, owned a pottery, which prospered during the Revolution, when "wares of all sorts were scarce and expensive." [79] Thomas Parke, of Dover, father of the poet and translator, John Parke, made hats.[80] A snuff mill had been established on Red Clay Creek near Yorklyn by 1782.[81] Distilleries must have existed, since a statute of 1779 forbade the manufacture of spirits from wheat, rye, or any grain, meal, or flour. [82] Silversmiths practiced their trade.[83] A clothing factory was established at Newark during the Revolution to equip the Delaware troops.[84]

VII. The Roads and Rivers

THE products of Delaware manufacturers, like those of Delaware farmers, were usually taken to market by water. Roads existed, but they were notoriously bad, fitted rather for the horseback

[76] Bishop, *History of Manufactures*, 109–111; Conrad, *History of Delaware*, II, 680–681, 733.

[77] Typed copy of will in HSD. See also George W. Marshall, *Memoir of Brigadier General John Dagworthy*, Papers of the HSD, X (Wilmington, 1895), 23–24.

[78] Bishop, *History of Manufactures*, I, 290; petition of nineteen residents of Sussex, 1781, Legislative Papers; Thomas Rodney, Journal, November 29, 1780, Brown Collection; James M. Tunnell, Jr., "The Salt Business in Early Sussex County," *Delaware History* (March, 1950), IV, 48–59.

[79] Montgomery, *Reminiscences*, 265.

[80] Benjamin Mifflin, *Journal of Benjamin Mifflin; the Record of a Tour from Philadelphia to Delaware and Maryland, 1762*, Victor H. Paltsits, ed. (New York, 1935), 16n.

[81] Conrad, *History of Delaware*, II, 465.

[82] *Laws*, II, 647.

[83] Jessie Harrington, "Delaware Silver," in Wilmington Society of the Fine Arts, *Antique Silver* (Wilmington, 1941); Montgomery, *Reminiscences*, 53.

[84] Thomas Rodney, Account of Shirts & Linnens Sent to the Factory for the Delaware Regiment, Rodney Collection, HSD.

rider than for the wagoner. "The Roads being bad we Came Sloe" [85] was a frequent complaint. Francis Asbury was obliged to get out of his carriage and walk.[86] Bridges and milldams frequently offered unusual hazards to the traveller,[87] while complaints were often made of the inadequacy of the ferries.[88] The two chief reasons for the poor state of the roads were the availability of cheaper water routes and the lack of any large communities between which a fast land transport might have been desired. New Castle County, however, did lie on the direct line between Philadelphia and the growing Chesapeake port of Baltimore. On this route too, waterways were used as far as possible, and to connect them a line of stages was established between New Castle and the Elk River in 1775.[89]

The river shipping, which this stage line principally served, was the most important type of transportation to the life of the three counties. Every navigable creek had landings—Fast Landing, Forest Landing, Johnny Cake Landing, such names they bore —where the farmers brought their produce. A letter book kept by Thomas Rodney from 1773 to 1775, when he was in the mercantile business at Dover, throws light on the river trade from the point of view of a Kent merchant. He bought manufactured goods and foreign imports in Philadelphia—nails, cinnamon, pepper, powder and shot, glassware, chinaware, snuff, tea, shoes, a well pump, skillets, stationery, chocolate, nutmeg, twine, sugar, tobacco, Peruvian bark (quinine), molasses, coffee, rum, rugs, English blankets, buckram. From Bowers Furbee in Kent he bought wheat and corn and sent them to John Brown at the Bird-in-Hand Wharf. To Redwood and Burket, Philadelphia merchants, he sent corn and offered bacon. From Levin and Joseph Derrickson and John Dagworthy, all of Indian River, Sussex, he ordered boards and shingles. On April 7, 1775, his sloop was ordered to get two hun-

[85] Jan. 29, 1770, Journal of Thomas Rodney, Rodney Collection. *Cf.* Honyman, *Colonial Panorama*, 12.

[86] Asbury, *Journal*, I, 353, 355.

[87] Thomas Rodney, Journal of a Trip to Philadelphia, Sept. 14, 1769, Rodney Collection.

[88] Philip Vickers Fithian, *Journal & Letters of Philip Vickers Fithian, 1773–1774; A Plantation Tutor of the Old Dominion*, Hunter Dickinson Farish, ed. (Williamsburg, 1943), 132–133, 144.

[89] Conrad, *History of Delaware*, II, 516.

dred bushels of corn from Caleb Luff of Kent and sell it at Egg Harbor, New Jersey [?], taking returns "in half price and Good Inch Board." On May 10 of the same year he sent wheat to John Depoister in Philadelphia and asked the latter to see that thirty hams and twelve "fouls" reached their purchasers.[90]

So many shallops were in the river trade that the Delawarean who happened to be in Philadelphia could always stroll down to the wharves with the reasonable hope of seeing a friendly shallop-man and hearing news from home. On September 13, 1769, Thomas Rodney, visiting in the metropolis, wrote: "After breakfast I walk'd Down Town to see If there were any of our County Shalloop men in Town. . . . I found David Pleasantons Shalloop [Pleasanton was from the same part of Kent as Rodney] Just unloading of Goods brought from a wreck Down the bay." [91] Nathaniel Luff, who later became Rodney's closest friend, was sent from Kent County to Philadelphia to school and was given by his father "an unlimited direction to draw on a shallopman, who came up at least once or twice a month, for what pocket money I wanted." [92] This constant shallop traffic provided also a convenient, if some-what uncertain, passenger service from Kent and Sussex to Wilmington and Philadelphia. By this means, Vincent Loockerman, of Dover, was able to leave home for Philadelphia on August 7, 1762, and return on August 9.[93] Enoch Anderson, Joseph Stidham, and others travelled from Lewes to Wilmington in 1776 in less than forty hours.[94] Mrs. Miers Clarke in 1790 sailed from Lewes to Philadelphia in twenty-eight hours.[95]

In 1774, Samuel Bush, of Wilmington, who had commanded a brig in the West Indies trade, bought a sloop of about thirty tons

[90] Thomas Rodney, bound MS. journal, HSD.

[91] T. Rodney, *Journal of a Trip to Philadelphia, 1769*, Rodney Collection.

[92] Luff, *Journal*, 11.

[93] Mifflin, *Journal of a Tour*, 17.

[94] *Personal Recollections of Captain Enoch Anderson, Papers of the HSD*, XVI (Wilmington, 1896), 19.

[95] "Aletta Clarke's Book," C. H. B. Turner, ed., *Some Records of Sussex County, Delaware* (Philadelphia, 1909), 355. It must be pointed out, however, that both Anderson and Mrs. Clarke were prevented by bad weather from getting away on the day they planned to sail and that both underwent nerve-racking experiences in connection with the trip. Other notes on the shallop trade occur in Read, *Read*, 38; in Mrs. F. B. Watkins, St. Georges and Appoquinimink (typescript), Corbit, Higgins, Spruance Papers; and in De Valinger and Shaw, *Calendar of Ridgely Letters*, I, 17.

and inaugurated a weekly service between Wilmington and Philadelphia. This new project was successful from the first and a freight service between these two ports was maintained by the Bush family for more than a century.[96]

In addition to the river traffic, there was also a considerable ocean trade from Delaware, chiefly based at New Castle and Wilmington. From these ports ships sailed along the coast and to the British Isles, southern Europe, Madeira, and especially the West Indies. Of the produce of the region, they carried out mainly flour, corn meal, and lumber, and imported coffee, molasses, wine, cotton, hides, limes, rum, sugar, and salt,[97] as well as immigrants and coin. A lighthouse to aid ships entering the Delaware capes was erected near Cape Henlopen in 1764 with money raised by lotteries. Burnt by the British in 1777, it was replaced by the Philadelphia Port Wardens in 1785.[98]

The non-import agreements and the Revolution seriously affected the maritime trade of Delaware. Through most of the war the British stationed patrol ships at the Delaware capes and frequently took American ships or forced them ashore.[99] After the capture of Philadelphia in 1777, the British commanded the bay and river along the whole coast of Delaware and ended all river traffic, at least all that was legal in the eyes of the patriots. When Philadelphia was evacuated in 1778, British and loyalist ships continued to raid Delaware Bay shipping and even ventured up the creeks to take shallops at their wharves. Local Tories dealt openly with the British at times, and lukewarm adherents of the patriotic cause were encouraged by the disruption of their customary trade to find a market where they could, even if with the enemy. By collusion the British were allowed to capture some local vessels. A state admiralty court was set up to take cognizance of such problems, but the guilt or innocence of the Delaware merchants was

---

[96] Memorial to George W. Bush, Bush Family Papers, HSD.

[97] Sutherland, *Population Distribution*, 276–278; account between Thomas Wiley and John Ferriss, St. Eustatius, Jan. 31, 1770, Ferris Family Papers; Bellas, *Delaware Cincinnati*, 55–56. One of George Read's brothers settled in the West Indies and another commanded a ship in the trade to those islands. Read. *Read*, 40.

[98] Albert E. S. Hall, Report of Condition of Henlopen Lighthouse, September 17, 1925 (typescript in HSD); Conrad, *History of Delaware*, II, 217.

[99] Anderson, *Personal Recollections*, 8–9; Montgomery, *Reminiscences*, 176–178, 181–183; *Pennsylvania Gazette*, May 31, 1775; April 17, May 8, 1776.

not easy to determine.[100] The people were often less judicial. A Wilmington mob broke into the home of Jonathan Rumford, a wealthy merchant suspected of loyalism. They scattered firebrands through the rooms and their leader, a blacksmith, crushed Rumford's skull with a hammer.[101] Yet earlier Rumford had been recommended by President Caesar Rodney to the French consul in Philadelphia as a purchasing agent for the French in Delaware, "because," Rodney wrote, "this State has a Port and Market which it is . . . my duty to encourage. . . ." [102] As the war continued, pressure was brought, unsuccessfully, on the Delaware government to lift the embargo, especially on the exportation of flour.[103]

By 1780 the depredations of the British on river and bay trade had become so serious that the legislature finally empowered President Rodney "to fit out barges to cruise on the bay and river of Delaware for the protection of the trade thereof." [104] Lieutenant Colonel Charles Pope, a former seaman and soldier, was made commander of the Delaware navy and, after finding difficulty in securing arms, he put to sea and had some success in protecting the bay trade.[105]

Before the war was over, petitions were reaching the legislature regarding the improvement of the maritime commerce of the state. Residents of the neighborhood of Duck Creek protested against a proposed obstruction to navigation on "so bold and valuable a water," where "from time immemorial" vessels carrying

[100] Frank Fletcher Stephens, *The Transitional Period, 1788–1789, in the Government of the United States* (Columbia, Mo., 1909), 97–98; T. Rodney, summary of case of Brig *Endeavour*, folder, "Legal Papers," Rodney Collection; Rodney, "Come all you Jolly Soldiers," folder "Original Poems," Brown Collection; testimony of John Brinckle, Jr., folder "T. Rodney, Letters sent by," *ibid.;* T. Rodney, statement in folder, "T. Rodney, 1779–1791," *ibid.; Governor's Register, State of Delaware,* I (Wilmington, 1926), 30–31, 36.

[101] Montgomery, *Reminiscences,* 168–170; T. Rodney, memo of what passed between J. R. and T. R., Dec., 1780, Brown Collection.

[102] Caesar Rodney to John Holker, Dover, July 26, 1780, Rodney Collection.

[103] T. Rodney to C. Rodney, Wilmington, Sept. 13, 1780, and C. Rodney to Adams, Clerk, and Rumford, Dover, Sept. 15, 1780, Rodney, *Letters,* 379–381; James Lovell to Elbridge Gerry, Nov. 20, 1780, Burnett, *Letters,* V, 453.

[104] *Delaware Archives* (Wilmington, 1911–1919), II, 920; *Minutes of the Council of the Delaware State from 1776 to 1792* (Dover, 1886), 562–563.

[105] *Delaware Archives,* II, 920–930; *Laws,* II, 771; *Governor's Register,* 35; *Minutes of Council,* 584–585, 668–669, 699, 720, 730; Rodney, *Letters,* 382–383, 406. There is a brief biographical sketch of Pope in Bellas, *Delaware Cincinnati,* 68–69.

fifteen hundred to twenty-five hundred bushels of grain had traded to Philadelphia, New York, and Boston. On this creek, they added, stood five excellent granaries containing nearly six thousand bushels, and from adjacent landings in the previous year forty thousand bushels of corn and wheat had been shipped, plus large quantities of barley and wood.[106]

In 1781, people living near the Indian River in Sussex asked that the placing of weirs in this stream be forbidden. The stream, they claimed, was navigable for twenty miles and before the British hindered trade it was "scarce inferior to any River or Creek in the State." [107] In the same year, two residents of Port Penn, on the Delaware near Reedy Island, asked the establishment of a lottery to raise funds for the improvement of their harbor, where ships often waited for a favorable wind. They asserted Port Penn possessed the best natural harbor on the Delaware, combining "the advantages of both Cork & Portsmouth." [108]

VIII. The Currency

BEFORE the Revolution Delaware perpetually suffered from a lack of currency with which to carry on her business. This was largely due to the fact that the colony consumed many English goods but produced little that could be sold in England, which resulted in what is generally known as an unfavorable balance of trade. In other words, England was perpetually draining Delaware of specie.[109]

To remedy this situation the government of the three counties

[106] Folder, "1778–Legislative, No. 2, Petitions, Resolutions, Amendments, Etc.," Legislative Papers.

[107] Folder, "1781 January–February, Legislative, New Castle Petitions," *ibid.*

[108] Folder, "1781 January–February, Legislative Petitions, Lotteries," *ibid.*

[109] Richard S. Rodney, *Colonial Finances in Delaware* (Wilmington, 1928), 14–16. This excellent monograph presents an exposition of the currency problem in Delaware up to 1792.

began to issue paper money in April, 1723. For the most part the Delaware bills of credit were secured by first mortgages on real estate made through loan offices in each county, new currency being issued to the mortgagees. They paid interest on their loans, and the interest payments helped to support the government. Some issues were retired by excise or property taxes.[110]

Thirty thousand pounds of paper currency, divided equally among the three counties, were issued under an act of September 2, 1775. It was explained that this issue was necessitated "through the scarcity of gold and silver in this government, occasioned by the frequent remittances thereof to Great Britain in discharge of the debts accrued by the importation of manufactures and merchandise from thence, and the constant sinking of the bills of credit emitted during the late war, and granted to his Majesty for the protection of his American dominions." Interest on this paper money could also be of help in supporting the government.[111]

In the year of this statute, however, the currency problem assumed an entirely different character from that of preceding years, for the Continental Congress, needing money to support its military effort, issued three million dollars of paper, of which each state was assigned a share to be paid in four annual installments beginning in 1779.[112] To support the credit of these bills, Congress asked the states to make them legal tender. Delaware complied on February 22, 1777,[113] and at the same time issued twenty-five thousand pounds in bills of credit.

This was the only paper money that Delaware ever issued as an independent state. As Congress continued to print more and more money without security, public confidence gradually declined and prices rocketed.[114] Since Continental currency was used to pay the mortgages on which the Delaware currency was

[110] *Ibid.*, 18, 27–28.
[111] *Laws*, I, 571–586.
[112] Albert S. Bolles, *The Financial History of the United States from 1774 to 1789* (New York, 1896), 40; *Journals of Congress*, II, 103, 221–223; III, 457–459.
[113] Bolles, *Financial History*, 150–153; *Laws*, II, 599–602; *Minutes of Council*, 50, 70, 94, 483–485; *Votes of the House of Assembly of the Delaware State*, October, 1776, pp. 12, 15–16, 19, 39–40; *ibid.*, January, 1777, pp. 36, 39–40.
[114] Petition of T. Rodney and G. Bedford to General Assembly, October, 1778, Rodney Collection; Lincoln, *Wilmington*, 88.

based, the local money, itself soundly backed, was involved in the depreciation. Finally, on November 4, 1780, Delaware suspended the status as legal tender of both continental and state issues, and this repudiation was made permanent in 1781.[115] Although a popular demand for paper money still existed in the state, the legislature refused to respond.[116]

Various attempts to prevent inflation through control of prices ended in failure. Delaware participated in two special conventions to adopt uniform price-fixing laws; extra-legal committees attempted to hold prices down, but no action to enforce any price laws seems ever to have been taken by the General Assembly.[117] As a result of a meeting in Wilmington in 1779, a petition was sent to the legislature complaining of "the Disorderly State of Our Trade, Occasioned Chiefly by Forestallers, Engrossers, and Monopolizers," and praying for relief for "the Useful Trader and the Industrious Manufacturer." [118] The requested law was enacted

[115] Rodney, *Colonial Finances*, 47–51; *Laws*, II, 608–618, 718–719; *Minutes of Council*, 578–579, 581–582, 586–587.

[116] A petition from Sussex County urged "the Emission of a Paper Currency" as "the only relief which now remains to Save the State from Ruin Anarchy and Distruction." Folder, "1782 January–February, Legislative Petitions," Legislative Papers. See also petitions for changing the depreciation rate of continental currency in folder, "1782 May–June, Legislative Petitions," *ibid.*

[117] Delaware appointed Caesar Rodney, Thomas Collins, and James Latimer to attend a convention in York, Pennsylvania, in March, 1777, to form "a system . . . for regulating the price of labour, of manufactures, . . . of internal produce, . . . and of goods imported from foreign parts, except military stores." *Minutes of Council*, 115; *Votes of Assembly*, October, 1776, 153. Thomas C. Cochran, *New York in the Confederation, an Economic Study* (Philadelphia, 1932), 30, claims no agreement was reached at York, but Allan Nevins, *The American States during and after the Revolution, 1775–1789* (New York, 1924), 617, states that a scale of prices was formulated. At any rate, the only reaction of the Delaware legislature was to pass an act regulating the prices charged by innholders and tavern keepers. *Delaware Laws*, II, 620; *Minutes of Council*, 115–117, 119, 122.

A price-fixing law passed the Legislative Council in 1778, but was not approved by the lower chamber. *Minutes of Council*, 194, 197, 199, 210, 220, 223, 229–230.

In 1779 Delaware again refused to pass a price-fixing law, though it was recommended by Congress, and would not enforce the price schedules. *Minutes of Council*, 508–509; Hubertis Cummings, "Robert Morris and the Episode of the Polacre *Victorious,*" *Pennsylvania Magazine of History and Biography* (July, 1946), LXX, 249–251. Delaware sent four representatives to a convention to fix prices called for January, 1780, but nothing was accomplished. *Minutes of Council*, 494–495, 500, 502–503, 505; Rodney, *Letters*, 335n. *Cf.* Thomas Rodney to John Dickerson [Dickinson], Dover, Sept. 1, 1778, Rodney Collection.

[118] Petition of October, 1779, Legislative Papers. David Bush, George Craighead, Joseph Bennett, Gunning Bedford, James Latimer, Thomas McDonough, and Joshua Clayton were among the sixty-odd signers.

in 1779, but the urgent necessity of securing supplies for the army occasioned its repeal in April, 1780.[119]

IX. The Social Life

ON the eve of the Revolution most of the free inhabitants of the Delaware counties were well supplied with the necessities of life, though they had few luxuries. "The manner and customs of the white people . . . were very simple, plain and social." "Almost every family manufactured their own clothes"; they ate home-produced beef, pork, poultry, wild game, butter, cheese, wheat, corn, and fruits; they drank milk, cider, small beer, and peach and apple brandy, but seldom used tea, coffee, or chocolate. Honey, instead of sugar, was their usual sweetening. Since even the largest farmers rarely sowed over twenty acres of wheat and thirty acres of corn, there were leisure hours "to play and frolic, at which times the young people would dance, and the older ones wrestle, run, hop, jump or throw the disc or play at some rustic and manly exercises. On Christmas Eve there was an universal firing of guns, and traveling round from house to house during the holiday, and indeed all winter there was a continual frolic at one house or another, shooting-matches, twelfth-cakes, &c." [120] Hunting was not only a pleasure, it increased many a larder as well.[121] Horse-racing and cock-fighting were also favorite pastimes; from the latter, indeed, comes the nickname of Delawareans, "Blue Hen's Chickens," a nickname earned by the courage of Delaware troops who, as

[119] Delaware *Laws*, II, 697, 701; *Minutes of Council*, 454, 456, 471–475, 510; Read, *Read*, 350.

[120] Undated letter of Thomas Rodney in *Proceedings on Unveiling the Monument to Caesar Rodney and the Oration . . . by Thomas F. Bayard at Dover . . .* (Wilmington, 1889), 20–21. In 1778, after taking part in a hot naval engagement all day, Enoch Anderson walked from Wilmington to New Castle to attend a ball. Anderson, *Personal Recollections*, 56–57.

[121] The legislature considered banning the "Ring-hunting of Deer with Dogs, whereby many of the Hogs and Sheep" were killed. *House Minutes*, 1769, 232, 235, 259.

legend has it, fought as bravely as the fighting cocks, brood of a blue hen, that belonged to one of their officers.[122] Card games were evening diversions for some, and excursions and bathing were popular in the summer.[123]

Thomas Rodney described a day's recreation in 1769 beginning with dinner at Duck Creek at three, after which he "play'd a Schore of Long Bullets then Sett of home—on the way Mett with a Large Company of people horse-Raseing—there were three half bloods Run the half Mile heats for a Saddle, which was won by a horse call'd the Crab—after that Tow Little three year old Mares Run and I think made a Much better Race than the first—This kept us So long, that I Didn't Reach home [Dover] Till Near Sun sett—after I come home I went to one of the Taverns and Spent three Hours at Cards, the Rema[in]ing part of the Evening past at home in Conversation with Mrs. Shee about her Courtship." [124]

Annual and semiannual fairs added a gay note to life in eighteenth-century Delaware. Planned to allow natives an opportunity to examine and purchase merchandise not otherwise obtainable in these counties which had no sizable city, these fairs became a grand frolic, with games, music, and dancing.[125] Young people looked forward to them as a time of display and flirtation. "Many a unhapy Lad," Thomas Rodney wrote, "will Retire with the Evening Sun of that day with a bleeding heart deeply wounded with Cupits Arrows, as it is Reported he will Make War that Day." [126] But gambling, drunkenness, fights, and riots could also be expected, which led a reforming element to seek an end to these moral dangers by abolishing the fairs.[127] During the Revolution, days of thanksgiving and of fasting, humiliation, and prayer were frequently observed in response to the recommendations of Con-

[122] William G. Whiteley, *The Revolutionary Soldiers of Delaware, Papers of the Historical Society of Delaware*, XIV, (Wilmington, 1896), 69. On December 7, 1776, the Council of Safety for Kent County banned "the Vile and indecent practices of Horse-racing and Cock-fiting" as Congress had recommended. Rodney, *Letters*, 145–146.

[123] Francis Asbury bathed in the ocean as early as April. Asbury, *Journal*, I, 314, 316, 360; T. Rodney to Sally Ridgely, Dover, April 20, 1767, Rodney Collection; T. Rodney, Journal of a Trip to Philadelphia, September 13, 1769, *ibid.*

[124] *Ibid.*, September 1, 1769.

[125] Montgomery, *Reminiscences*, 218–220; Read, *Read*, 322.

[126] T. Rodney to S. Ridgely, Dover, April 20, 1767, Rodney Collection.

[127] Lincoln, *Wilmington*, 74–75.

gress.[128] Thanksgiving Day was usually celebrated in December.
There were few organized social groups in pre-Revolutionary
Delaware. Masonic lodges were being formed at Cantwell's Bridge,
Wilmington, and Dover, which were allied to the Grand Lodge of
Pennsylvania. Other lodges were later established at New Castle,
Duck Creek Cross Roads, Newark, and Georgetown, the latter,
later moved to Laurel, being attached to the Grand Lodge of
Maryland. A Grand Lodge of Delaware was not established until
1806.[129]

Informal social gatherings and the close ties of blood and con-
jugal relationship took the place later occupied by clubs. The
upper class was composed of the landed gentry, the rich merchants, and their associates, the Anglican clergy, the physicians,
and the lawyers. The ties of wealth and position which united
this group were continually being reinforced by intermarriage.
George Read married a daughter of the Rev. George Ross, rector
at New Castle. A daughter of the Rev. Thomas Crawford, Anglican missionary at Dover, was the mother of Caesar Rodney,
whose niece married Dr. John Brinckle. James A. Bayard, an attorney, and Dr. Joshua Clayton married the daughter and adopted
daughter, respectively, of Richard Bassett, wealthy proprietor of
Bohemia Manor. The Rev. Sydenham Thorne, of Milford, was a
planter of wealth as well as a missionary.[130]

The dirt farmers and the mechanics, the bulk of the population,
were the middle class of society. Their standing was determined
not so much by their wealth as by their way of life, which frequently startled the socially prominent by its simplicity. One
Dr. Thomas, for example, owned three thousand acres and gave all
his time to farming, refusing to practice medicine. Though he was
by some "considered the best informed man in New Castle
County," since he dressed like a common farmer and kept no company, he "was therefore nothing thought of." [131] Benjamin Mifflin

[128] *Minutes of Council*, 39, 332, 336–338, 451–453, 522–524, 580, 582, 585–586,
680, 682–683, 750; *Votes and Proceedings of Assembly*, 1782, pp. 8, 14.
[129] Conrad, *History of Delaware*, II, 437–438; J. Hugo Tatsch, *Freemasonry in
the Thirteen Colonies* (New York, 1933), 158–166.
[130] Conrad, *History of Delaware*, II, 675, 678; petition of Thorne, June, 1786,
and counter-petitions, folder, "1786 May–June, Legislature, Petitions, Misc.," Legislative Papers.
[131] T. Rodney, Journal of a Trip to Philadelphia, Oct. 25, 1790, Brown Collection.

was shocked to find his uncle, William Shurmer, living "in a Loansom Cottage a small Log House that serves for Kitchen, Parlour, Hall & Bed Chamber," with nothing to offer a guest but "rum, Water & Brown Sugar." [132]

Into this class commonly fitted the Scotch-Irishman, but he was a newcomer, progressing up the social ladder and subject to the usual human prejudices against the rising man. It may have been a matter of social distinction quite as much as of religious or racial feeling that prompted David Varnum to declare "he had as lief be under a tyrannical King as under a tyrannical Commonwealth, especially if the d—d Presbyterians had control of it." [133]

The proud Delawarean of English stock could not always forget that his Scotch-Irish neighbor was but one step removed from such indentured servants as Margaret Ferguson and Mary Caulfield, who ran away from the employment of William Stark and Joseph Tatnall in 1776, taking with them "a cambret riding habit, faced with blue peelong," an "old taffety gown, of a straw color, one other cotton and linnen gown, of a light green color, two calicos and one linsey short gown, 3 striped linsey petticoats, a gray coating cloak, with a cape, each a black bonnet. . . ." [134] Most of such servants were Irish, but not all. Amer Grubb, of Brandywine Hundred, advertised for a twenty-year-old "Dutch-servant lad," Henry Nibble, who ran away April 2, 1776, and William Brobson sought an "English servant man, named John Alderson, a barber by trade." [135]

In spite of outward similarities in their condition, the indentured servants were by no means in as bad a state as the slaves. True, a slave might be manumitted, and manumissions were common in Delaware, but his physical appearance remained a mark of his bondage. Furthermore, in most cases his rearing was so primitive that he had little hope, in the short span of a lifetime, of winning any social recognition. He was almost always illiterate and had little chance of learning to read or write. Economically, many vocations would remain closed to him whatever his legal status.

[132] Mifflin, *Journal*, 16.
[133] Scharf, *History of Delaware*, I, 225.
[134] *Pennsylvania Gazette*, April 24, 1776.
[135] *Ibid.*, July 19, 1775; April 17, 1776.

Politically he could exert no power, for the franchise was denied him.

The indentured servant, in contrast, could look forward to his freedom in a fixed and certain time, and the possibility that his past status might be put aside altogether. He was free to move where he pleased. Land was cheap and most occupations were open to him. In his youth, he might well have received in the old country a better education than his master's children received in America —particularly if he were Scotch-Irish.

X. The Churches

THE Scotch-Irishman enjoyed not only economic opportunities in Delaware, but also the consolations of his faith. Indeed, on the eve of the Revolution Presbyterianism was the second most popular sect in the three counties. No church was officially established. Penn's charter of 1701 guaranteed freedom of worship to every monotheist and the right to hold office to every Christian.[136] In spite of the latter privilege, however, the Assembly of the lower counties, by an act of 7 George II, required its members to take an oath specifically denying the Roman Catholic faith.[137]

This colonial law was rooted, of course, in the historical enmity of Englishmen for the Catholic countries of France and Spain, but it betrayed, too, the overwhelmingly Protestant complexion of the land. Largest in number were the Anglicans, though most of them were unchurched. Quakers were few in number but great in their cultural influence. Growing Baptist and Catholic groups, a single Lutheran church, a few rural Nicholites, and, still within the Anglican communion, a people called Methodists complete the religious census of pre-Revolutionary Delaware.[138]

[136] Francis N. Thorpe, ed., *The Federal and State Constitutions, Colonial Charters, and Other Organic Laws* . . . (Washington, 1909), I, 558.
[137] *Laws,* I, 155.
[138] Elizabeth Waterston, *Churches in Delaware during the Revolution, with a Brief Account of their Settlement and Growth* (Wilmington, 1925) is a general reference for this section.

The Church of England was handicapped in the lower counties, as elsewhere in the colonies, by the lack of a bishop in America. Since the Anglican priest must be ordained by a bishop, clergymen had to come from England. There were never enough English missionaries to serve the colonies, while the expense and trouble of an ocean voyage hindered the missions from producing their own ministry by sending young men abroad for education and ordination. Furthermore, the want of a bishop to confirm the believers prevented most Anglicans from becoming communicants in the church.[139]

In the absence of a sufficient number of missionaries each clergyman was forced to assume responsibility for an area larger than he could effectively serve. For a long time there was but one Anglican priest in each county, with the result that only a very small number of the people could possibly be reached on any one Sunday.[140] In 1776 there were five priests in Delaware—Aeneas Ross at New Castle, Philip Reading in Appoquinimink Hundred, Samuel Magaw at Dover, Sydenham Thorne near Milford, and Samuel Tingley at Lewes. These men were supported in part by the Society for the Propagation of the Gospel, the Anglican missionary society, and in part by their parishioners. Every congregation was ordered to provide a glebe farm for the support of any minister appointed after 1765, and several ministers augmented their incomes through teaching.[141]

The Revolution proved a particularly difficult time for the Anglican clergy. Four of the five priests in Delaware had been born in the colonies, and one of them, Aeneas Ross, was the brother of one signer of the Declaration of Independence and the brother-in-law of another. But their colonial birth, which might have predisposed these men to sympathy with the Revolution, was countered by other factors: England was the source of the most dependable part of their income; prayers for the royal family were a part of the Anglican services; and at ordination each priest had taken an oath of loyalty to the king.

---

[139] Rightmyer, *Anglican Church in Delaware*, 140.

[140] *Cf.* letters of Charles Inglis, Samuel Magaw, and Samuel Tingley in William Stevens Perry, *Historical Collections Relating to the American Colonial Church,* V (1878), 118, 124, 125, 127, 137.

[141] Rightmyer, *Anglican Church in Delaware*, 136.

Three of these priests—Ross, a patriot, Tingley, a loyalist, and Magaw, whose attitude toward the Revolution is not certainly known—continued to officiate during the Revolution.[142] In doing so, Tingley met a difficult problem. Prayers for the royal family would not have been tolerated by his neighbors; yet if he did not officiate his "flock would unavoidably be scattered." To satisfy all, he cleverly changed the words of the service, and "instead . . . of saying, . . . O Lord, save the King, . . . said, O Lord, save those who thou hast made it our especial Duty to pray for." [143] This to him meant the king; let others think of whom they would.

The other two priests, Thorne and Reading, were not so subtle nor so successful in avoiding persecution. Thorne was called before the Kent County Committee of Correspondence on September 11, 1775, for refusing to observe a day of fasting and prayer which had been declared by Congress and for uttering "certain Words and Expressions tending to Cause Divisions, and excite Unusual Jealousies. . . ." [144] Thorne later declared he had been called before this committee four times, but had suffered nothing worse than personal abuse. He held no formal services after 1777 when he was prohibited from praying for the king. Reading, who also suffered much abuse for his loyalism, held no services after August, 1776.[145]

The Anglican laity, like the clergy, were divided on the Revolution. Downstate the congregations were to a large degree loyalist. Samuel Tingley wrote: "the members of the Church in my Mission have proved loyal, excepting a few families, who, tho' they always professed themselves Churchmen, have proved that . . . they are Churchmen by profession, but Presbyterians by trade, i.e., no friends to Church & state." [146] And Samuel Magaw testified: "I do not believe there can be any where a stronger attachment

[142] *Ibid.*, 24, 63–65, 91, 170–171; Lewis W. Gibson, An Historical Sketch of "The Church at Dover," MS., Church Papers, HSD; Richard S. Rodney, "Immanuel Church, New Castle," *Historical Magazine of the Protestant Episcopal Church*, XII (1943), 21.

[143] Samuel Tingley to the Secretary of the S.P.G., New York, March 5, 1782, Perry, *Collections*, V, 135.

[144] MS., Transactions of Kent Committee of Correspondence, September 7, 1775, HSD.

[145] Rightmyer, *Anglican Church in Delaware*, 43, 67, 169–170.

[146] Tingley to Secretary of S.P.G., New York, March 5, 1782, Perry, *Collections*, V, 134–135.

to the Parent Country, or a more warm regard for that Religion which we jointly profess, than among the greatest number of those to whom I have been appointed to Minister." [147] The division of the Churchmen, as the Anglicans were called, is revealed by the fact that such leading patriots as George Read, Caesar Rodney, and John Clowes, and such banned loyalists as Boaz Manlove, Thomas Robinson, and Luke Shields were all members of the same persuasion.[148]

Whereas the Revolution placed the Anglican church in an anomalous position, the Presbyterian church on the other hand flourished. The Presbytery of New Castle, with jurisdiction over Delaware and parts of Pennsylvania and Maryland, had been organized in 1717. But a division of this presbytery which had taken place in 1735, resulted in the establishment of the Presbytery of Lewes, including the churches of Kent and Sussex and of several counties on the Eastern Shore of Maryland. After about seven years the two presbyteries were again joined, only to be separated once again in 1758 and remain apart until 1810.[149]

Like the Anglicans, the Presbyterian ministers often were expected to cover impossible distances and to divide their time between two or more churches.[150] "Here are Numbers of starving Souls crying to us for the Bread of Life," pleaded the Lewes Presbytery in 1773, "and we are unable to assist them." [151] The lack of these ministers was probably due in part to their small stipends [152]

---

[147] Magaw to Secretary of S.P.G., Philadelphia, October 7, 1776, ibid., 128.

[148] Rightmyer, op. cit., 168.

[149] J. L. Vallandigham and Samuel A. Gayley, History of the Presbytery of New Castle . . . 1717 to 1888 (Philadelphia c. 1888), 17–18; Records of the Lewes Presbytery, MS. (Presbyterian Historical Society, Philadelphia), I, 1. The year 1758 also marked the end of a schism in Presbyterianism that had torn the New Castle Presbytery in two. John W. Christie, "Presbyterianism in Delaware," H. Clay Reed, ed., Delaware: A History of the First State (New York, 1947), II, 649.

[150] Records of the Presbytery of New Castle upon Delaware, MS. (Presbyterian Historical Society), III, 354, 361.

[151] Records of Lewes Presbytery, I, 95–96.

[152] William McKennan, pastor of the Red Clay Creek Church, was for some time paid only nine pounds a year. John D. Blake, A History of the Red Clay Creek Presbyterian Church, typescript, HSD. In 1779 the New Castle Presbytery, facing "the melancholy Prospect of the Interests of Religion, declining amongst us for want of a due support to Ministers," especially in view of "the great Depreciation of the Currency," enjoined the people to provide support "equivalent to what they used to give. . . ." Records of New Castle Presbytery, IV, 140.

which some ministers augmented by farming, practising medicine, or teaching school.[153]

The Presbyterians, however, were free of one of the problems that beset the Anglicans in supplying an adequate number of clergymen. The Presbyterian minister was licensed and ordained by a local presbytery and so needed to make no expensive and dangerous ocean voyage. Strict insistence was placed, however, on an adequate education as a preparation for the ministry, and to that end the "log college" in Pennsylvania, the College of New Jersey, later Princeton, and Dr. Francis Alison's academy at New London, later moved to Newark, were established.[154]

In the Delaware State the greatest concentration of Presbyterians was in New Castle County, where they had first landed. Neither they nor their ministers felt any love for England or its Hanoverian monarch; this in part explains why New Castle was the most decidedly Whig county in Delaware, for "the Presbyterians . . . almost all, without exception, proved fiery advocates for independency." [155] Four of the most prominent Presbyterian ministers in the three counties, William McKennan of Red Clay Creek, Joseph Montgomery of New Castle and Christiana, John Miller of Dover, and Mathew Wilson of Lewes, were intimately allied to the Revolutionary cause. McKennan's son was a captain in the Delaware Regiment.[156] Montgomery delivered a sermon on July 20, 1775, in which he stated that "a defensive war is lawful," "revolutionary principles justify resistance against unlawful power," and the choice must be made either to fight for liberty or "submit our necks to the yoke"—stronger statements than the Continental Congress was making at this time. He later became an army chap-

---

[153] John Montgomery Forster, *A Sketch of the Life of the Rev. Joseph Montgomery* (Harrisburg, 1879), 29; *Delaware Gazette*, April 17, 1790; *Delaware Register*, II, 191–193; Patrick Lyon, *The Narrative of Patrick Lyon* . . . (Philadelphia, 1799), 14.

[154] On January 11, 1775, John Rankin, "a young Gentleman from ye Accademy of New Ark" applied to be received as a candidate for the ministry. But since he had no college degree the presbytery was of divided opinion and decided to ask the synod: "May Presbyteries license Persons to preach ye Gospel who have not obtained a Degree from some College?" Records of New Castle Presbytery, IV, 107.

[155] Tingley to Secretary of S.P.G., New York, March 5, 1782, Perry, *Collections*, V, 135.

[156] Bellas, *Delaware Cincinnati*, 63.

lain and a member of Congress from Pennsylvania.[157] John Miller also anticipated independence, preaching, prior to July, 1776, on the text, "We have no part in David, nor any inheritance in the son of Jesse: to your tents, O Israel!" [158] Two of his sons served as army surgeons, one dying in the service in 1777.[159] Mathew Wilson was an ardent republican, who wrote and spoke against the Stamp Act. Later, after the colonists protested the tea monopoly, he refused to drink tea and even published an article discussing the injurious effects of tea-drinking and recommending seventeen vegetable substitutes.[160] Among the many Presbyterian laymen who distinguished themselves by civil or military activities during the Revolution were Colonel John Haslet, who was killed at Princeton, John McKinly and Nicholas Van Dyke, presidents of the state, James Tilton, George Monro and Henry Latimer, army surgeons, Colonel David Hall, and Major John Patten.

The pacifist Quakers of Delaware could not, of course, present any list of military heroes, but they too had their martyrs of the Revolution. One such was John Cowgill, a farmer of Little Creek, Kent County, who had refused to accept continental money, since he, like many Friends, felt that to do so would be to sustain the continental army which was supplied through the issue of this money. Although threatened by a patriotic assembly, he would not submit. His horse was stolen, his cattle and sheep driven away, his grain taken. On his way to meeting he was seized by a company of armed men who ordered him into a cart, conducted him to Dover and forced him to parade through the streets with a placard on his back. Again warnings were issued to him and again he refused to heed them. His grain was refused at the mill; his children were turned out of school. "When we went to bed at night," his

---

[157] The speech referred to was printed with a dedication to Colonel Samuel Patterson, Major Gunning Bedford, and other Delaware officers. Forster, *Life of Montgomery*, 25–28, 30–32.

[158] Edward F. Humphrey, *Nationalism and Religion in America, 1774–1789* (Boston, 1924), 100.

[159] *Delaware Register*, II, 114; Samuel Miller, ed., *Medical Works of Edward Miller . . . with a Biographical Sketch* (New York, 1814), xiii; T. Rodney, MS. poem, "An Epicedium on Doctr. J. M.," folder, "Original Poems of T. Rodney," Rodney Collection.

[160] *Delaware Register*, II, 192–193. Thomas Read, the minister at Old Drawyers, was another ardent rebel.

daughter wrote, "we did not know what would be the issue before day and in that way we lived for several years." [161]

The Quakers were most numerous in Wilmington and to the northwest and in Kent County, particularly in the neighborhood of Duck Creek.[162] Their suffering in the Revolution arose from their desire to be neutrals, to take no part in wars or revolutions. Warner Mifflin journeyed from Kent to Philadelphia to urge both Howe and Washington to lay down their arms. He refused passes in crossing from one army to another and by his courage and sincerity won the admiration but not the compliance of the generals.[163] Retreating from participation in the great events of the times, the Quakers devoted themselves to mending their own fences. They expelled slaveholding from their society, attacked drunkenness, promoted temperance, urged plainness of speech, behavior, dress, and furnishings, and inquired into the morals and the education of their youth.[164] Years later a Quaker woman asserted that "many of the important testimonys which was maintained by frds. and was almost peculiar to them as a people; are now picked up and become matter of deep interest to those very people, who reviled and persecuted frds. on account thereof—Peace Societys, Temperance Societys,—Abbolition Societys. . . ." [165]

As the Quakers marked time, the Baptists in Delaware were actively proselyting. Their oldest church was that at the Welsh Tract, near Newark, founded by a group of Welshmen who came from Pembroke and Carmarthen counties via Pennsylvania.[166] This church, a member claimed, "was the principal, if not sole, means

[161] Mary Corbit to John Cowgill, Cantwell's Bridge, June 18, 1825, Corbit, Higgins, Spruance Papers.

[162] Joseph Oxley, an itinerant Quaker, visited Wilmington in about 1770, finding that "the chief part of the inhabitants of this town, which is a very improving one, are under our denomination." Rufus M. Jones, *The Quakers in the American Colonies* (London, 1923), 524. In addition to the meetings in New Castle and Kent counties, there were small meetings at Lewes and Cool Spring in Sussex. Conrad, *History of Delaware*, II, 714, 720.

[163] Justice, *Warner Mifflin*, 41–69, 102.

[164] Jones, *Quakers in American Colonies*, 565–574.

[165] Sarah Cowgill to Mary Corbit [Appoquinimink, n.d.], Corbit, Higgins, Spruance Papers.

[166] Richard B. Cook, *The Early and Later Delaware Baptists* (Philadelphia, c. 1880), 14.

of introducing singing, imposition of hands, ruling elders, and church covenants into the Middle States." [167] Welsh Tract served as the mother church for most of the other Baptist churches which appeared in New Castle and Kent counties—*e. g.*, at Wilmington, Duck Creek, Cow Marsh, Mispillion—before the Revolution. The faith was brought to Sussex County from Virginia during the Revolution by Elijah Baker and Philip Hughes.[168]

The Baptists in Delaware won some new members from the Presbyterians and the Quakers, but most of their proselytes were from among the great unchurched body of Anglicans. Their activities in 1779 inspired Asbury to one of his rare witticisms: "I found the Baptists were fishing in troubled water, (they always are preaching water to people,) and are striving to get in all the houses where we preach. . . . I met with a woman who warmly contended for dipping, as though it had been for life. Another began with me about going to their houses; and said, we must all live in heaven. I said, there will be no rebaptizing there. She said, we must imitate our Lord. I said, our Lord rebuked the wind and walked upon the sea." [169] The rector at Lewes, Samuel Tingley, called a plague on both houses in 1782: "I have . . . had to encounter for three years past with the enthusiastic notions of Ignorant methodists and anabaptists, some of whose absurdities has as direct a tendency to overturn all order and decency in the Church, as the base principles and practices of those who call themselves Whigs (a soft term for rebels) have in the state." [170]

The most noted Baptist in Delaware was Morgan Edwards, Welsh-born, Anglican-reared historian of the church and a founder of Brown University. Leaving the active ministry in 1772, he moved from Philadelphia to a farm in Pencader Hundred where he remained for the rest of his life. Edwards is reputed to have been the

[167] Morgan Edwards, "History of the Baptists in Delaware," *Pennsylvania Magazine of History and Biography*, IX (1885), 52.

[168] Cook, *op. cit.*, 15, 22–26, 28, 34; Edwards, *op. cit.*, 51, 60–61; Conrad, *History of Delaware*, II, 627, 659.

[169] Asbury, *Journal*, I, 315–316. The next year Asbury "appointed brother Wyatt to keep the ground against the Baptists, and to supply our places here instead of the traveling preachers that are going to conference; for John's people intend to come a fishing about, when we are gone." *Ibid.*, I, 361.

[170] To Secretary of S.P.G., New York, March 5, 1782, Perry, *Collections*, V, 139.

only Baptist preacher in America who was a loyalist sympathizer.[171] In Delaware, however, the Baptists were such humble folk that they caused little stir in politics.[172]

Certain other faiths existed in Delaware at the beginning of the Revolution. A Swedish Lutheran Church still carried on the worship known to the first settlers at Wilmington. The preaching, however, was now in English, the language of the old country having been forgotten by the parishioners.[173] Lawrence Girelius, the pastor, "an accomplished gentleman and scholar of a high order," [174] was the last to be secured from Sweden. During the Revolution militia were quartered in the church and services were discontinued. Girelius threatened to return to Sweden as the inflation made his salary of £140, later raised to £200, insufficient; nevertheless he remained till 1791.[175]

The few Catholics in Delaware at this time were mostly unchurched, although priests occasionally came from Maryland to minister to them. Just before the Revolution, in 1772, a chapel was built in New Castle County, at Coffee Run, near Mt. Cuba.[176] An unusual group called the Nicholites, holding some Quaker principles, dwelt in western Kent and on the Eastern Shore of Maryland. They were "sprung from one Nicols, a visionary, but I hope a good man," according to Asbury, who found them in 1780 under the

[171] Cook, *Delaware Baptists*, 59–60; A. H. Newman, *History of the Baptist Churches in the United States* (New York, 1894), 278–279; Horace W. Smith, *Life and Correspondence of the Rev. William Smith, D.D.* (Philadelphia, 1879– 1880), I, 293; Moses Coit Tyler, *The Literary History of the American Revolution, 1763–1783* (New York, 1897), II, 387–391; Edwards, "History of Baptists in Delaware," 45–46.

[172] Of the minister at the Welsh Tract Church after 1777, Edwards wrote: "He is popular among one class of hearers, and were he to labor at finding out the fixed meanings of words, the right way of pronouncing, accenting, and tacking them together in concords, he might be tolerable to classes of some refinements. As it is, he grates their ears so with barbarisms as to check their attention and hurt their feelings." Edwards, *op. cit.*, 58.

[173] Nelson W. Rightmyer, "Swedish-English Relations in Northern Delaware," *Church History* (June, 1946), XV, 11.

[174] Montgomery, *Reminiscences*, 131.

[175] Rightmyer, *op. cit.*, 11–13. Cf. *The Records of Holy Trinity (Old Swedes) Church*, Horace Burr, trans., *Papers of the Historical Society of Delaware*, IX (Wilmington, 1890), 510–513.

[176] Eugene J. Kraemer, "The Catholic Church in Delaware," Reed, *Delaware*, II, 681; Rightmyer, *Anglican Church in Delaware*, 41, 55, 138.

leadership of James Harris and left a description of them: "They clothe in white, take everything from nature, and condemn all other societies that do not conform to the outward: If a man were to speak like an archangel; if he sung, prayed, and wore a black, or a coloured coat, he would not be received by these people. . . . They oppose family prayer as much as any sinners in the country. . . ." [177]

XI. The Methodists

ANOTHER faith arose like the Nicholites in rural Delaware and the Maryland Eastern Shore on the peninsula which became known as its American cradle. Sired by John Wesley, carried to the New World by Francis Asbury and his precursors and successors, it grew amid the suspicions and persecutions of a war-racked land. Its mission "was not . . . to the great and noble, . . . to the cultured, the fashionable, the aesthetic," but "to the masses, just as God made them, . . . covered with wounds and blood—steeped in ignorance and sin. . . ." It found its clergy in the fields and at the wayside, required of them little but conviction, and sent them forth to the mass of people, the great unchurched, untended peninsular body. "I sighed for the backwoods," one preacher cried, "which were a Paradise to me compared with this suffocating borough [Wilmington]." In their backwoods the Methodist preachers, "normal specimens of a God-made race," wept or shouted, thundered "the dread maledictions of Jehovah, in sorrowful threats of a lake of literal fire and brimstone," and convulsed "an audience by their ludicrous caricatures of the solemn visaged hypocrite, or by their mimicry of the insane and grotesque antics of the silly despisers of God." [178]

[177] Asbury, *Journal*, I, 350. *Cf. ibid.*, 344; Kenneth Carroll, "Joseph Nichols and the Nicholites of Caroline County, Maryland," *Maryland Historical Magazine*, XLV (1950), 47–61; Carroll, "More about the Nicholites," *ibid.*, XLVI (1951), 278–289.

[178] Robert W. Todd, *Methodism of the Peninsula* . . . (Philadelphia, c. 1886), 12, 25.

Methodism was introduced into Delaware shortly before 1770 by Robert Strawbridge, an Ulsterman and an independent itinerant, and Captain Thomas Webb, a one-eyed veteran of the British army.[179] In 1772 Francis Asbury, greatest of the early Methodist evangelists sent to America by John Wesley, appeared in various places in Delaware. He preached in Wilmington, "though there were but few to hear." In New Castle he "met with opposition, and found the Methodists had done no great good." The tavern-keeper who received him "lost his company" by doing so; though it was "open for dances and balls" Methodists were refused permission to meet in the courthouse. When a year later Asbury returned, he reported many of the people "devoted to pride, vanity, and folly," and when he reappeared in New Castle in 1774, he discovered "Satan was there, diverting the people by a play." [180]

The success of the church downstate more than compensated, however, for any indifference shown in Wilmington and New Castle. Here its real growth dates from 1778, when Asbury fled to Kent County from Maryland where he had refused to take a required oath of loyalty which pledged him to bear arms if called upon.[181] From 1775, when Wesley published his *Calm Address to the American Colonies*, a strong loyalist argument, all of his ministers became suspect in the eyes of American rebels. Caesar Rodney, for instance, was convinced that the Methodist ministers were raising a force of Tories on the Maryland line in 1777.[182] In April, 1778, a hundred Tories under Cheney Clow, a "back-sliding Methodist," began a counter-revolution in western Kent and threatened to march on Dover.[183] A Methodist missionary, Martin Rodda, for dis-

---

[179] James M. Buckley, *A History of Methodism in the United States* (New York, 1898), I, 136; Rightmyer, *Anglican Church in Delaware*, 116; William W. Sweet, *Methodism in American History* (New York, c. 1933), 52, 57. The visits of George Whitefield in 1739 and later stirred up great excitement but led to no permanent Methodist associations.

[180] Asbury, *Journal*, I, 27–28, 81, 112.

[181] In Delaware "the clergy were not required to take the State-oath: though, with a clear conscience, I could have taken the oath of the Delaware State, had it been required; and would have done it had I not been prevented by a tender fear of hurting the scrupulous consciences of others." *Ibid.*, I, 272.

[182] C. Rodney to G. Washington, Middletown, Sept. 6, 1777, Rodney, *Letters*, 219.

[183] Harold B. Hancock, *The Delaware Loyalists, Papers of the Historical Society of Delaware*, New Series, III, (Wilmington, 1940), 34; Freeborn Garrettson, *The*

tributing the king's proclamation in Delaware, was forced to take refuge on a British ship.[184] Consequently, Asbury found it wise during much of the two years he spent in Delaware, to remain in partial seclusion. Admitted to the home of a devout Anglican, Judge Thomas White, father of Senator Samuel White, he debated "whether to deliver myself into the hands of men, to embrace the first opportunity to depart, or to wait till Providence shall further direct." [185] He decided on the last course, but when Judge White, himself, was seized by the state authorities, Asbury was temporarily deprived of refuge. During the five weeks White was detained, Asbury travelled about on back roads, hiding in swamps and with strangers. At White's home Asbury met a man who was to become the most prominent Methodist convert in Delaware, Richard Bassett of Bohemia Manor, landowner, lawyer and militia officer, as well as a future senator and governor.[186]

Despite his difficulties, Asbury did succeed in kindling a spiritual fire that soon began to burn bright. "The congregations were attentive and affected, . . . although . . . rude and unpolished," he wrote on August 2, 1778. On October 1 "there was a gracious melting in the congregation," and an "untaught audience felt the weight of Divine truth." To be sure there were times when the audience was "ignorant, hardened," "under the influence of a spiritual torpor," "proof against the power of the word," times when he had to turn out "the disorderly members," yet he found his "spirit at liberty in preaching to those untaught people, who behaved with seriousness and attention," and he entertained the hope that "as the gospel of Jesus Christ meets with indulgence in this free State, . . . it will prove a general blessing; and that Delaware will become as the garden of the Lord, filled with plants of his own planting." [187]

Other Methodist preachers also flocked to the state, and "melting times," faintings, and prostrations became common occurrences as

---

Experiences and Travels of Mr. Freeborn Garrettson . . . (Philadelphia, 1791), 77.

[184] Sweet, *Methodism in America*, 91–92.

[185] Asbury, *Journal*, I, 272.

[186] Buckley, *History of Methodism*, I, 217–220; Sweet, *Methodism in America*, 88–89; Robert E. Pattison, *Life and Character of Richard Bassett, Papers of the Historical Society of Delaware*, XXIX, (Wilmington, 1900), 12–13.

[187] Asbury, *Journal*, I, 280, 281, 283, 284, 286, 290, 292.

the thrill of the power of God's word entered the monotonous lives of the peninsular farming folk. Freeborn Garrettson, a native of the Eastern Shore, swept like the wrath of God through the peninsula, breathing such eloquence that many a humble auditor became frenzied or collapsed, unable to withstand the shock of this new world of emotion. In 1778 Garrettson entered Dover, hitherto "a proverb for wickedness," and was invited to preach in the academy. As he alighted from his horse, a crowd gathered, shouting, "He is one of Clowe's men! Hang him! Hang him!" But the Lord interposed, Garrettson reported later, just as "I was in a fair way to be torn to pieces." Instead of suffering the hangman's rope, he was safely escorted to a stage at the academy's door, the people flocking round, "both within and without." After singing and prayer, he preached on the text: "If it bear fruit well, and if not, then after that thou shalt chop it down." "We rarely see such a weeping company in a new place," he reported. "One woman was powerfully wrought upon, who sat in her window more than a quarter of a mile off"; even the ringleader of the once-threatening mob was converted.[188]

"Under a large spreading tree" at "Muskmelon" on another occasion, Garrettson "gave out, 'One thing I know, whereas I was blind now I see,'" to which there was much "weeping and mourning among poor sinners," and many conversions. An officer in the audience "threw up his commission and became a pious follower of Christ." And again, at Marshy Hope, "the word ran through all the congregation, and there was a great shaking among the people. Among the rest, a woman was struck, and cried aloud for mercy, till she fell to the ground. Her husband was much offended. . . ." [189]

Organization followed evangelism. In 1779, a year in which Asbury reported, "It affords me some satisfaction to find that the people in these parts appear to advance in religion," the Methodists formed a Delaware Circuit, with a reported membership of 795. With the organization a year later of two more circuits, this membership was increased to 1135.[190] A preliminary conference of preachers of the northern circuits, held in April, 1779, prepared for

[188] Garrettson, *Experiences and Travels*, 93–96.
[189] *Ibid.*, 86, 90–91.
[190] Asbury, *Journal*, I, 305; *Minutes of the Methodist Conferences 1773 to 1794* . . . (n.p., c. 1794), 33, 40; Conrad, *History of Delaware*, II, 606–607.

a second conference at Fluvanna, Virginia, where Asbury, under the title of General Assistant, was given power to determine issues in America as Wesley did in England.[191]

The purpose of this action was to unite the Methodists, for those in the South seemed to be schismatic. Asbury, who desired to maintain good relations with the Anglicans, was determined that the Methodist preachers, themselves, should not administer the sacraments but should instead resort to the Church of England for baptism and communion. He became very friendly with Samuel Magaw, the rector at Dover, who treated him "with exceeding great kindness." "The people of these parts (the most wealthy not excepted)," declared Asbury, "are for the most part, very courteous and friendly." [192] He frequently attended Magaw's services and also those of another Anglican rector, Sydenham Thorne, and Magaw, Thorne, and Hugh Neill, formerly of Delaware but now rector of an Eastern Shore parish, all attended a Methodist quarterly meeting in November, 1779, with a willingness "to give . . . all the assistance they could by word and deed." Magaw and Neill also attended quarterly meetings in 1780. The reaction of the Presbyterian ministers was, however, quite different, for they were usually very unfriendly. Asbury heard about one minister, probably Mathew Wilson of Lewes, who went so far as to proclaim a fast "to let the people know what the Methodists were," telling them that the Methodists "must be sent of the devil." [193]

Although willing to preserve a connection with the Anglican church, Asbury gradually came to realize that the common assumption of a connection between Methodism and Tory sympathies made necessary the development of a distinctly American Methodist organization, to be in no way connected with wartime politics. When talking with a Presbyterian minister in 1779, Asbury was embarrassed by charges made against the Methodists and "could not attempt a vindication of those amongst us who had dipped deep in politics." [194] Asbury's efforts to this end in Delaware were not with-

[191] Asbury, *Journal*, I, 309; *Minutes of Methodist Conferences*, 27–29; Sweet, *Methodism in America*, 93–94.
[192] Asbury, *Journal*, I, 307–308; Buckley, *History of Methodism*, I, 225; Rightmyer, *Anglican Church in Delaware*, 117–118.
[193] Asbury, *Journal*, I, 327, 333, 362, 409; see also, 312, 313, 340, 353, 358, 361.
[194] *Ibid.*, 308. *Cf., ibid.*, 318.

out reward, for in 1780 he observed that "prejudices wear off; . . . bad as these people were, they never persecuted us, as they have done at some other places.[195] Surmounting the charge of Toryism, winning the adherence of such prominent men as the Whites, Bassett, and Allen McLane,[196] and, most important of all, developing a device, the circuit with its itinerant preachers, by which to reach a people otherwise without spiritual solace, the Methodists grew steadily, quite disappointing a Kent Countian who, on hearing of the construction of Barratt's Chapel, had commented: "It is unnecessary to build such a house, for by the time the war is over, a corn-crib will hold them all." [197]

Methodist success may also be partly attributed to the careful attention they gave to the young. Asbury recommended that all the ministers conduct meetings with children as "an important but much neglected duty." In proposing such a meeting himself, he requested "parents to send a note with each [child], letting me know the temper and those vices to which the child might be most subject." Naturally much interested in education, he and Magaw planned the establishment of a school in Dover,[198] and the Methodist conference recommended the inauguration of Sunday schools in order to provide free reading instruction to poor children, both white and black.[199]

The welfare of colored people was important to early Methodism. Ministers were required "to leave nothing undone for the spiritual benefit and salvation of the negroes, within their respective

[195] *Ibid.*, 356. Yet within a month he wrote: "I am in heaviness through the deadness of the people, and the lies of the wicked about us—of which there appear to be enough; and it does seem now as if they could freely shed our blood. . . ." *Ibid.*, 359.

[196] Henry Boehm, *Reminiscences, Historical and Biographical, of Sixty-Four Years in the Ministry* (New York, 1865), 88; Buckley, *History of Methodism*, I, 220–221; Pattison, *Bassett*, 12–13. On Sunday, February 4, 1781, Asbury wrote: "I preached [in Dover], and had some of the Council and members of the Assembly to hear me. I spoke plainly; intending my discourse as a vindication of the doctrine of the Methodists." Asbury, *Journal*, I, 420.

[197] Buckley, *op. cit.*, I, 210. In 1780 the Methodists had eight ministers in Delaware, whereas the Anglicans, the largest sect in membership, had but five. Rightmyer, *Anglican Church in Delaware*, 119.

[198] Asbury, *Journal*, I, 340, 410, 412, 413.

[199] "Let persons appointed by the bishops, elders, deacons or preachers, to teach (gratis) all that will attend, and have a capacity to learn; from six o'clock in the morning till ten; and from two o'clock in the afternoon till six. . . ." *Minutes of Methodist Conferences*, 146. *Ibid.*, 104.

circuits," "to embrace every opportunity of inquiring into the state of their souls," to unite the sincere with the Methodist society, "to meet such in class, and to exercise the whole methodist discipline among them." Travelling preachers were ordered in 1780 to free any slaves they might own; "slave-keeping" was declared "contrary to the laws of God, man and nature and hurtful to society; contrary to the dictates of conscience and pure reason." [200] The Conference also disapproved "the practice of distilling grain into liquor" and ordered members not to operate distilleries.[201] Sternly advocating habits of early rising and industry, preachers were told to "make conscience of rising at four, and if not, yet at five, and is it not a shame for a Preacher to be in bed till six in the morning." [202]

Before he left his refuge in Delaware, Asbury noted definite signs of progress: "Before, the people were swearers, drunkards, fighters, horse-racers, and such like; but the Lord hath done great things for them." On each return to Delaware he noted further improvement.[203] His view is supported by a Methodist historian who claims that at this time, "the greatest revival of religion had been on the southern shore of Maryland and in some parts of Delaware." [204] But, "in this our labour," wrote Asbury, "we have to encounter hunger, heat, and many restless nights with mosquitoes, unwholesome provisions, and bad water: but all this is for souls; were it for silver, I should require a great sum." [205]

XII. The Schools

IN pre-Revolutionary Delaware the pattern of settlement on farms and in small towns made the support of schools as difficult as that of

---

[200] *Ibid.*, 38, 62, 103–104.
[201] *Ibid.*, 39, 62.
[202] *Ibid.*, 37.
[203] Asbury, *Journal*, I, 317, 325, 344, 409. "I think," he wrote on January 14, 1781, "for ignorance of God and religion, the wilds and swamps of Delaware exceed most parts of America with which I have had any acquaintance; however, God is able of these stones to raise up children unto Abraham." *Ibid.*, 418.
[204] Buckley, *History of Methodism*, I, 231.
[205] Asbury, *Journal*, I, 313.

churches. Indeed, many Delawareans received no formal education at all. One writer suggested that less than half of the people could keep accounts or write.[206] While no one can determine the exact amount of illiteracy, the number of crude "X's" on petitions to the legislature through the several following decades gives evidence that a large proportion of the people could not even sign their names.

Public, tax-supported education did not exist. Such schooling as was available depended upon religious societies and their ministers, upon private teachers, and upon a few schools, formally or informally established. Of all these elements the church was the most important, for here the responsibility for education had traditionally rested since the time of Swedish and Dutch colonization. The ministers, however, were too few, the funds available too small, and the people too scattered for church-sponsored education to reach the masses.

Anglican missionaries were granted some funds for parish libraries and for the distribution of tracts to the people, and it is likely that some of them augmented their small stipends by teaching.[207] Quakers, lacking a clergy, had to hire schoolmasters. In the 1740s, shortly after their settlement in Wilmington, they established a school where boys and girls were taught in separate departments. Other Quaker schools appeared, at least briefly, on Duck Creek and on White Clay Creek.[208]

Presbyterians also took much interest in education. A school founded by the Rev. Francis Alison at New London, Pennsylvania, in 1743, was moved first to Cecil County, Maryland, and then to Newark, Delaware, by his successor, the Rev. Alexander McDowell. At Newark it was chartered by the Penns in 1769 as the Newark Academy, a non-sectarian institution.[209] A former student

---

[206] Todd, *Methodism of the Peninsula*, 16.

[207] Rightmyer, *Anglican Church in Delaware*, 163.

[208] Montgomery, *Reminiscences*, 322; Conrad, *History of Delaware*, II, 615; Lyman P. Powell, *The History of Education in Delaware* (Washington, 1893), 43, 138–139; William C. Dunlap, *Quaker Education in Baltimore and Virginia Yearly Meetings with an Account of Certain Meetings of Delaware and the Eastern Shore Affiliated with Philadelphia* (Philadelphia, 1936), 250, 253, 310–312.

[209] Powell, *Education in Delaware*, 72–75; *A Brief History of the University of Delaware* (Newark, 1940), 6. The 1769 charter is in the Memorial Library, University of Delaware. *Cf.* George H. Ryden, "The Relation of the Newark Academy of Delaware to the Presbyterian Church and to Higher Education in the American Colonies," *Delaware Notes*, ninth series (Newark, 1935), 7–42.

and teacher in this academy, the Rev. Mathew Wilson, later conducted a school in Lewes.[210] In 1773 the New Castle Presbytery declared that a plan recommended by the Synod of Philadelphia for "the Education of poor and pious youths" was "impracticable," but agreed to help such youths gain an education fitting them for the ministry "when any such" appeared "to need . . . Assistance." [211]

Individual Presbyterians, without ecclesiastical position or support, were also important in the history of Delaware education. Usually well educated, the Scotch-Irishman was in great demand as a teacher. Sometimes Scotch-Irishmen purchased as indentured servants were used as tutors. Planters in need of a tutor for their children are said to have exclaimed, when they saw an immigrant ship come up the river, "Let us go & buy a School Master." Other farmers hired a teacher by the year and boarded him around in turn. "The office & character of such a person is very mean & contemptible here," wrote George Ross, early in the eighteenth century, "& it cannot be other ways, 'til the public takes the Education of Children into their mature consideration." [212]

Many teachers opened their own schools. A Scotchman called Master Wilson taught classical and elementary subjects in Wilmington in 1760.[213] John Filson, who later achieved fame as a Kentucky surveyor and writer, had an elementary school there before and after the Revolution but gave it up because a wounded arm prevented him from disciplining his pupils.[214] John Thelwell, a devout Methodist, taught in Wilmington for half a century. He occupied innumerable town offices, apparently needing them all to make a decent living. In his school first the British Horn Book, then Dilworth's speller, Gough's arithmetic, and the Bible were standard texts, and a prayer and a hymn were the opening exercises. "The rattan or the ferule seemed to be in perpetual motion, and were as common in his seminary as gymnastics are at this day. . . ." [215]

[210] Delaware Register, II, 192; Delaware Gazette, April 17, 1790.
[211] Records of New Castle Presbytery, III, 347.
[212] Perry, Collections, V, 47.
[213] Montgomery, Reminiscences, 241.
[214] John Hamilton, "Some Reminiscences of Wilm't'n and My Youthful Days—&c., &c.," Delaware History, I (July, 1946), 89; Powell, Education in Delaware, 47.
[215] Hamilton, "Reminiscences," 90; Montgomery, Reminiscences, 227–229. Reference to other schoolmasters is found in extracts from the minutes of the Wilmington Monthly Meeting in Dunlap, Quaker Education, 252–253.

The most pretentious school in Wilmington was the Wilmington Academy, which was established in the 1760s and was chartered as a public grammar school for New Castle County in 1773. Lawrence Girelius, pastor of the Lutheran Church, was the first president of its board of trustees, and among the early members of the board were Bishop White, Thomas McKean, Dr. William Smith, Joseph Shallcross, Thomas and Vincent Gilpin, George Read, and Dr. Nicholas Way. The classes, held in its stone building surrounded by a fine grove of trees, were under the direction of one Robert Patterson when the Revolution began. He drilled the youth of the town in military tactics and later himself joined the army. Classes were suspended during several of the war years, when the building was occupied at times by each army. Public annual examinations of the students were held, with testing and recitations during the day and the enacting of scenes from Shakespeare in the evening.[216]

A part of the market square in New Castle was set aside by the assembly in 1772 for the erection of a schoolhouse and was placed under five trustees.[217] A schoolhouse was erected at Christiana Bridge in 1769 at a cost of more than one hundred pounds.[218] Joseph Coleman was brought to Dover by Asbury in 1780 to set up a school there.[219] Nathaniel Luff was taught by the Rev. Charles Inglis and other less competent men in Dover.[220] A grammar school existed at the head of the Bohemia River, on the Maryland line, in 1775.[221] In 1768 there was not a grammar school in Sussex County and consequently the man was rare who could "write a tolerable hand or spell with propriety the most common words. . . ." A schoolhouse had been built in Lewes and several attempts made to

---

[216] Montgomery, *Reminiscences*, 293–295; Scharf, *History of Delaware*, II, 686; Rightmyer, *Anglican Church in Delaware*, 164–165; *Pennsylvania Gazette*, May 1, 1776; T. Rodney to C. Rodney, Wilmington, May 7, 1782, Rodney Collection. Caesar A. Rodney's tuition here in 1782 cost less than two shillings a quarter. T. Rodney to Trustees of Wilmington Grammar School, May 8 and August 8, 1782, Brown Collection. *Cf.* E. Miriam Lewis, ed., "The Minutes of the Wilmington Academy, 1777–1802," *Delaware History* (Sept., 1949), III, 181–226.

[217] David Finney, John Thompson, George Read, Thomas McKean, and George Monro. *Laws*, I, 516–517.

[218] Memorandum in folder, "Delaware Schools," HSD.

[219] Rightmyer, *Anglican Church in Delaware*, 120, 162.

[220] Luff, *Journal*, 3–6. *Cf.*, *Calendar of Ridgely Family Papers*, I, 20.

[221] Samuel D. Alexander, *Princeton College during the Eighteenth Century* (New York, *c.* 1872), 29–30; Samuel Miller, *Memoirs of the Rev. John Rodgers, D.D.* (New York, 1813), 96 ff.

establish a Latin school, but the "extreme poverty" of the people caused each attempt to fail.[222]

Girls as well as boys were taught in many of the schools. Next door to the Wilmington Academy lived Major John Patten's sister, who "had in charge a number of misses from distant places to be educated here." John Thelwell's sister Debby, a "worthy woman but with no literary pretensions," "assisted and kept the girls in order." Miss S. Hanson was "celebrated for the excellent government of misses" and had many girls from far points under her care.[223] Mrs. Elizabeth Way, mother of Dr. Nicholas Way and friend of Benjamin West, taught needlework, including "the art of shirt-making." A strict disciplinarian, she used switches and cat-o'-nine-tails freely and insisted on proper posture. If a pupil's "head leaned down, Jamestown-weed burs strung on tape were ready for a necklace"; if a pupil's back stooped, a steel the length of the waist was at hand which fastened by a strap and included a piece which went around the neck to hold the chin up. "A morocco spider worn on the back, confined to the shoulders by a belt, was more usual." [224] Master Wilson had girls in his school, although he thought few of them should proceed in arithmetic further than simple division; "only tom-boys, with big slates," Wilson felt, "would care to cipher in the Double Rule of Three." [225] A tradition claims that Lewes had the oldest school for girls in the colonies; at any rate Thomas Lloyd of Philadelphia sent his daughters there to finish their education.[226]

Vocational education was provided by the apprenticeship system. Bartis Comegys, of Kent County, Maryland, apprenticed his seventeen-year-old son, John, to Thomas Rodney for four years to learn the "Art and Mistery of Shop and book-keeping," binding the contract with a money payment. Rodney was to furnish "meat, drink, washing, lodging and waring apparrel" and a "new sute of Cloaths," in addition to the usual apparel at the end of the term of

[222] John Andrews to S.P.G. [Lewes], August 4, 1768, Rightmyer, *Anglican Church in Delaware*, 86. Thomas Penn ordered in 1734 that the income from the Great Marsh, a Lewes commons, be applied to education. Scharf, *History of Delaware*, II, 1230.

[223] Montgomery, *Reminiscences*, 229, 293, 315.

[224] *Ibid.*, 239–240.

[225] *Ibid.*, 241; Scharf, *History of Delaware*, II, 684.

[226] Powell, *Education in Delaware*, 60–61.

apprenticeship. John was to behave "well and Truly, and Honestly and soberly." [227]

The most important preparatory school in the lower counties was the Newark Academy, to which King George and Dr. Johnson contributed, when agents were sent abroad to solicit funds.[228] In 1768, one year before it secured a formal charter, the founder, Dr. Alison, then vice-provost of the College of Philadelphia, wrote that the academy had sixty boys under the care of a rector and two assistants, who taught "the Languages, . . . Arithmetick, Euclid's Elements, . . . Practical branches of the Mathematicks, & Logick." Students preparing for the ministry went on to college, but those interested in "law or Physick" were generally content with the proficiency in liberal arts which they acquired here. The students paid ten to fifteen pounds a year for lodgings and three pounds ten shillings for tuition. "Hence farmers can educate their children, so as to fit ym. for almost any station in life, yt. could not hope for such advantages, were they obliged to educate ym. in this City, tho here they can finish their Education." [229]

Through the Presbyterian connection, which was, however, declining, the academy drew students from a considerable distance. Of nine graduates in 1775, four came from Delaware, two from Virginia, two from North Carolina, and one from Pennsylvania.[230] The success of the fund-raising mission of Williamson and Ewing to England and Scotland, plus other gifts, including one of land from Morgan Edwards, the Baptist minister, augured well for the future of the academy. In 1777, however, the academy was closed, as Newark came to be on the battle line. After serving for a time as a shoe factory, it was reopened in approximately 1780 under William

[227] Indenture, April 11, 1774, Brown Collection.

[228] In 1772 Dr. Hugh Williamson solicited funds in the West Indies for the Newark Academy. George E. Hastings, *The Life and Works of Francis Hopkinson* (Chicago, c. 1926), 58. Cf. *Pennsylvania Gazette*, October 11, 1775; W. B. Sprague, *Annals of the American Pulpit* (New York, 1858), III, 217; Beverly McAnear, "The Raising of Funds by the Colonial Colleges," *Mississippi Valley Historical Review*, XXXVIII (1951–1952), 591–612.

[229] F. Alison to Ezra Stiles, Philadelphia, May 7, 1768, F. B. Dexter, ed., *Extracts from the Itineraries and Other Miscellanies of Ezra Stiles* . . . (New Haven, 1916), 433.

[230] *Pennsylvania Gazette*, October 11, 1775. *Ibid.*, January 2, 1775, carries a notice of a lottery for the benefit of the academy.

Thomson.[231] In that year, the charter having been carried away by the British, the legislature received petitions begging it to "constitute a public Seminary" in Newark, where the academy had an acre of ground and a stone building large enough for eighty to one hundred boys. This town, it was argued, was in little danger of attack by the enemy, being distant from navigable water—the war was still going on—and it was healthy and moral. A public seminary would be "conducive to polish the genius of youth & for the Support & Maintenance of that Freedom & native Liberty which God & Nature hath Bestowed." [232] In 1781, the trustees informed the legislature that although board members had been sent to South Carolina, the West Indies, and Europe to solicit funds, in addition to their "private Contributions," their efforts "through various Accidents" had "proved ineffectual." Consequently, the state was asked to undertake the "Patronage of this Institution" and was urged to "erect it into a College upon a broad and catholick Bottom, securing equal Privileges for all Denominations of Christians. . . ." [233] Some residents of Newark urged again in 1782 that the legislature undertake to support the academy, which at this time had twenty-seven students.[234] In spite of these requests, the state took no action.

All of the schools were not as satisfactory as the Newark Academy seems to have been. The proprietors of the school at Christiana Bridge, "Fully Sensible of the Great Loss our Children Sustains by Employing of the present Master John Maulroy on account of his Irregular Conduct," appointed two of their members to find another teacher.[235] Nathaniel Luff studied Latin for two years in Dover but found when he went to Philadelphia at the age of fourteen that he knew so little he had to begin all over. The boys there laughed at his ignorance; Dr. Alison examined Luff and found he did not know even the meaning of "parsing." Yet the tuition was

[231] Powell, *Education in Delaware*, 75–77.

[232] Folder, "1780 March–April, Lewes, Education (Newark Academy)," Legislative Papers.

[233] Petition of January, 1781 (Memorial Library, University of Delaware, Newark). The signers of this first suggestion of a state college were Mathew Wilson, Thos. Read, Willm. McKennan, Alexr. McDowell, John Evans, Jno. McKinly, John Thompson, Thos. McKean, John Ewing, and Jos. Montgomery. An authorized copy of the charter was in the hands of the trustees.

[234] Petition of June 5, 1782 (Memorial Library, University of Delaware).

[235] Resolution, December 18, 1782, folder "Delaware Schools," HSD.

twice as high in Dover as in Philadelphia: "double price for errone-
ous principles." Luff explained that in Dover "a few men anxious for
the promotion of their children were excessively gulled by tutors—
themselves unacquainted with the learned languages and sciences,"
who taught nothing but bad habits.[236]

Frequently young men of the lower counties were sent, like Luff,
to other colonies for part of their schooling. Four Delawareans were
graduated from Princeton before the Revolution,[237] and still more
from the College of Philadelphia. Ministerial, legal, and medical
students went especially frequently to neighboring areas for schooling or apprenticeship. The clergy were more itinerant than the
lawyers and physicians; only a small part of the clergy of Delaware
had been born or reared in this state.

Among the lawyers, George Read was educated at New London,
Pennsylvania, in the academy of Francis Alison, and then read law
in Philadelphia. John Dickinson went to the Inns of Court in London, as did Benjamin Chew. Nicholas Ridgely studied with Robert
Goldsborough, in Cambridge, Maryland. David Hall and John
Vining read law in New Castle and Dover, respectively. John Parke
attended the Newark Academy and the College of Philadelphia,
before reading law in New Castle.[238]

Of the physicians, Henry Latimer, George Monro, and John R. B.
Rodgers went to Edinburgh to study. Joshua Clayton, James Tilton,
and Nicholas Way attended the College of Philadelphia. John
Brinckle studied in Philadelphia with William Shippen, Nathaniel
Luff with George Glentworth, and Charles Ridgely with Phineas
Bond. Some received all their training in Delaware: James Sykes,
Jr., went from the Newark Academy to study with Joshua Clayton,
Edward Miller from the same school to Charles Ridgely, and James
McCallmont to Mathew Wilson.[239] Dr. Nicholas Way also took
many students, especially from South Carolina.[240]

The only printing press in the lower counties before 1776 was

[236] Luff, *Journal*, 5–7.
[237] Alexander, *Princeton in the Eighteenth Century*, 29, 46, 189, 191.
[238] The general source for this paragraph is Scharf, *History of Delaware*, especially the chapter on "The Bench and the Bar," I, 508–610.
[239] The general source for this paragraph is Lewis P. Bush, "Medicine and
Medical Men," Scharf, *History of Delaware*, I, 470–507.
[240] Montgomery, *Reminiscences*, 303.

kept by James Adams, a Scotch-Irishman of Londonderry birth, who had come to Philadelphia before 1753 and worked there for Franklin and Hall. He set up in business for himself in Philadelphia in about 1760, but apparently to avoid competition moved to Wilmington in 1761. Here he printed laws and other government materials, almanacs, religious works, and educational books. When the British invaded Delaware in 1777 he moved his press to Doylestown, Pennsylvania, but he returned to Wilmington after the British evacuated Philadelphia in 1778. In 1762 he established the first and only pre-Revolutionary Delaware newspaper, the *Wilmington Courant,* but it was printed for less than a year. No copies of it are known to survive.[241]

Very little literature of artistic value had been produced in the lower counties. John Dickinson, reared in Kent, had become famous through his *Letters from a Farmer in Pennsylvania to the Inhabitants of the British Colonies,* which appeared in a Philadelphia newspaper in 1767–1768, were immediately copied by all but a few colonial journals, went through at least eight pamphlet editions, and, in the year of first publication, were republished in London, Dublin, and Amsterdam. Their appearance, it has been said, "constituted the most brilliant event in the literary history of the Revolution." [242] The author, however, was at this time making his home at Philadelphia, though he still held property in Delaware, to which he was to return.

John Parke, of Dover, who became a colonel in the Revolution, published in 1777 a series of eulogistic poems, commemorating Colonel John Haslet, also of Dover, General Mercer, and other Revolutionary heroes. Parke, the son of a hatter and Kent County sheriff, had attended Newark Academy and the College of Philadelphia and had studied law with McKean at New Castle. He is

[241] Dorothy Hawkins, "James Adams, the First Printer of Delaware," *Papers of the Bibliographical Society of America,* XXVIII (1934), pt. 1, 29–30; Dorothy Hawkins, A Checklist of Delaware Imprints up to and including 1800 . . . (M.S. thesis, Columbia University, 1928), typescript in Wilmington Institute Free Library, vi, ix, x, 73; Clarence S. Brigham, *History and Bibliography of American Newspapers, 1690–1820,* I (Worcester, 1947), 79.

[242] Tyler, *Literary History of the Revolution,* I, 234–239. Dickinson also wrote a popular poem which he called "A Song for American Freedom" and which became known as the "Liberty Song." It was published in the *Boston Gazette* in 1768. *Ibid.,* I, 239–241.

best known for his translation of the lyrics of Horace, which was published in 1786.[243]

It is more difficult to discover what was being read in Delaware than what was being written. Charles Ridgely's father allowed him to buy a set of the *Universal History* for eight pounds in Philadelphia in 1753. Thomas Rodney tells of reading Plutarch, Dryden, and a life of Peter the Great in September, 1769.[244] Thirty-five Delawareans subscribed to the first American edition of Blackstone, published in Philadelphia 1771–1773.[245] Newton was also known, for in Dover on August 29, 1769, Thomas Rodney was "alarm'd with the News of a Comett," and rushed "Next Door to Doctr. McCalls, . . . also a mathematician and there . . . Examined Sr. Isaac Newton to Know If he had Spoke of Any to Appear about this time. . . . Doctr. T[ilton] & Att[orney] V[ining] . . . Came there too."[246] Philadelphia newspapers circulated through the lower counties. Delawareans advertised in them, and the assembly recognized their availability by ordering notices to be placed in them.[247] Drama made at least one appearance in Delaware, for Asbury wrote, May 21, 1774, "At Newcastle on *Saturday*, Satan was there, diverting the people by a play."[248]

XIII. The Causes of Revolution

LIFE in the lower counties fostered few causes for revolution; few of the quarrels that rent other colonies had any grounds for existence here. There were neither Indians nor Indian lands in Delaware. There was no frontier to quarrel with the seaboard. The counties were so nearly equal in size and population that there was

[243] Hugh H. Brackenridge, *The Death of General Montgomery at the Siege of Quebec, to which are added Elegant Pieces, commemorative of distinguished characters* (Philadelphia, 1777). John C. French, "John Parke," *DAB*, XIV, 210–211.

[244] *Calendar of Ridgely Family Papers*, I, 73, 74; T. Rodney, Journal, 1769, Rodney Collection.

[245] Typed list from fourth volume in folder "Delaware General File," HSD.

[246] T. Rodney, Journal, 1769.

[247] *House Minutes*, October 26, 1768, pp. 164–165.

[248] Asbury, *Journal*, I, 112.

little complaint of sectional discrimination. There was no established church and little discrimination against any religious group. Proprietary power was not as serious an issue here as it was in the province to the north. The crown had never vetoed local legislation; indeed it appears that the acts of the colonial assembly were not even sent to England.[249] The dominant agricultural economy served to ally the people rather than to produce unfriendly vocational divisions among them.

The causes of Revolution in Delaware arose not from any internal development peculiar to this little colony but out of her close association with her neighbors and her connection with the civilization of a river valley. The commerce on the great waterway that coursed along the side of Delaware and bore her merchandise and her people to Philadelphia stimulated cultural, social, familial, and religious ties which disregarded colonial boundaries.[250] When, for example, in Philadelphia the Whartons' interest in Indian trade and western land speculation suffered hardships from the British trans-Appalachian policy after 1763, Delawareans who were intimately acquainted with Samuel Wharton and whose legislature later made him its delegate to Congress were moved to resentment.[251] If parliament's attempt to restrict American commerce injured the trade of the port of Philadelphia, the Brandywine millers were directly affected, and so were Delaware mariners like Hugh Montgomery, Delaware rivermen like Samuel Bush, Delaware grain growers like Caesar Rodney, and even lumber dealers like John Dagworthy, not to mention the innumerable wagoners and shallopmen and innkeepers whose names are forgotten. British revenue acts also affected the same group and, of course, many others.

---

[249] "Your Majesty has a Negative upon our Laws," the colonial assembly admitted in a petition to the king, October 27, 1768. *House Minutes,* 166 ff. Yet Charles M. Andrews wrote H. Clay Reed that to his best knowledge the laws of the lower counties were not submitted to the king. Information from Dr. Reed.

[250] This argument has been further developed in the author's "The Philadelawareans; a Study in the Relations of Philadelphia and Delaware in the Late Eighteenth Century," *Pennsylvania Magazine of History and Biography,* LXIX (1945), 128–149.

[251] See Samuel Wharton to George Read, Philadelphia, August 2, 1766, Read, *Read,* 30–33, and other letters and references to their friendship in this book and in the Papers of the Read Family of New Castle County, Delaware (Library of Congress). Samuel Wharton was elected to Congress from Delaware on February 2, 1782.

Whatever patriotic sentiments found their way into Philadelphia papers found their way also into the homes of literate Delawareans, for these were almost the only journals that they read. If an unwise Townshend's taxes provoked a "Pennsylvania Farmer" to protest, Delawareans living near his great Kent County estates would not remain ignorant of his words. And indeed when —and if—a seamstress in Philadelphia stitched a tri-colored banner of stripes and stars, Delaware was interested, for was she not the former daughter-in-law of the minister who occupied the most influential pulpit in Delaware and niece of the state's most potent political figure? [252]

Even though the white stock of the lower counties was overwhelmingly British in origin, its ties to neighboring colonies were closer than to the mother country. Three generations of Englishmen had tilled Delaware soil since the great migrations in the days of the Duke of York and William Penn. Here by the river, as they turned over American loam, they turned over too their English heritage. Warmed by a new world's sun and enlivened by its rain, the seeds of this heritage produced a new crop, a new national character. Here was a new man, an American. Like his English forefather, he was full of loyal sentiments of love for a king he had not seen, and of respect for a crown whose power he had not known; but a sight of the royal visage or a touch of the royal power might cure him of this sentimental attachment as though it were scrofula.

No such sentimental attachment existed for the eighteenth-century immigrants, the Scotch-Irish. These Derrymen and men of Armagh and of Newry and of Belfast had fled in bitterness of heart from an alien king. Ulster had bloomed, the fruit had been plucked, and those who tended it had been forsaken. They were determined not again to lose the fruit of their toil. Whatever provincial particularism these migrants lacked was compensated for by their distaste for a transoceanic tyranny—whether it be the tyranny of king or of parliament.

---

[252] George H. Genzmer, "Betsy Ross," *DAB*, 175. John Ross, son of the Rev. Aeneas Ross of New Castle, and nephew of George Read, was killed in January, 1776, in a gunpowder explosion at Philadelphia while he was on patrol duty as a soldier in the militia.

Here beside Hudson's South River under the kindly but weak control of Penn, the colonists had learned to govern themselves. Their small land seemed forgotten amid the richer colonies about them; their prospects seemed relatively prosaic. Great planners and schemers looked beyond, to the Kanawha, the Wyoming, the Mohawk, to unbounded western horizons. Yet the mild prosperity of the Delaware counties continued to attract settlers, not only from overseas, like the Scotch-Irish, but a steady seepage from neighboring colonies—a Read from Maryland, a Rogers from Virginia, a Vining from New Jersey, a Bennett from Pennsylvania.

As early as the beginning of the eighteenth century, when in Penn's assembly the growth of Philadelphia and the interior regions threatened the equilibrium between the province and the lower counties, the particularism of the latter was made manifest by their refusal to continue the union, by their insistence on having a separate assembly through which they could run their affairs in their own way. After this was achieved in 1704, little interference from outside disturbed the course of the political life of the lower counties. They had no resident governor of their own and no council. A Penn or his delegate usually made a yearly trip from Philadelphia to New Castle, where he established himself at some inn for the duration of the assembly's session. Generally he ratified the new legislation with no more than a minor quibble over a phrase, accepted a gift of perhaps two hundred pounds for support "As a Proof of the Esteem of the House, to which he was much obliged," [253] and then returned to Philadelphia. The political feuds which existed in the lower counties were largely between "ins" and "outs," between "court" and "country" factions, apparently formed around important persons and their friends and foes. Ruled for decades by a government exceeded in its independence only by Connecticut and Rhode Island, these people who had become thus accustomed to governing themselves as freeborn Englishmen, resented as unconstitutional the enlivened imperial interest of Britain's parliament after the Seven Years' War. "In freedom we're born and in freedom we'll live," the Delawareans sang with John Dickinson. [254]

[253] *Votes and Proceedings,* June 9, 1766, pp. 71–72.
[254] "A Song for American Freedom," Tyler, *Literary History,* I, 240.

A particularistic, agrarian, conservative civilization, self-directing, intolerant of interference from outside; a mercantile aristocracy and intelligentsia, closely allied to similar groups throughout the Delaware Valley, prospering amid imperial neglect; a large, enterprising, educated Scotch-Irish minority, nursing unhappy memories of parliamentary coercion—this was the odd combination of factors readying the lower counties for revolution. Only the spark was wanting to make this tinder flame.

Yet, with a small population and without western lands to bring dreams of an expanding, independent commonwealth, Delaware, in a consciousness of her weakness, was unlikely to initiate any precipitate action to part from the British Empire. Her role, instead, was to wait upon her sister colonies and join them when she approved their action. Once revolution had occurred, Delaware, realizing she could not stand alone, sought equality in a close union. This the Federal Constitution seemed to provide, and consequently Delawareans were almost of one mind in supporting it—were, indeed, the first to grant it ratification. Since the revolution in Delaware was so closely linked to the national struggle, its story must be narrated mainly in terms of events on the larger scene.

XIV. The Stamp Act and the Townshend Duties

THE first occasion which united Delaware with the other colonies in protesting laws of parliament was a call issued by the Massachusetts House of Representatives on June 8, 1765, for a congress of delegates of the colonies to meet in New York in October. The purpose was to "consult together on the present circumstances of the colonies, and the difficulties to which they are and must be reduced by the operation of the acts of parliament, for levying duties and taxes on the colonies"—that is, the Sugar Act (1764), which strengthened parliament's control of American commerce, and the Stamp Act (1765), which taxed legal documents and some others—"and to consider of a general and united, dutiful, loyal and humble representation of their condition to his majesty and to the parliament, and to implore relief." [255]

This was Delaware's first opportunity to unite with the other colonies in protest against parliamentary action. Since the House of Assembly had adjourned before receiving this call and was not likely to be summoned into special session by the proprietary governor, the assemblymen in each county prepared a letter appointing Jacob Kollock of Sussex, Caesar Rodney of Kent, and Thomas McKean of New Castle a committee to represent them at the New York meeting.[256] All of the eighteen assemblymen signed the necessary credentials, with the exception of the three delegates, who were also members of the assembly. The three accrediting letters show obvious marks of collaboration. Although each of the delegates was from a different county, the same group was nominated in each letter. Furthermore, the Kent and Sussex letters, dated September 13 and 17, respectively, were all but identical in wording. The New Castle letter, dated September 21, was stronger in tone. Where the other two letters admitted the signers were "sensible of the impropriety of assuming the functions of assemblymen during the recess," the New Castle members claimed they were "assured of the hearty approbation of any future house of assembly of this government," and boldly complained of "the weighty and oppressive taxes imposed upon the good people of this government by the divers late acts of parliament, and of the great infringement of the liberties and just established rights of all his majesty's colonies on this continent." All three documents suggested a petition to king and parliament, but New Castle added a qualifying note: the petitioners should, "dutifully, yet most firmly," assert "the colonies' right of exclusion from parliamentary taxation," and they should request "that they may

---

[255] "Journal of the Stamp-Act Congress," in Hezekiah Niles, ed., *Principles and Acts of the Revolution in America* (New York, 1876), 156.

[256] This is probably the earliest example of a current Delaware custom of sharing its three Congressional posts among the three counties. In 1954 Delaware's three Congressmen were Senator John J. Williams of Sussex, Senator J. Allen Frear of Kent, and Representative Herbert Warburton of New Castle. This practice, however, was not followed during the Revolution.

not, in any instance, be stripped of the ancient and most valuable privilege of a trial by their peers." [257]

This is an early example of a continuing factor in Delaware politics: the comparative forwardness of New Castle County. There are several possible explanations for this fact. First, since New Castle contained a larger proportion of Scotch-Irish and a smaller proportion of men of English stock than did the other counties,[258] it had fewer cultural and sentimental ties to the British crown than did Kent and Sussex and hesitated less at a separation. For the same reason it was not so well satisfied with the cultural pattern set up in colonial America as were these two other counties. A French migration to New Castle County in the 1790s and the coming of the south Irish, Germans, and other peoples in the nineteenth and twentieth centuries have perpetuated this peculiarity of New Castle County.

Second, New Castle County was the home of the mercantile interests of Delaware. Here were the colony's leading ports and manufacturing industries. Since it was the merchant class who first felt the weight of restrictive British legislation, they could be expected to represent the earliest and strongest opposition to it. Traditionally too, the merchant class, like the European bourgeoisie, were particularly receptive to new ideas and change.

Third, New Castle County was in greater proximity to Philadelphia and therefore to the newest trends in American thought. Situated on the land route from the cities of the middle colonies to Maryland, Virginia, and the South, it was frequently crossed by travellers. In short, it was on the main road of intercolonial culture and close to that culture's center and its largest city.

How one resident of New Castle County felt about the Stamp Act and its probable effect on intercolonial relations is revealed in a letter of George Read to an English friend. The political disputes hitherto confined to parties in the respective colonies, he advised, had "all resolved into one, and that with the mother-country. The stamp-act . . . hath raised such a firment among

[257] *Ibid.*, 160–161.

[258] This comparison leaves the Negroes out of consideration. They were most numerous in Sussex (Greene and Harrington, *Population before 1790*, 123), but were of no political importance in the eighteenth century.

us . . . that I know not when it will subside." "Just complaints" must be answered by repeal of the law, else Americans will consider themselves destined "to become the slaves of Great Britain by the Parliament's making laws to deprive them of their property without their assent, by any kind of representation. This will naturally lead them into measures to live as independent of Great Britain as possible. . . ." [259]

When Congress met in New York on October 7, 1765, to protest the Stamp Act, Delaware's Rodney and McKean were in attendance. Their credentials were accepted, being evidence of no more informal an election than had occurred in New York or New Jersey. The third Delaware delegate, Jacob Kollock, did not attend.

The date of the meeting was also the thirty-seventh birthday of Delaware's elder delegate. "Caesar Rodney is the oddest looking man in the world," John Adams was to write of him nine years later. "He is tall, thin and slender as a reed, pale; his face is not bigger than a large apple, yet there is sense and fire, spirit, wit, and humor in his countenance." [260] A great part of Rodney's sense, fire, and spirit were to be employed in Delaware's cause during the next two decades, as this landed gentleman of Kent, grandson of the speaker of Delaware's first colonial assembly and himself the speaker of its last, served as soldier, Congressman, and governor.

With the thirty-one-year-old McKean, Rodney supported James Otis, a Whig, for the chairmanship. Although, according to John Adams, "none supported Otis with more uniformity and decision" than these two delegates from Delaware, the results of the election gave the chairmanship to the conservative Timothy Ruggles.[261]

---

[259] Read continues, "They will, gradually, go into the making of woollens and ironmongery, your two great branches of manufactory; and although from the high prices of labor in general among us they will be greatly impeded in the first attempts, yet the necessity of persevering will surmount and possibly remove that difficulty. The spirit hath seized them already and prevails surprisingly. Home-spun cloth is worn as well by the beaux as the men of gravity of all ranks, and though only fashion with the first, it will soon grow into habit, which, when once fixed, will not be readily changed. From this consideration alone every friend to the mother-country and the colonies ought to wish and to afford a helping hand to obtain an alteration in the late system of politics in England." To Richard Neave, Jr., [c. August, 1765], draft, Read, Read, 29–30.

[260] C. F. Adams, ed., Works of John Adams (Boston, 1856), II, 364.

[261] J. Adams to J. Morse, Quincy, Nov. 29, 1815, ibid., X, 184.

After the congress had declared its opposition to taxation without representation and to recent commercial restrictions and had recorded its support of trial by jury and its loyalty to the king, it petitioned king and parliament for a redress of grievances. Rodney and McKean supported these measures whole-heartedly, but Chairman Ruggles timidly refused to sign the petition. McKean, according to his own account, pressed Ruggles "so hard that he at last said 'it was against his conscience,' on which word I rung the change so loud, that a plain challenge was given by him and accepted, in the presence of the whole corps; but he departed the next morning before day, without an adieu to any of his brethren." [262]

The proceedings in New York were followed eagerly by at least some people in Delaware. One of Caesar Rodney's cousins, John Rodney of Lewes in Sussex County, wrote: "I do not know that Ever I was so desirous of seeing anything of a publick Nature as I have been to see the Petition and Memorial to the King and both houses of Parliament." He wanted to visit Caesar on the latter's return to have "my Curiosity Intirely gratified on such a Momentus Occasion, to wit, to see the mode the manner the Arguments and Remonstrances of that most Important Congress, in whose hands we have as it were Intrusted our Liberties." Commenting later on a repeal of the Stamp Act, John wrote that it "would be perhaps the best piece of News that ever America was favoured with," but the act's enforcement "would certainly terminate in Our Ruin for the Consequence I apprehend would be, either to submit to that detestable Act, or to be Envolved in an open Rebellion, both of which is Shocking even to think of." [263] When in the spring of 1766 the Stamp Act was repealed, Delaware rejoiced. New Castle, a traveller reported, "was illuminated on the joyful

[262] McKean to John Adams, Philadelphia, August 20, 1813, Adams, *Works*, X, 60–61. Rodney explained to his brother that he was "in an Assembly of the greatest Ability I ever Yet saw" and was awed by a talk of "Petitioning and addressing That Body of the great legislature of the Empire for Redress of Grievances," at once setting "forth the Liberty we have, and ought to Enjoy, (as freeborn Englishmen) according to the British Constitution," and yet avoiding "any Infringement of the prerogative of the Crown, and the Power of Parliament." Rodney, *Letters*, 25-26; Niles, *Principles*, 162–168.

[263] Rodney, *Letters*, 26–27.

Occasion . . . and really made a pretty Appearance from the Water." [264]

At an adjourned session of the Delaware assembly in May, 1766, Rodney and McKean reported on the congress and received legislative approval.[265] The assembly had already undertaken some independent action. In the previous October it had appointed George Read, Charles Ridgely, and David Hall a committee to draw up resolutions "relating to the Liberties and Privileges of the Inhabitants of this Government and setting forth the Grievances the said Inhabitants Labour under from some late Acts of Parliament." [266] These resolutions, approved by the assembly in June, 1766, by which date the Stamp Act had been repealed, declared that (1) this government has "with the greatest Cheerfulness" contributed men and money to the king when requisitions were made; (2) its people are "entitled to all the inherent Rights and Liberties of his Majesty's Subjects in Great Britain, or elsewhere"; (3) taxation by consent is a fundamental British right, confirmed by the "Magna Charta" and various statutes; (4) this consent can only be given by the colonial legislatures; (5) "Trial by Jury . . . is the Interest and invaluable Right of every British Subject in these Colonies"; (6) the extension of Admiralty Court jurisdiction is subversive of the rights of colonists; and (7) the people have "Hearts filled with the utmost Respect and Gratitude to his Majesty," are zealous in his service, "and bear the truest Allegiance to his Person." [267]

Upon McKean's motion, these critical, if loyal, resolutions were accompanied by an address of thanks to the king for the repeal of the Stamp Act, an address written by a committee composed of McKean, Rodney, and Read—whose ages at the time averaged only thirty-four.[268] The king was properly impressed. He "was so well pleased with it," the lower counties' London agent, Dennys De Berdt, informed the assembly, "that he read it over twice." And well George III might have been pleased, for the address was

---

[264] Hastings, *Francis Hopkinson*, 128.
[265] *House Minutes*, May 27, 1766, pp. 34–41. They were later allowed £140 for their services. *Ibid.*, June 2, 1766, p. 51.
[266] *Ibid.*, Oct. 23, 1765, p. 10.
[267] *Ibid.*, June 3, 1766, pp. 54–55.
[268] *Ibid.*, May 30, 1766, p. 50.

loaded with such saccharine phrases as, "the Clouds . . . are dissipated," "Hearts are animated," and "Affection is unbounded," for "the best of Kings" from "the most loyal subjects." [269] In the general rejoicing, however, passage of the Declaratory Act, asserting parliament's power to "bind the colonies and people of America in all cases whatsoever," seems to have been overlooked.

The success of the address won for its young authors appointment and reappointment as a committee of correspondence to communicate with agent De Berdt, who received a piece of plate as a reward for his efforts.[270] This combination of McKean, Rodney, and Read was very soon engaged in writing a second address to the king, this time in protest against the Townshend Acts. By these acts parliament in 1767 imposed duties on certain imports, including tea. When the assembly met in the following year, McKean recommended an inquiry into "how far the Inhabitants . . . are affected by the Operation of" these acts "for the express purpose of raising a Revenue." [271] Three days later the house unanimously approved resolutions declaring that the Townshend Acts deprived the colonists "of the Exclusive Right of taxing themselves" and thus were subversive of the Assembly's "natural, constitutional and just Rights and Privileges," and "pernicious to American freedom." The petition of protest framed by Rodney, Read, and McKean acknowledged "all possible obligations" and "all due Subordination" to the "most gracious Sovereign" in the usual turgid style, but regretted New York's loss "of her Legislative Authority," and the passage of Townshend duties: although parliament is "confessedly the wisest and greatest Assembly upon Earth, . . . our Fellow-subjects of Great-Britain cannot . . . represent us." "When it is considered," the petitioners cleverly added, "that your Majesty has a Negative upon our Laws, and the sole Execution of them, that our Governor is only during your Royal Pleasure, and all Honors and Distinctions are derived from the Crown, it is humbly hoped that the Dependence of this Colony on the Mother Country will appear to be sufficiently secured." [272]

[269] *Ibid.*, June 5, 1766, pp. 59–61; Oct. 26, 1767, p. 121.
[270] *Ibid.*, June 5, 1766, p. 61; June 6, 1766, p. 65; Nov. 1, 1766, p. 106; Oct. 24, 1769, p. 234.
[271] *Ibid.*, Oct. 21, 1768, p. 156.
[272] *Ibid.*, Oct. 24, 1768, pp. 157–158; Oct. 27, 1768, pp. 166–170.

On the same day the assembly's speaker, John Vining, sent a letter to Peyton Randolph, speaker of the Virginia House of Burgesses, informing him of Delaware's "Intentions of co-operating . . . in prudent Measures" and of its earnest "desire to keep up a Correspondence" with the Virginia legislature.[273]

But it was not the words of petitions but the action of non-importation associations which made the colonial point of view effectively felt in England. No boycott agreements had been entered into in Delaware, because, according to George Read, "we had no traders among us who imported goods from Great Britain, except in very small quantities and in vessels belonging to Philadelphia, which was sufficiently guarded by the agreement of its own citizens." As chief spokesman for the Philadelphia–Delaware mercantile connection, Read addressed an appeal to the people of lower New Castle County to maintain their "natural connection" to Philadelphia, for some of the merchants there, complaining that Maryland's non-import agreement was less inclusive than Pennsylvania's, threatened to dissolve the association, lest the people of Delaware "form a connection in the way of trade with the Marylanders, introduced by going there to purchase excepted articles, which trade may continue after all contests with the mother-country are over." The people of upper New Castle County, Read added, especially those of Wilmington, New Castle, Christiana, Newark, Newport, and Hamburg Landing, "have resolved to support the Philadelphia agreement." [274]

The extant text of Read's proposed agreement, dated August 17, 1769, provided that no goods were to be imported contrary to the "spirit and intention" of the pact of the Philadelphia merchants, that anyone in the British dominions who imported articles contrary to this pact was to be blacklisted, and that any signer violating the agreement was to "have his name published in the public news-papers as a betrayer of the civil rights of America, and be forever deemed infamous, and a betrayer of his country." [275]

Within a year more stringent regulations for enforcement of the agreement were adopted at a meeting at Christiana of representa-

[273] *Ibid.*, Oct. 27, 1768, pp. 179–182.
[274] Undated letter in Read, *Read*, 80–82.
[275] Read, *Read*, 82.

tives of several New Castle County towns. Two persons in each town were appointed "a committee of inspection to watch the trade." They examined goods brought into Delaware and reported the sale of embargoed goods to a general committee which determined further action. Usually violators were made to appear in person before the general committee, of which Read was chairman, and were required to make a public declaration of regret for their actions, promise not to repeat them, and pay the proceeds for the sale of these goods to a fund for the poor of the county.[276]

The passage by the assembly of further resolutions on imperial relations was occasioned in 1769 by the arrival of a letter from the Virginia Burgesses enclosing a set of resolutions presented to them by Washington and written by George Mason. The Delaware assembly resolved that the sole right of taxation was vested in it; that the people might petition their king and could join with other colonies in doing so; and that trials for crimes committed in Delaware by residents should be heard in Delaware and the king should be asked to save his subjects from the fear of being carried overseas for trial. A petition incorporating these resolutions was immediately presented and approved.[277]

In 1770, in deference to colonial protests, all the Townshend duties except the tea tax were repealed, and friction between this colony and the mother country decreased somewhat, in spite of such incidents elsewhere as the Boston Massacre (1770) and the *Gaspée* affair (1772). But early in 1773 the mismanaged and boycotted East India Company was given special favors, including monopoly of the tea trade with America, to restore its dwindling fortunes. This action encouraged efforts of Massachusetts and Virginia radicals to keep the colonies from slipping into any easy compliance with parliament. As a result of communications from Massachusetts and Virginia,[278] on October 23, 1773, the assembly appointed a committee of correspondence to consist of the usual trio, Rodney, Read, and McKean, plus two less ardent politicians, John McKinly and Thomas Robinson. McKinly was a Scotch-Irish physician of Wilmington who was later elected first president of

[276] *Ibid.*, 83.
[277] *House Minutes*, June 17, 1769, pp. 215–219.
[278] Thomas Rodney, Notes, in folder "Letters to and from T. Rodney," Brown Collection.

Delaware. He was so moderate a patriot that his later capture by the British inspired few efforts to save him. Robinson, a prominent Sussex landowner, became an outright Tory, the most notable one in Delaware, and fled to the British.[279]

XV. The Delaware State

THIS committee of correspondence, keeping in touch with the New England situation, seems to have been responsible for the quick action taken in 1774, when news of the Coercive Acts, especially the Boston Port Bill punishing Boston for the Tea Party, became known in Delaware. The similarity of the resolutions passed at mass meetings held at each county seat revealed the committee's directing hand.[280] These resolutions called the Boston Port Bill "unconstitutional" and "dangerous to the liberties of the British colonies"; recommended a collection for the poor of Boston; set up a committee of correspondence for each county;[281] and asked Speaker Rodney to call assembly members together for the purpose of choosing delegates to a Continental Congress. Although Rodney had no constitutional right to issue such a call, he was probably asked to do so because Governor John Penn's refusal to act in Pennsylvania made any action by him for Delaware improbable.[282]

---

[279] Rodney, *Letters*, 38n.; James H. Peeling, "The Public Life of Thomas McKean, 1734–1817" (Ph.D. thesis, University of Chicago, 1929), 22. *Cf.* Harold Hancock, "Thomas Robinson: Delaware's Most Prominent Loyalist," *Delaware History*, IV (1950), 1–36.

[280] Rodney, *Letters*, 38–42; G. Read to C. Rodney, New Castle, June 29, 1774, Leon de Valinger, Jr., ed., "Rodney Letters," *Delaware History*, I (1946), 102.

[281] The MS. "Book of the Proceedings and Transactions of the Committee of Correspondence for Kent County, begun July 20th, 1774," is in folder entitled "Kent Co. Transactions" at the Historical Society of Delaware. These transactions reveal the opposition of the two southern counties to holding the convention of assemblymen at New Castle and thus foretell removal of the capital to Dover. The downstaters felt that the committee in New Castle County was too forward. These transactions also disclose that Kent County sent two hundred pounds for the relief of the Boston poor.

[282] Peter Force, comp., *American Archives* . . . (Washington, 1837–1853), 4th series, I, 419–420; Allan Nevins, *The American States during and after the Revolu-*

At Rodney's request, the assemblymen convened in an unofficial meeting at New Castle in August, 1774, and elected Read, McKean, and Rodney delegates to Congress. They were ordered to pledge allegiance to the king; to claim for the assembly the sole right of levying taxes; to forbid the carrying of Delawareans abroad for trial; to condemn the Boston Port Act; to seek intercolonial cooperation; and to arrange an embargo on exports to and imports from Britain.[283] After participatng in the first Continental Congress in Philadelphia, which drafted a petition to the king and organized an association to boycott imports from Britain,[284] the delegates reported back to the assembly on March 15. The next day they were reappointed by the assembly as delegates to the second Congress.[285]

Formal resolutions and instructions are often dull reading, but those relating to Delaware's representation in the early Continental Congress are of unusual interest in that they demonstrate that "radical change in the principles, opinions, sentiments, and affections of the people," which, according to John Adams, "was the real American Revolution." [286] The delegates to the second Congress were instructed in March, 1775, to avoid "everything disrespectful or offensive to our most gracious Sovereign," and to look toward the reestablishment of relations between the colonies and Great Britain on a constitutional basis. At the same time they were instructed to insist that each colony have an equal voice in the deliberations of Congress.[287]

---

tion, 1778–1789 (New York, 1924), 47, 60; Rodney, *Letters,* 42–43; Read, *Read,* 88–90; [James Tilton], *The Biographical History of Dionysius, Tyrant of Delaware, by Timoleon* (Philadelphia, 1788), 10–11; Thomas Rodney, Essay on the Revolution, by Hermes, Brown Collection.

[283] Rodney, *Letters,* 43–45; Worthington C. Ford, *et al.,* eds., *Journals of the Continental Congress* (Washington, 1904–1937), I, 21–22.

[284] Committees of inspection were chosen by the people of New Castle and Kent "in the respective Hundreds" to cooperate with the Continental Congress in the boycott of British goods. Proceedings of Kent Committee of Correspondence, Nov. 22, 1774; Arthur M. Schlesinger, *The Colonial Merchants and the American Revolution, 1776–1783* (New York, 1918), 460, 502–503, 574; *Pennsylvania Packet,* Jan. 2, 1775; Margaret W. Willard, ed., *Letters on the American Revolution, 1774–1776* (Boston, 1925), 18.

[285] T. McKean to his wife, March 16, 1775, McKean Papers (Historical Society of Pennsylvania, Philadelphia), VI, 1.

[286] To H. Niles, Quincy, Feb. 13, 1818, Adams, *Works,* X, 283.

[287] Rodney, *Letters,* 55–57.

When later that spring fighting broke out in Massachusetts, the Delaware assembly agreed to bear its share of the expense of a continental army. Consequently new instructions to Read, Rodney, and McKean included an order to join with the representatives of the other colonies in military preparations in addition to the old admonitions to seek reconciliation with England and an equal vote with other colonies.[288]

The Delaware delegates were bound by these instructions when, on June 7, 1776, Richard Henry Lee proposed his famous resolution of independence. Because the Delaware delegates and some others were thus restricted, consideration of Lee's resolution was postponed to July 1. "It appearing in the course of these debates," wrote Jefferson, that Delaware and five other colonies "were not yet matured for falling from the parent stem, but that they were fast advancing to that state, it was thought most prudent to wait a while for them." [289]

The maturing process was now moving forward rapidly. With Rodney in the chair and McKean on the floor, on June 15 the assembly voted new instructions which consisted of but two sentences, one of which merely repeated the injunction to insist on an equal vote for Delaware. The other sentence, however, was unprecedented, for, omitting all reference to reconciliation and peace, it ordered the delegates to concur with those from other colonies "in forming . . . compacts, . . . concluding . . . treaties, . . . and in adopting such other measures as shall be judged necessary for promoting the liberty, safety, and interests of America. . . ." [290] The assembly obviously intended the delegates to follow their own desires in voting on Lee's resolution. "McKean has returned from the Lower Counties with Full Powers," exulted John Adams.[291] McKean exercised his "Full Powers" on July 1 by

[288] Rodney, *Letters*, 57–58, 72–73; Instructions to Delegates to the Continental Congress, March 22, 1776, Miscellaneous Papers—Three Lower Counties (Historical Society of Pennsylvania). The continued stress on reconciliation is attributed by James Tilton in his *Biographical History of Dionysius*, page 22, to a victory of moderates in the Sussex and New Castle elections.

[289] John H. Hazelton, *The Declaration of Independence* (New York, 1906), 123; Julian Boyd, ed., *The Papers of Thomas Jefferson*, I (Princeton, 1950), 313.

[290] Read, *Read*, 164–165; Rodney, *Letters*, 92.

[291] Edmund C. Burnett, ed., *Letters of Members of the Continental Congress* (Washington, 1921–1936), I, 491.

voting for independence, but Read split the Delaware vote by opposing McKean. Rodney's ride through "thunder and Rain" brought him to Philadelphia on July 2 in time to support McKean and place Delaware on the side of Lee's resolution.

Adams' exultation was undoubtedly increased if he learned from McKean that the Delaware assembly had coupled its grant of new instructions on June 15 with a second step toward independence, the suspension of government under the crown. Realizing that some "temporary authority" must be established, the assembly had resolved unanimously that all officeholders should hereafter act "in the name of the government of the counties of New Castle, Kent, and Sussex, upon Delaware, as they used" to do "in the name of the King, until a new government shall be formed." [292] The new government was not formed until after a state constitution was adopted on September 20; [293] meanwhile Delaware was governed under the terms of the July 15 resolution by its old colonial officials, the one notable change being that Caesar Rodney, as speaker of the assembly, had replaced Governor John Penn as the chief executive.[294]

On July 29 Delaware celebrated its independence on Dover Green, where the Declaration of Independence was read and the committee of inspection marched two by two around the square, "followed by the Light Infantry in slow time with music." Then a circle was formed round a fire in the middle of the Green, and the president of the committee cast a portrait of King George into the flames, declaring, "Compelled by strong necessity, thus we destroy even the Shadow of that King who refused to reign over a free people." "Three Huzas again," the chronicler related, "and the greatest joy in every countenance except a few long faces." [295]

Meanwhile the assemblymen had met at Speaker Rodney's call

---

[292] Force, *American Archives*, 4th series, VI, 884; Rodney, *Letters*, 92. One of the petitions opposing any change in the government is in the folder entitled "Delaware, re Slavery, Militia, Lottery, etc.," in the HSD. *Cf.* Thomas Rodney to an unnamed captain, Dover, June 1, 1776, in folder "Letters sent by T. Rodney," Brown Collection.

[293] *Proceedings of the Convention of the Delaware State held at New Castle on Tuesday the Twenty-seventh of August, 1776* (Wilmington, 1927), 26.

[294] Rodney, *Letters*, 93n.

[295] Thomas to Caesar Rodney, Dover, July 30, 1776, De Valinger, "Rodney Letters," *Delaware History*, III (1948), 109.

and decided that ten delegates should be chosen by each county to form a constitutional convention. In a hotly contested election the conservatives won full delegations in Kent and Sussex and secured part of the New Castle delegation, aided perhaps by the appearance of the British at New York, the imminent possibility of their presence on the Delaware, the departure of some of the militia, and the irritation aroused by the overly zealous action of warm rebels. Caesar Rodney, ill rewarded for his valiant service, was defeated by a Kent faction led by Dr. Charles Ridgely. The defeat of Rodney, the ardent advocate of independence, and the election of Read, a moderate who had but a month earlier opposed independence, manifested the conservative nature of Delaware.[296]

In spite of Rodney's fear that the convention might be tempted to seize all power in its hands, even to the extent of choosing new delegates to Congress, it wisely restrained its powers, functioning as a governing body only in reference to pressing matters concerning conduct of the war.[297] It is interesting to note that this constitution, by which Delaware was to be governed for sixteen years, was the first to be written by any state through a device now generally considered correct, the election of a special convention for that purpose.[298] The convention's action was final,

[296] Rodney had rejected a suggestion of his brother that the Kent Committee of Inspection check on individuals whose patriotism appeared to be lukewarm. See the thorough discussion of the election in H. Clay Reed's excellent monograph, "The Delaware Constitution of 1776," 16–22. Cf. the correspondence of Caesar Rodney with his brother Thomas in Rodney, Letters, 99–105; [Tilton], History of Dionysius, 25–26; Hamilton, Anglo-American Law, 23–24.

[297] Rodney, Letters, 105–106, 116–117, 125–126; Reed, "Constitution of 1776," 34–36. McKean thought, with good reason, that the conservative majority in the convention, having set the next general election for October 21, when many of the radical patriots would be out of the state with the army, were willing to bide their time in the assurance that they would control the new government. Ibid. John Haslet wrote: "I am much mortified at the amazing revolution of sentiment in the two lower counties. Mobile vulgus. Not less astonishing is the system of government formed by their representatives so republican. . . . The hand of McK[ea]n was in it. What must their constituents think of it, hooping and hollowing for the King?" Haslet to Caesar Rodney, "Camp at Tapan," Nov. 12, 1776, typed copy at HSD from Sparks MSS., 52 (Widener Library), Misc. Papers, Revolution, II, 82.

[298] Claude H. Van Tyne, The American Revolution, 1776–1783 (New York, 1905), 140; Roger S. Hoar, Constitutional Conventions; Their Nature, Powers, and Limitations (Boston, 1917), 4. A contrary opinion is expressed in Walter F. Dodd, Revision and Amendment of State Constitutions, Johns Hopkins University Studies in Historical and Political Science, extra vols., new series, no. 1 (Baltimore, 1910), p. 15.
Andrew C. McLaughlin called this device "the thoroughly correct method for

the constitution being made effective by the election of legislators that fall in accordance with its terms and without any opportunity for the voters of the state to record their specific approval of it.

The authorship of the constitution has been variously attributed both to McKean and to Read,[299] but on no very solid basis. Although Read, as speaker of the convention and of the committee which prepared a draft of the constitution, and also as leader of the moderate or conservative faction which was the majority, exerted great influence, the final draft was more probably a co-operative work to which many minds contributed.[300]

This constitution gave the lower counties a new title, "The Delaware State." [301] It provided for a bicameral legislature to be called the General Assembly,[302] the upper house of which was to be known as the Legislative Council and the lower house as the House of Assembly. The Council was to consist of nine members, three from each county, chosen in alternate years for three-year terms; the House of Assembly was to have twenty-one members, seven from each county, chosen annually—similar to the colonial assembly. The right of franchise was to remain, as before, with all freeholders owning "fifty acres of land or more well settled, and twelve acres thereof cleared and improved, or . . . otherwise worth Forty Pounds. . . ." [303] Money bills were to originate in the lower house, but they might be "altered, amended, or rejected by the legislative council." A president was to be elected for a three-year

the manifestation of the principle that government is the creature of the people." "The American people," he adds, "discovered and put into use the representative constitutional convention, the basic American institution, . . . a method of establishing government on the basis of popular power; and in the long course of history I don't think you will find any greater political achievement." "Some Reflections on the American Revolution," *Aspects of the Social History of America* (Chapel Hill, 1931), 55–56.

Allan Nevins incorrectly asserts that this was not an especially elected constitutional convention. *American States*, 128.

[299] Conrad, *History of Delaware*, I, 151; Read, *Read*, 186–187.

[300] J. B. McMaster and Frederick Stone, eds., *Pennsylvania and the Federal Constitution, 1787–1788* (Lancaster, 1888), 254–255; Peeling, Life of McKean, 66; Reed, "Constitution of 1776," 24n.

[301] The constitution of 1776 may be examined in *Laws*, I, appendix, 82–91; *Proceedings of the Convention, 1776*, pp. 26–35; and Thorpe, *Federal and State Constitutions*, I, 562–568.

[302] In abandoning the unicameral colonial system, Delaware was probably influenced by other states which had already adopted constitutions providing for bicameral legislatures.

[303] *Laws*, I, 148.

term by the General Assembly, and a privy council of four members, two elected by the House and two by the Council, was to advise him. Among the president's powers was the right, with the advice of the privy council, to lay an embargo "not exceeding thirty days" during a recess of the General Assembly and to embody the militia and act as their commander-in-chief. Elections to state and county offices were to be held annually on the first of October, and the legislature was to convene on the twentieth of the same month. The delegates to Congress were to be "chosen annually, or superseded in the meantime" by the General Assembly, through a joint ballot of its members. All legislators were required to take a Trinitarian oath. The importation of slaves from Africa was completely forbidden, and their importation from elsewhere for sale was likewise banned. The English common law was adopted, as was as much of the English statute law "as had been heretofore adopted in practice." The "establishment of any one religious sect . . . in preference to another" was forbidden; clergymen continuing "in the exercise of the pastoral function" were not to be allowed to hold any civil office. The consent of five-sevenths of the House and seven-ninths of the Council was necessary for amendment, with certain sections, as that regarding slaves, declared to be unamendable. A Declaration of Rights and Fundamental Rules of the Delaware State, based on the Pennsylvania and Maryland bills of rights, had been adopted by the convention before it completed the constitution.[304]

XVI. The Revolution

FROM 1776 to 1781 Delaware was constitutionally an independent nation, allied in war against Great Britain with twelve other former colonies. The chief problems of her government were those

---

[304] *Laws*, I, appendix, 79–81; Max Farrand, "The Delaware Bill of Rights of 1776," *American Historical Review*, III (1898), 641–649; George Read to Caesar Rodney, New Castle, Sept. 17, 1776, Rodney, *Letters*, 119–120. This letter also summarizes the constitution very conveniently. Reed, "Constitution of 1776," corrects an error by Farrand regarding the source of the Delaware bill of rights.

involved in making its new political organization effective and in maintaining cooperation with the other states in the face of a common enemy.[305]

A particularly stubborn problem that bothered the new state government was a lack of unanimity in the support of the Revolutionary cause. The moderation and essential conservatism of the central and southern parts of the state, removed from the ways of travellers and the paths of new ideas, fostered a certain changeless loyalty to the old order, which, in its quietest aspects, irritated the radical rebels.[306] Although investigations were carried on by committees of inspection,[307] they were not sufficiently effective to prevent an armed insurrection in Sussex County in the spring of 1776. The militia were called out and an investigation ordered, but continental troops quelled the outbreak.[308] Some, George Read for one, feared this action by an out-of-state authority would do more harm than good.[309]

Although in February, 1777, the General Assembly ordered the death penalty for active Tories, in April Congress expressed alarm at "the spirit of Toryism" in Sussex County and in near-by parts of Maryland.[310] The investigating committee set up by the legislature found "criminal Intercourse" with the British widespread and "a considerable Part" of the people of Sussex "unfriendly and disaffected to the present Constitution of Government in this State, and to the independency of the United States in general." [311] Con-

[305] The story of the Delaware troops is related by Christopher L. Ward in *The Delaware Continentals* (Wilmington, 1941).

[306] This problem has been studied by Harold B. Hancock in his *The Delaware Loyalists, Papers of the Historical Society of Delaware*, new series, III (Wilmington, 1941). Note also the articles and documentary material which Professor Hancock has subsequently published in *Delaware History* magazine.

[307] See subpoena for Thomas Rodney from Kent County Committee of Inspection and Observation, September 7, 1775, Brown Collection, and T. Rodney to C. Ridgely, Dover, Sept. 12, 1775, Ridgely Papers (DSA).

[308] Anderson, *Recollections*, 7–16; Hancock, *Delaware Loyalists*, 14; [Tilton], *History of Dionysius*, 21–22.

[309] G. Read to Robert Morris, New Castle, Nov. 8, 1776, Read, *Read*, 212–213. Probably the excessive zeal of the radicals and the interference of outside authorities helped the conservatives win the election of the constitutional convention in the summer of 1776 and of the legislature in the fall. *Cf.* C. Rodney to T. Rodney, Philadelphia, August 21, 1776, Rodney, *Letters*, 104.

[310] *Journals of Congress*, VII, 275.

[311] Report of commissioners to examine for signs of disaffection in Sussex (signed by John Thompson and Thomas Collins) to President McKinly and the Privy Council, May 30, 1777, Papers of the Continental Congress (Library of Congress, Washington), LXX, 605; *Votes of Assembly*, 1777, p. 144; *Minutes of Council*, 130.

tinental troops were again sent to Sussex, there to be joined by militia, and some suspected loyalists were removed from the state. The British capture of Philadelphia in the fall of 1777 increased the danger of the situation, but it also had its advantages to the cause of revolution since it drove patriots to greater exertion.

Caesar Rodney, as militia commander and as chief executive of Delaware, led the struggle against loyalism with such success that Thomas McKean wrote his wife, "the Inhabitants of Delaware are said to be on the verge of total Revolution to Whiggism." [312] In April, 1778, shots were exchanged in Kent County between a patriot force and Tories under Cheney Clow.[313] Then in June, a law was enacted confiscating the estates of forty-six specified Tories, as well as of all others who had aided the British and not asked for pardon by August 1 of that year.[314] Another law, the Test Act, designed to test political opinion, required all male whites to take an oath of allegiance to the revolutionary government. Those who refused to take the oath would not be allowed to vote, hold office, or serve as jurymen. But in 1788 the Test Act was repealed, ostensibly to enfranchise the Quakers, and within the two years following its repeal political privileges were restored to refugee loyalists who had drifted back to the state.[315]

Though the number of Delaware loyalists was large, the natural moderation and conservatism of the people made the number appear greater than it actually was. Rodney's leadership routed some of the official apathy and indecision, and if not all and perhaps not even a majority of Delawareans were converted to "Whiggism," still through the middle years of the Revolution a Whig group did direct state policy.

The record of the Delaware troops in the Revolution is a glorious tale, but since their achievements lay far beyond the bounds of the state, their activities play little part in its domestic history. The colony's first contribution to the Continental Army was a battalion

[312] McKean Papers, VI, 11. *Cf.* T. McKean to John Adams, Philadelphia, Nov. 15, 1813, Adams, *Works,* X, 81–82.

[313] Hancock, *Delaware Loyalists,* 34–35; Charles Pope to Caesar Rodney, Grog Town, April 14 and 16, 1778, Rodney, *Letters,* 259–260.

[314] *Laws,* II, 636–643. *Cf.* Hancock, *op. cit.,* 62–64, for descriptions of these men.

[315] Hancock, *Delaware Loyalists,* 32; *Laws,* II, 928–929, 968–969.

(also called a regiment) commanded by Colonel John Haslet and raised at the beginning of 1776. Later that year a second regiment under Colonel Samuel Patterson was sent to New Jersey to join the "flying camp," a group of soldiers with short enlistments who were delegated to form a highly mobile band to protect the middle states. Provision was made for a third battalion to be commanded by Samuel West in September, 1776, but this unit seems never to have entered continental service. During the fall the organization was started of a battalion which was to serve under the command of Haslet after the expiration of all earlier enlistments in 1777. When Haslet was killed at Princeton, David Hall received the command and led the battalion till he was wounded at Germantown. A small but gallant remnant of this unit served throughout the war and was disbanded at Christiana in October, 1783.[316] Another regiment, commanded by Henry Neill, passed three months of the year 1780 in uneventful service in Kent County, Maryland.[317] Units of the militia were called out at various times to suppress loyalism and trade with the enemy and to repel the British march across Jersey in 1776 and the advance from the Chesapeake in 1777.

The Delaware soldiers in the continental service were not drafted, but were volunteers, often stimulated to enlist by the offer of a bounty, the amount of which tended to increase as the war went on.[318] Officers were promised half-pay for life, while the widows of those who died in the service were to be pensioned.[319]

---

[316] William G. Whitely, *The Revolutionary Soldiers of Delaware* (Wilmington, 1875), 130–148; *Delaware Archives* (Wilmington, 1911–1919), I, 81–85, 88–89.

[317] *Delaware Archives*, II, 631–632; *Minutes of Council*, 560–561, 567–568.

[318] Read favored conscription, but McKean opposed it. Read, *Read*, 307–308; *Minutes of Council*, 148, 186–190, 247–248, 411, 419, 426–429.

[319] *Minutes of Council*, 434–436, 809–811; *Votes of Assembly*, 1782–1783, p. 25; *Laws*, II, 771–772, 785–786. The organization of the armed forces is the main subject of the "Minutes of the Delaware Council of Safety, 1775–1776," edited by Leon de Valinger, Jr., in *Delaware History*, I, 55–78.

XVII. The Invasion

THE first General Assembly chosen under the constitution of 1776 did not immediately select a chief executive, appointing instead a Council of Safety to guide the state during the legislature's December adjournment.[320] Delegates to Congress were, however, chosen at once. Read was reelected, but Rodney and McKean were replaced by John Dickinson, "the Pennsylvania Farmer," and John Evans, of Newark. By returning the only delegate who had in the previous summer opposed independence and by dropping the two who had favored it, the assembly indicated its conservative character. Further evidence is to be found in the fact that Dickinson, as a Pennsylvania delegate, had also opposed the Lee resolution and had refused to sign the Declaration. Colonel Haslet, with the army in Jersey, wrote to Caesar Rodney: "I was astonished, tho I expected it, when I heard of our new delegation; how meditated, deep and powerful is their [the controlling faction's] malice. . . . They were obliged to go a begging in order to replace you." [321] "A-begging" indeed it was. After the assembly's questionable action in thus ignoring two ardent patriots, Delaware was left unrepresented in Congress for some months, for Read, as speaker of the Legislative Council, was too busy to attend Congress frequently, and Evans and Dickinson refused, pleading illness.[322] As substitutes for Evans

[320] The fifteen members of this council were James Latimer, John McKinly, Abram Robinson, John Lea, and Nicholas Van Dyke, of New Castle County; Caesar Rodney, James Sykes, Thomas Collins, John Banning, and Richard Bassett, of Kent; and David Hall, Jacob Moore, John Wiltbank, John Rodney, and James Rench, of Sussex. *Minutes of Council*, 24; *Votes of Assembly*, October, 1776, pp. 17–20, 30.

[321] New Brunswick, Nov. 19, 1776, typed copy in Haslet Papers, HSD, from Sparks MSS. See J. H. Powell, "Speech of John Dickinson Opposing the Declaration of Independence, 1 July, 1776," *Pennsylvania Mag. of Hist. and Biog.*, LXV (1941), 458–481, and "The Debate on American Independence, July 1, 1776," *Delaware Notes*, XXIII (1950), 37–62.

[322] John Evans to G. Read, Jan. 6, 1777, and J. Dickinson to Read, New Castle, Jan. 20, 1777, Read, *Read*, 251–254. Dickinson was at this time writing to Read: "This winter is the only time that will be allowed us to think of peace before we suffer indescribable calamities," Kent, Jan. 22, 1777, *ibid.*, 255.

and Dickinson, the assembly chose James Sykes, a Kent County landowner, and Nicholas Van Dyke, a New Castle lawyer. This action did little immediately to improve Delaware's representation, for the new delegates were slow in attending. When Sykes finally arrived in Congress, he found himself ill at ease and out of place. "I am by no means fit for my task," he wrote to Read. "I am in a most disagreeable situation, a stranger to every person, unable to speak my sentiments in Congress, and no colleague to confer with on any subject that may concern our State." [323] After two weeks the awed delegate came home, never to return.

The assembly which made such a poor choice of Congressmen showed little better judgment when finally, in February, 1777, they chose a president for the state. Their choice, John McKinly, Irish-born Wilmington physician and militia officer, was said, by an enemy, to have been "a mere patch upon the back" of George Read. The dominant faction probably supported him because his moderate views made him acceptable to the Kent and Sussex conservatives, while his ancestry and his religion gained him popularity with the Scotch-Irish Presbyterians of New Castle County.[324]

McKinly's administration was brief for it was sharply terminated in September by a British invasion of northern Delaware and his own capture. The Delaware counties themselves were too small to interest the British very much, but their strategic position near the colonial capital and metropolis of Philadelphia brought them into the front line of the war. In the early winter of 1776, a British march across Jersey toward Philadelphia had been stopped by Washington at Trenton. Thereafter the British had to be content for some months to disrupt Philadelphia shipping by a naval patrol at the Delaware capes.

In the summer of 1777, however, General Howe, the British commander, attempted to reach Philadelphia by a new maneuver. Embarking an army at New York on a fleet of over 160 ships, he sailed down the Jersey coast to Cape Henlopen, which he reached

[323] *Ibid.*, 261.

[324] [Tilton], *History of Dionysius*, 27–28. Haslet reported to Rodney from camp: "I am informed the Arch-Politician [Read] has refused the Government, & intends it I'm told for the blundering Bri[gadi]er [McKinly]. he will then govern the Old Woman and the State; and, retired behind the scene, will be blamed for nothing." Nov. 12, 1776, typed copy in HSD from Sparks MSS.

on July 29. The obvious procedure here was to turn north through the Delaware bay and river toward Philadelphia. But Howe was deterred from this step by reports of fortifications on the Delaware. Consequently he continued south to the Chesapeake and then moved north through its waters, wider and less defensible than the Delaware.

At the northern end of the Chesapeake Bay, on the shores of the Elk River, the British army was finally landed. From the Elk, Howe marched northeastward into Delaware. As the British troops moved up the road which led around the foot of Iron Hill from Glasgow to Newark, they met a detachment of American light infantry awaiting them near Cooch's Bridge in the woods beside the road.

Here on the morning of September 3, a hot skirmish occurred. The Americans gradually withdrew as additional units of British came to the aid of the German mercenaries who had led the march and received the first fire from the woods. A British attempt to outflank the Americans was turned back by marshy soil. Eventually the rebels slipped away and rejoined Washington.[325]

The American commander had brought his forces south from New York through Philadelphia to Wilmington to meet the invaders, of whose movements accounts had been brought to him by scouts along the coast. On the road between Newark and Wilmington he ordered entrenchments prepared, but the British escaped him here. Howe rested his troops for several days after the skirmish at Cooch's Bridge, and then started out from Newark north to Pennsylvania, instead of taking the normal route to Philadelphia, which lay through Wilmington. Washington wheeled his army about and hurried up the Brandywine to defend its crossing at Chadds Ford, a few miles north of the Delaware line. But here again Howe performed the unexpected. He sent a very strong left flank across the Brandywine at an undefended ford north of Washington. The surprised Americans were badly defeated in the major battle that followed and were forced to retreat farther north into Pennsylvania, leaving the road to Philadelphia, and, incidentally, all of northern Delaware, open to the enemy.

Immediately after the battle, a British contingent was rushed to Wilmington, where they captured President McKinly and

[325] Edward W. Cooch, *The Battle of Cooch's Bridge* (Wilmington, 1940).

seized a ship in the Christina loaded with official state records and funds and other valuables. They did not, however, occupy Wilmington or any part of Delaware for long. After Philadelphia was taken, Howe turned his attention to opening the Delaware River. A bloody battle secured for the British its guardian forts—they lay above the Delaware counties—and then Wilmington was abandoned, a month after its seizure, for the British felt no need to scatter their forces through the Delaware Valley when their naval strength gave them control wherever they chose to exert it. For months to come, no Delawarean who lived near navigable water was free from danger of British raiders.

The invasion and the capture of McKinly necessarily upset the functioning of the new Delaware government. In the president's absence his powers constitutionally devolved upon the speaker of the upper house, the Legislative Council. But this official, George Read, had been in Philadelphia, attending the Continental Congress. Until Read could return to Delaware by a perilous trip through New Jersey, Thomas McKean, as speaker of the House of Assembly, the lower chamber, tried to carry on in a state "without a head, without a shilling." [326]

With New Castle town exposed to British might on the river, the county polls were moved inland to Newark in October, 1777, and the legislature then chosen dared not meet in New Castle but began a peregrination through the state which eventually ended with the establishment of Dover as the new capital. Not only in New Castle were the elections disrupted; no returns at all were presented from Sussex, where the radicals, shouting of Toryism, had driven conservatives from Lewes "with a great show of arms." New Castle returned a radical slate, while Kent chose moderates, and the resultant impasse led to the adjournment of the first meeting of the legislature without the passage of a single act. New elections in Sussex returned radicals, but since holdover conservatives still controlled the upper house, the legislature remained ineffective.[327] A new election to Congress indicated the increasing radical strength, for Van Dyke alone was reelected,

[326] McKean to Read, Lunn's Tavern, Sept. 26, 1777, Read, *Read*, 279–280; *ibid.*, 274–276; McKean to C. Rodney, Oct. 15, 1777, Rodney, *Letters*, 241–243; [Tilton], *History of Dionysius*, 32.
[327] [Tilton], *History of Dionysius*, 32–33.

with the champions of independence, McKean and Rodney, supplanting Sykes and Read.[328]

Radical strength in the lower house dominated another joint meeting of the General Assembly when in March, 1778, it proceeded to the choice of a new president. McKinly's three-year term was, of course, not over, but he "had little prospect of exchange shortly," and Vice-President Read, dependent for his livelihood on his legal practice, had asked to be relieved of duties "alone sufficient to employ the whole time of any individual." In this desperate hour Caesar Rodney was chosen president by twenty votes out of twenty-four. His new responsibilities were recognized a year later, when he was relieved of his Congressional post. McKean and Van Dyke were then reelected to Congress, and Dickinson became the third delegate, in place of Rodney.[329]

During the first year of Rodney's term, the military situation of Delaware was eased considerably. An American division, including the Delaware regiment, took up winter quarters in Wilmington in December, 1777, and remained there until June, 1778. In this month the British evacuated Philadelphia in order to concentrate their forces at New York. This action moved the front lines of the war far from Delaware, except for the continued threat of naval raids from the British ships that continued to patrol the capes and sometimes entered the bay.[330]

XVIII. The Articles of Confederation

THOUGH Delaware's military problems were now much relieved, important political problems were yet to be decided. During Rodney's presidency, however, steps were taken toward a solution of these problems too.

[328] *Minutes of Council*, 162–165.
[329] *Ibid.*, 205–207, 255–259, 261–262.
[330] Ward, *Delaware Continentals*, 212–213, 236–237, 256–261, 512–517.

These steps grew out of developments in the famous Congress of 1776. In June of that year, before his opposition to a declaration of independence had temporarily discredited him, John Dickinson had been appointed chairman of a Congressional committee to prepare a plan of union. Although letters of Read, Rodney, and others prove the great importance they attached to this problem at the time,[331] the plan was not completed and submitted to the states until November, 1777.[332] There was such confusion, incident to the British invasion, in Delaware at the time that no official copy reached the executive in time for presentation to the General Assembly until the fall of the next year.[333] By the summer of 1778 every state had ratified these Articles of Confederation except New Jersey, Delaware, and Maryland, and New Jersey joined the van months before Delaware took action. Recent investigation indicates that Maryland's long delay—until 1781—was prompted in part by the interest of influential citizens in western land speculations unrecognized by the states, especially Virginia, which claimed these lands. Since the Articles provided that no state should be "deprived of territory for the benefit of the United States," these speculators had little chance of getting their claims recognized, for they largely came from states having no claim to the lands in question, and certainly Virginia would favor its own land-grabbers rather than non-Virginians. Consequently, it was to the advantage of these Maryland speculators to try to delay ratification of the Articles in the hope that either the objectionable clause would be deleted or that Virginia would relinquish its vast western claims.[334]

The headquarters of these land speculators was Philadelphia, and since that city was the focus of Delaware's mercantile interests, it would have been strange had Delaware, with no land claims itself, not supported the speculators. Indeed, Samuel Wharton, the speculators' leading lobbyist,[335] served as a delegate to Congress from Delaware in 1782 and largely occupied himself with the

---

[331] Rodney, *Letters*, 93, 102.
[332] *Journals of Congress*, IX, 907.
[333] Read, *Read*, 304; Rodney, *Letters*, 272, 290.
[334] *Cf.* Merrill Jensen, "The Cession of the Old Northwest," *Mississippi Valley Historical Review*, XXIII (1936), 27–48.
[335] A. Lee to S. Adams, Philadelphia, April 21, 1782, Burnett, *Letters*, VI, 331.

problem of claims to western lands. A Philadelphian, he was elected to Congress largely through the influence of his bosom friend, George Read.[336]

In a letter of March, 1778, to McKean, Read expressed his doubt of the wisdom of that clause in the Articles which denied the federation power to deprive states of territory. Bounds, he felt, must be put to their claims so that all the states could share land not already ceded by the Indians to the king, adding that the income from this land would pay the war debt and that the small states should not be assessed to protect the ungranted, limitless expanse of the large states.[337] But McKean, answering that a state grown too large would divide of its own choice and that Delaware could apply for western townships for her soldiers, favored immediate ratification.[338]

The irritation arising in other states by January, 1779, at the delay in ratifying the Articles, was expressed by a New Hampshire delegate, who wrote: "All the States are represented [in Congress]. I wish I could say they were Confederated, but our Froward Sister M[aryland] and her little Crooked Neighbour [Delaware] still stand out." [339]

Toward the end of January a committee of Delaware's Legislative Council composed of Read, Richard Bassett, and John Clowes, whom Read had once called "the Wilkes or McDougal of Sussex," reported on the Articles.[340] Read probably wrote the report and three of the four resolutions based on it, for they resemble

[336] Richard Neave, Jr., to G. Read, London, July 11, 1765, Read, *Read*, 29; S. Wharton to G. Read, Philadelphia, Aug. 2, 1766, *ibid.*, 32–33; T. Rodney to C. Rodney, Wilmington, Feb. 9, 1782, Rodney, *Letters*, 432–433. Read once collected debts in Delaware for one of Wharton's firms. Will Spencer to Thomas Duff, New Castle, Oct. 1, 1764, Papers of the Read Family of New Castle County, Delaware (Library of Congress). *Cf.* John A. Munroe, "Nonresident Representation in the Continental Congress," *William and Mary Quarterly*, 3rd series, IX (1952), 166–190. James Madison wrote that citizens of Delaware were "interested in the claims of the land companies," but I have found little evidence of any such financial interest. Burnett, *Letters*, VI, 341.
[337] Read, *Read*, 305.
[338] *Ibid.*, 308–309; Burnett, *Letters*, III, 149; Peeling, *Life of McKean*, 84–85.
[339] Burnett, *Letters*, IV, 6, 7.
[340] Read, *Read*, 39. John Wilkes (1727–1797) was a famous British radical pamphleteer, who was jailed on a libel charge and twice expelled from parliament. *Dictionary of National Biography*, XXI, 242–250. Alexander McDougall (1732–1786) was a Scotch-born New York merchant, soldier, and politician, called the "Wilkes of America," who was jailed for libel in 1770. *DAB*, XII, 21–22.

his earlier comments to McKean. These resolutions asked that the
boundaries of states claiming to extend to or beyond the Mississippi
be limited, that Delaware receive a share of western lands ungranted at the beginning of the Revolution, and that controversies
regarding private land rights to Delaware soil be settled in Delaware courts.[341] The General Assembly reasoned that, although the
Articles were "in divers respects unequal" and disadvantageous to
Delaware, "the interest of particular states ought to be postponed
to the general good of the union," with the hope "that the candor
and justice of the several states will, in due time, remove, as far
as possible, the objectionable parts." The delegates to Congress
were consequently ordered to sign the Articles of Confederation.
They did so as soon as they came to Congress. McKean's signature on February 22 completed official ratification, and on May 5
Dickinson and Van Dyke, late arrivals at Congress, added their
signatures.[342] When Congress filed the resolutions on February 29,
it stipulated that the filing should "never be considered as ad-
mitting any claim . . . set up or intended to be set up," a provision
obviously intended to foil any stratagem by which the three dis-
sident small states of New Jersey, Maryland, and Delaware could
gain a foothold for an attack on the ownership and control of the
western lands.[343] All three states opposed this action of Congress
and Maryland continued her lone opposition to the Articles until
1781, when upon her acceptance they became the basis of a confederation of united states of which Delaware was one.

XIX. The Factions

LOCAL politics in Delaware in the 1780s involved an almost con-
tinuous political feud between two factions, neither one of which
was ever well enough organized to be called a party. Just as British

[341] Read, *Read,* 347–349.
[342] Rodney, *Letters,* 293–294; *Journals of Congress,* XIII, 236; XIV, 548.
[343] *Ibid.,* XIII, 236–237.

invasion forced into prominence the most radical leaders in the state, those who most ardently supported a severance of the old ties, British abandonment of Philadelphia allowed a more conservative leadership to prevail. Consequently when Caesar Rodney's term as president of Delaware expired, John Dickinson, who had opposed the Declaration of Independence, was elected to succeed him. As chief executive, Rodney had distinguished himself by his active support of the war and his close cooperation with Congress. Dickinson's short term gave the erstwhile "penman of the Revolution" opportunity to display his interest in issues broader than the narrow bounds of Delaware and to attempt to assume a real legislative leadership.[344] Born in Maryland, trained for the law in England, long resident in Pennsylvania, merchant and political philosopher, it is not strange that Dickinson's thinking was not confined to strictly local issues. When a delegate to Congress in 1779 he wrote Rodney that he was "bound to prefer the general Interests of the Confederacy to the partial Interests of Constituent Members, how many soever they be & however respectable and meritorious." [345]

The increasingly conservative tendency in Delaware politics was again exhibited in the election of delegates to Congress in 1782, when Thomas McKean, Caesar Rodney, Philemon Dickinson, and Samuel Wharton were chosen.[346] This was indeed the strangest aggregation of delegates ever to represent Delaware —only one, Rodney, being a resident of Delaware, and he fast declining in physical vigor. Though McKean had been representing Delaware for years,[347] he had long ago moved to Pennsylvania and was now chiefly interested in the affairs of that state. Philemon Dickinson, the president's brother, was a landholder in Delaware but a resident of New Jersey. Samuel Wharton was a

[344] See the excellent article by John H. Powell, "John Dickinson, President of the Delaware State, 1781–1782," *Delaware History,* I (1946), 1–54, 111–134.

[345] Rodney, *Letters,* 301.

[346] Four delegates were chosen rather than the usual three after a recommendation to this effect by President Dickinson, who pointed out that inasmuch as according to the Articles, now in operation, it was necessary to have a minimum of two delegates if a state were to vote in Congress, a larger delegation should be chosen to ensure attendance. *Minutes of Council,* 700.

[347] McKean had served as president of Congress from July 10 to November 5, 1781.

Philadelphia merchant and an old friend of John Dickinson and George Read. Since the interests of the mercantile and landed aristocracy of Delaware transcended state boundaries, it was natural for them to seek dependable men of like mind to represent them regardless of where such men might reside.

Delawareans of this class, however, found it inconvenient to attend Congress, and for long periods the state was unrepresented there. The interests of able politicians were often more attracted to the state legislature, which in some ways was a more powerful and effective body than Congress. It was also true that Congressmen were paid by the state which they represented, and Delaware had been very slow in recompensing its delegates. Nicholas Van Dyke, who was a delegate to Congress from 1777 to 1782, wished to be rid of this obligation, but yet, "I cannot reconcil it to my Concience," he wrote a friend, "to retreat until this War ends, unless my Place could be filled by a better Hand. Such in our State do not incline to serve. . . . They prefer their own Ease & Interest to the Promotion of the Good of their Country." [348] Madison suggested that Delaware chose interested men from out of state as its delegates to avoid the expense of paying them.[349]

Whether because of physical proximity which enabled frequent attendance at Congress, or wealth which supported it, or patriotic zeal which encouraged it, or personal interest which demanded it, this strange delegation, with the exception of Rodney, the sole Delaware resident, gave the state a more regular representation in Congress than it had been accustomed to. But in spite of long and detailed instructions advising these men in the case of "doubts or difficulties" to "communicate them fully to the President of this State," so that he might consider asking the legislature for further direction, they did not enjoy popular support.[350] The Scotch-trained physician, Dr. Henry Latimer, who later became a Senator, protested that the appointment had been "made after he left the assembly and that he should not have voted" for Dickinson and

[348] Van Dyke to Thomas McKean, Feb. 14, 1781, McKean Papers, I, 43. His criticism was directed at John Dickinson and George Read, who had refused election to Congress on what Van Dyke thought were weak excuses.

[349] Read, *Read*, 379–380, quoting from Madison, *Papers*, II, 901.

[350] *Minutes of Council*, 713, 715–717.

Wharton, whose selection was "very Surprizing . . . Especially the Latter." [351] Wharton, attacked in the Philadelphia papers because he had stayed in England until 1778, finally found it necessary to deny to the General Assembly that he had ever been a Tory and to insist that he had remained in England at the instigation of Franklin, to whom he had made regular reports.[352]

In 1783 state pride asserted itself and the legislature passed a resolution prohibiting the election of nonresidents as delegates.[353] Wrote Timoleon: "The disgrace of being represented in Congress by foreigners had . . . become so generally impressed upon every man of the least delicacy that it was now no difficult task to appoint residents of the state, instead of our delegates from abroad." [354] Thus Rodney, the only delegate who had not attended Congress, was the only one to be reelected. The remainder of the new delegation consisted of three newcomers to Congress: Dr. James Tilton, the fiery democratic patriot and original of "Timoleon"; Eleazer McComb, merchant, banker, and state auditor; and Gunning Bedford, Jr., a young lawyer and Princeton graduate, who had been state attorney-general. Their attendance record was poor, though Congress finally had to pass a resolution to get rid of Tilton and Bedford, who insisted on staying after their term had expired.[355]

Again a rising state pride forced a change of policy, this time in respect to the executive. Whereas in 1782 John Dickinson had been elected president over his own protestations with his own the one dissenting vote, in 1783 when he announced his election as president of Pennsylvania, the news was given an unfriendly reception in the legislature. He offered to resign as president of Delaware, but the lower house, the House of Assembly, which had just been elected and may be assumed to represent an aroused popular state consciousness, would not consider it; since the president of Delaware had assumed the presidency of Pennsylvania the Delaware chair was vacant, this house declared, resignation or no

[351] Thomas to Caesar Rodney, Wilmington, Feb. 9, 1782, Rodney, *Letters*, 432–433.

[352] Wharton to Simon Kollock, Philadelphia, June 10, 1782, Legislative Papers.

[353] *Minutes of Council*, 786.

[354] [Tilton], *History of Dionysius*, 39.

[355] *Journals of Congress*, XXVI, 137–140.

resignation. Hold-over conservatives in the upper house, however, spared Dickinson the indignity of ejection. He was allowed to resign, and so, soon after, did John Cook, Kent farmer and tanner, who, as speaker of the upper house, had been serving as acting president in Dickinson's absence.

The conservatives are said to have tried to secure the election of ex-President McKinly or Chief Justice William Killen, but the opposition was too strong for them. Philadelphia journals had effectively screamed their alarms into Delaware: Was Delaware a state or a rotten borough? Would not the election to Congress of Wharton, a man who had stayed in England through the years when the outcome of the Revolution was most doubtful, be considered by the most notorious Tories as an invitation to return to America in glory? And had not this nonresident selection occurred in Delaware under the administration of Dickinson, a man who would as readily abandon Delaware for Pennsylvania as he "would leave his chair of ease"? It was of no immediate use for Dickinson to declare that he had made no secret of his continental point of view, that he had not sought preferment in Delaware but had it thrust upon him. Once reaction had started, it gained momentum, receiving further impetus from a successful conclusion of the war. When a new chief executive was chosen, it was "an independent governor," Nicholas Van Dyke.[356]

In contrast to the more forceful Rodney and Dickinson, Van Dyke was a strict constructionist. George Read, at the request of Charles Thomson, secretary of Congress, tried to persuade Van Dyke to take a more active leadership. Meeting with failure he declared that what Delaware needed was "more energy in all the parts and persons of government." The president continued to maintain, however, that an executive who attempted to use "a

---

[356] See *Freeman's Journal* (Philadelphia), Dec. 25, 1782. The story of the Delaware Congressional delegation of 1782, of its replacement in 1783, and of Dickinson's resignation is treated in detail in Munroe, "Nonresident Representation in the Continental Congress." See also [Tilton], *History of Dionysius*, 38–39. It should be noted here that the terms "conservative," "radical," and "moderate" have no exact meanings and are used only for want of better means of denoting the factions, not parties, in Delaware politics of the 1770s and 1780s. "Radical" refers to the faction more actively supporting a complete break with England; "conservative" and "moderate" refer to the faction more eager to hold to old political institutions. Since only ill-organized cliques existed in politics at this time, men could easily change sides, and then, as always, there were strange bedfellows.

constructive or implied power" would meet with "disgust and much trouble." [357]

By the fall of 1783 the conservative faction was again gaining strength, especially in New Castle, for many people who had previously refused to take the oath of loyalty, were now, with the fighting long past, beginning to qualify and to vote. So close and bitter was the voting that the results were contested in Kent and Sussex, a new election for councillor being ordered in the latter county.[358] A year later the radicals regained their power, aided perhaps by such measures of the conservatives as the dismissal and replacement of many magistrates, largely on political grounds. The year 1785 again saw the radicals victorious, though the conservatives carried Sussex for the first time since early in the Revolution.[359]

The Sussex shift of political power foreshadowed a future trend in Delaware politics. The war was now several years in the past; the radicals who had seized control during that time and swung Delaware from its usual calm course were now deemed a bit bumptious. That they were often Scotch-Irish Presbyterians diminished their prestige in the eyes of most Delawareans of English stock, especially those in the two southern counties. Here, too, many moderates and loyalists who had withdrawn from politics during the war were now actively participating in elections once again.

In 1786 the more conservative faction won control of the lower house. Their strength was shown to some extent in the choice of delegates to Congress, Gunning Bedford, Sr., war veteran and brother-in-law of George Read, Nathaniel Mitchell of Laurel, like Bedford later a Federalist governor, and Thomas Rodney being preferred over many other candidates, including three former Congressmen, Nicholas Van Dyke, John Patten, and William

[357] Read, *Read*, 398–406, 411–412.

[358] [Tilton], *History of Dionysius*, 39–41. *Votes and Proceedings of the Legislative Council of the Delaware State*, 1783–1784 (Wilmington, 1787), 25–27, 33, 34. This assembly chose John Vining, John McKinly, Henry Latimer, and Thomas Rodney delegates to Congress, but none of them attended under this appointment.

[359] [Tilton], *History of Dionysius*, 41–44. John Vining, Gunning Bedford, Jr., James Tilton, and Samuel Patterson were elected to Congress in October, 1784, and the first two, plus John Patten, William Peery, and Thomas Rodney, in November, 1785.

Peery.[360] Van Dyke's term as president had expired, so Thomas Collins, Kent landholder of Belmont Hall near Smyrna, militia officer, and brother-in-law of John Cook, was unanimously elected president, a testimony to his popularity with all sides.

Again in 1787, the conservatives were successful, but only after a hotly contested election in Sussex. On the first return its representation had been divided between the two factions in an effort to avoid a pitched battle. New elections were soon ordered, and the polls were moved from Lewes, home of much of the radical strength, to a more central location in the interior. Here the conservatives were victorious in an exciting election, in which it was said that armed bands, led by Nathaniel Mitchell and cursing all Irishmen and Presbyterians, wandered about the country near the polls to frighten the opposition.[361]

XX. The Federal Constitution

SUCH intrastate turmoil contrasts markedly with the national unity which was being sought in 1787 not far north of New Castle County. The convention which sat at Philadelphia planning a new nation culminated a series of efforts designed to make an effective government of the league of states united by the Articles of Confederation.

As early as 1781, the very year in which the Articles were

---

[360] *Minutes of Council*, 999, 1001–1004. Bedford resigned, and Dyre Kearny, a Kent attorney, was chosen to replace him. *Ibid.*, 1013, 1038–1040. The two Gunning Bedfords, Senior and Junior, were cousins.

[361] [Tilton], *History of Dionysius*, 64–70, 74–79; Thomas Rodney to Jacob Broom, Poplar Grove, Jan. 27, 1788, Brown Collection. See also petitions and records of testimony in folders entitled, "1787, October–November, Legislature, Petitions," and "1788, January–February, Legislature, Petitions," Legislative Papers. Kearny, Mitchell, and Isaac Grantham, a New Castle County politician and ex-soldier, were elected Delaware's last delegates to the Continental Congress, Thomas Rodney and John Patten having also been nominated. The *Minutes of Council*, 1080 and 1086, state that Rodney, not Grantham, was a delegate, but Kearny's letter in Burnett, *Letters*, VIII, 685, seems to prove Grantham's appointment. Perhaps Rodney was first chosen, but resigned, and Grantham was elected to his place; there is, however, no evidence of this in the *Minutes of Council*.

adopted, Congress, hitherto dependent on the states for appropriations, asked for power to levy a 5 percent ad valorem tariff on imports. Delaware agreed, but Rhode Island was reluctant, while
Virginia changed her mind after originally complying. As a result, the impost was never collected.[362] Again in 1783, Congress
asked for power to impose tariffs, coupling with this request another asking that each state should for twenty-five years establish
revenues to pay its quota of an annual requisition of one and a
half million dollars, these revenues to be separate from all other
state taxes. Delaware's compliance was swift and, for a time,
unique. Wrote Madison: "Delaware is the only one among those
which have bestowed a consideration on it [the revenue plan] that
has acceded in toto." [363] But New York's failure to agree to the
tariff defeated this second effort of Congress to bolster its weak
financial position.[364]

In 1784, to facilitate the negotiation of favorable commercial
treaties, Congress sought a fifteen-year control over commerce,
including the power to prohibit the import or export of goods carried in the vessel of a country not having a trade treaty with the
United States, and the power to forbid foreigners from bringing
into this country goods not produced in their native land or its
colonies. Delaware acted more slowly on this proposition but finally
in 1786 granted her approval. Still the Congress of the Confederation was unable to exercise this power, for too few states joined
Delaware in fully complying with the recommendation.[365]

In this same year when other attempts to increase the power
of Congress seemed to have failed, Virginia proposed a convention
of all states to discuss the general condition of interstate commerce and to formulate appropriate and desirable legislation for
submission to Congress. For this meeting Delaware chose five
commissioners, whose distinction testifies to the importance at-

[362] Minutes of Council, 628, 660, 682; Merrill Jensen, The New Nation (New
York, 1950), 58, 63–66.
[363] Burnett, Letters, VII, 259; Minutes of Council, 825–827, 829, 845.
[364] Only four states in addition to Delaware ever granted the requested revenues.
All but New York accepted the tariff. Journals of Congress, XXXI, 518, 523; E.
Wilder Spaulding, New York in the Critical Period, 1783–1789 (New York, 1932),
174.
[365] Journals of Congress, XXXI, 907–908; Minutes of Council, 954; Votes of
Legislative Council, 1785–1786, pp. 114, 118, 130.

tached to their mission. George Read, leader of the state bar and the state's most influential politician, had frequently refused other political posts on the plea of the demands of his business, but he agreed to accept this appointment. Richard Bassett, wealthy landholder of New Castle and Kent counties and of the Eastern Shore, and John Dickinson, who was back in Delaware once more, along with Jacob Broom, Wilmington manufacturer, and Gunning Bedford, Jr., prominent lawyer, completed the delegation.[366]

Broom and Bedford did not go to Annapolis, where the convention met on September 11, 1786, but the other three did attend, and Dickinson was chosen chairman of the meeting. Only five states were represented, and, after three days of discussion, the delegates present decided that more than power to regulate commerce was needed to revive the government. Consequently a report was sent to Congress and to each of the states recommending that a convention meet in Philadelphia on the second Monday in May, 1787, to consider all the ills of the Confederation.[367]

George Read thought this proposed convention so important that he asked for the postponement of a session of the United States Court of Appeals for Admiralty Cases, of which he was a judge, so he could attend the General Assembly's next meeting, explain the proceedings at Annapolis, and urge the election of delegates to the Philadelphia Convention.[368] The General Assembly approved the recommendation and passed the desired act, instructing its delegates to discuss "such alterations and further provisions, as may be necessary to render the Federal Constitution adequate to the exigencies of the Union." Read saw to it that the following important qualification was added to these instructions: "So always and provided, that such alterations or further provisions, or any of them, do not extend to that part of the fifth article of the confederation of the said states . . . which declares, that *in determining questions in the United States in Congress assem-*

[366] *Minutes of Council*, 969–971.

[367] This report quoted the instructions of the Delaware delegates at Annapolis to emphasize the fact that Delaware had been the only state which had ordered its delegates to frame an act to be submitted to Congress for its approval and to the state legislatures for their confirmation. *Journals of Congress*, XXXI, 677–680; *Minutes of Council*, 1001, 1025; Read, *Read*, 430. Delaware's copy of the report is among the Executive Papers in the State Archives.

[368] Read, *Read*, 421–423.

bled, each state shall have one vote." He had already explained to
Dickinson the necessity for such a clause to "relieve the commissioners of the State from disagreeable argumentation, as well as
prevent the downfall of the State, which [otherwise] would at
once become a cypher in the union." [369] It was the support of this
provision by the small states in the Constitutional Convention
that secured them half a loaf, namely, an equal vote in the United
States Senate, although they failed to secure a similar equality in
the House of Representatives.

The group chosen to represent the state at Annapolis—Read,
Dickinson, Bassett, Broom, and Bedford—were again chosen as
delegates to the Philadelphia Convention. Picture them as they
appeared to a Georgia delegate upon arrival in Philadelphia in the
summer of 1787. Read at fifty-four enjoyed an excellent reputation as a man of character and learning, but was a tiresome orator
with feeble voice and poor articulation. Though Dickinson, because of his renown as a writer and scholar, was paid "the greatest attention whenever he spoke," William Pierce, the Georgian,
found him "an indifferent Speaker," who labored "with an affected
air of wisdom . . . to produce a trifle," one whose language was
"irregular and incorrect" and whose "flourishes" were "like ex-
piring flames, . . . [which] just show themselves and go out—
[with] no traces . . . left on the mind to chear or animate it."
Bassett was forty-two, "gentlemanly," "a religious enthusiast,"
"a Man of plain sense," with "modesty enough to hold his Tongue."
Broom, the youngest Delaware delegate, was thirty-five, "a plain
good Man, with some abilities, but nothing to render him con-
spicuous, silent in public, but chearful and conversible in private."
Bedford, then about forty and "very corpulent," was "a bold and
nervous Speaker," with "a very commanding and striking manner,"
but "warm and impetuous in his temper, and precipitate in his
judgment." [370]

[369] Read, *Read*, 438–440; *Minutes of Council*, 1035–1036, 1038–1040; George H.
Ryden, *Delaware—the First State in the Union* (Wilmington, 1938), 8–11. Read
said his distrust of the large states arose especially from their greediness for western
lands: "I consider the acts of Congress hitherto, as to the ungranted lands in most
of the larger States, as sacrificing the just claims of the smaller and bounded States
to a proportional share therein, for the purpose of discharging the national debt
incurred during the war."
[370] William Pierce, "Character Sketches of Delegates to the Constitutional Con-

The details of the convention of 1787 are at once too familiar and too involved to be recounted here. In general, the Delaware delegates favored a strong national government as long as Delaware shared equally with the other states in the control of that government. To emphasize this last point, Read reminded the convention that he and his colleagues were instructed (by a clause he, himself, had written) to withdraw if the equal status of the states was altered.[371] Impetuous Gunning Bedford lost his temper and threatened that the small states would seek foreign allies rather than a union in which they lost their equal suffrage. Dickinson spoke privately to Madison of the same possibility. He proposed a compromise on representation through a bicameral legislature, just such a compromise as was finally adopted, and this the Delaware delegates apparently did not consider inconsistent with their instructions. Delaware's small size and population and its consequent weakness, its desire to share in the public domain, its intercolonial connections and particularly its dependence on the port of Philadelphia, were factors which led Delawareans to seek a strong government. In a strong government, the Constitutional compromise on representation was the best guarantee of an abiding influence on policy that Delawareans could hope for. Consequently the Delaware delegates who had, through Read's influence on the legislature, shackled themselves by instructions to insist on an equal vote—to prevent "disagreeable argumentation"—could feel free to support the best arrangement they could get.[372]

At the first Delaware assembly session after the convention had completed its task, President Collins presented the Constitution

---

vention," Max Farrand, *The Records of the Federal Convention of 1787* (New Haven, 1911–1937), III, 92–93.

[371] Farrand, *Records*, I, 37. George H. Ryden's pamphlet, *Delaware—the First State in the Union*, discusses the part played by the Delaware delegates in the convention.

[372] The sentiments voiced by each of the five delegates can be traced handily through the index at the back of Vol. IV of Farrand, *Records*. Read was most nationalistically minded, favoring a complete consolidation, in which the states would be wholly obliterated. It is not odd that he became a Hamiltonian Senator. Dickinson wanted a strong government, but insisted that much power should remain in the states. Bedford was even more conscious of state rights; he and Bassett opposed giving Congress a veto over state legislation. Broom, the manufacturer, said little, but when delegates despaired of any agreement he insisted the convention must produce some results, if only by a bare majority.

and recommended it "as a subject of the most important consideration, involving in its adoption not only our prosperity and felicity,
but perhaps our national existence." [373] His plea was supported by
four petitions, with 171 signatures, urging the calling of a convention to ratify the Constitution.[374]

A resolution led to an election on November 26, 1787, at which
each county chose ten delegates to the ratifying convention. The
number of delegates was the same as to the General Assembly, and,
indeed, in Sussex belated elections to the Assembly and Council
were also held on November 26. In general, the radical faction
carried New Castle, while the conservatives were victorious in
Kent and Sussex. The defeated candidates in Sussex complained
of unfair practices, but, though they memorialized the convention,
they did not ask action, for they did not want to waste time when
both factions were known to be in favor of the Constitution.[375]

When the convention met in Dover on Monday, December 3,
1787, President Collins addressed it and presented a copy of the
Constitution. Nothing is known of the discussion which took
place during the next few days, but on December 7 by a unanimous
vote Delaware became the first state to ratify the Constitution.
The death knell of the Confederation had been sounded—and in
the small capital of one of the smallest of the states which had
joined together in that Confederation less than seven years earlier.
Within two weeks ratification by Pennsylvania and New Jersey
made the Delaware Valley bloc complete.

While proximity to Philadelphia and the convention may have
encouraged the rapid action of these three states, the influence of
the close interrelations fostered by the Delaware River must not
be underestimated—after all, Georgia, far to the south, was the
fourth state to ratify. The economic and cultural connections of
the counties in three states and on both shores of the Delaware
must have prepared their people for closer union. Jersey, like
Delaware, ratified unanimously, without factional opposition, and
for the same reasons, its small size, its interest in western lands,

[373] *Minutes of Council*, 1065.
[374] *Ibid.*, 1079; Ryden, *Delaware—the First State*, 17; petitions in DSA.
[375] [Tilton], *History of Dionysius*, 73–75. *Cf.*, folder "Convention to ratify United
States Constitution, 1787," DSA.

sound money, and the sanctity of contracts, and its dependence on out-of-state ports.[376]

The conservative group which had dominated Delaware for several years and had led her into the new government soon secured the election of George Read and Richard Bassett to the United States Senate and of John Vining to the House of Representatives. It is significant that the new government was considered important enough to be worth the time of three of Delaware's most eminent men, at least some of whom had refused to serve the Confederation. They recognized the value of a strong union; the smallness of Delaware fostered nationalism among thoughtful men of all factions. So, from amidst an election victory of his opponents, Dr. James Tilton, a leader of the radical faction, the Republican party-to-be, surveyed the future under the new government with much hope. "Although every other means under Providence should fail us," he declared, "we hope at least to derive some consolation from the New Federal Constitution. From hence we may expect some standing institutions to walk by. Fraudulent retrospective laws will be no more. . . . And although it should be long, before Virtue shall become triumphant over Vice, good men will nevertheless be more out of the reach and power of unjust and wicked oppressors than Heretofore." [377]

[376] Ryden, *Delaware—the First State*, 24–29; Richard P. McCormick, *Experiment in Independence* (New Brunswick, 1950), 272–278.
[377] *History of Dionysius*, 100.

Part II

Post-Revolutionary Patterns

I. Problems of Peace

EIGHT years of combat had won for Delaware a recognition of her independence; more years of political maneuvering had united her with the other former colonies, first in a loose league and then under a strong national government. Of the changes which had occurred in the life of the people of Delaware during these years, some were a result of the Revolution, some were a forecast of the future development of the state.

"The American War is over," Benjamin Rush wrote, "but this is far from being the case with the American Revolution." Patriotic conservative Delawareans, regaining political control in the Confederation period, regarded some aspects of the continuing revolution without favor. Weakened by the defections of loyalists, the Anglican landed gentry were concerned that the poorer classes, especially the Scotch-Irish, had derived encouragement from the strife to contest control of the three counties. Yet the levelling influences of the Revolution had brought no extension of the franchise, though these influences were evident in the prohibition of slave importation in the 1776 constitution, which when considered in connection with the Pennsylvania abolition law of 1780 betokened an attack on slavery.

Peace had meant the reopening of the Delaware River trade and made the Philadelphia market again accessible to Delaware lumber, wheat, corn, and flour. The war had encouraged economic self-reliance, and the end of British restrictions removed all legal hindrances to industrial development. Delaware's hitherto-sound paper currency had, however, been ruined by the collapse of the continental issue, and the weakness of the Confederation made the future price structure uncertain. The opening of western lands threatened to draw farmers away from Delaware and to divert the flow of immigrants from the state unless industrial development was quickened and agricultural methods reformed.

The rapid growth of Methodism forced its adherents to adopt a form of organization, and their numbers represented an imminent political force whose support would be needed by those who would control the destiny of Delaware. A shattered Anglican church needed to reorganize if it were to regain and retain its old prestige. Finally, since the security of the state would rest not only on the morality, but on the education and intelligence of its citizens, the schools and the press needed to be developed to combat the ignorance and backwardness which had heretofore prevailed far too widely.

II. Agriculture

BEFORE the Revolution, during the Revolution, and after the Revolution the majority of Delawareans were farmers. Fortunately we have a thoughtful survey of their vocation in the report made by Dr. James Tilton in 1788 to the Philadelphia Society for Promoting Agriculture, which had forwarded to him a series of forty-eight queries posed by a French scientist.

The depreciation of the currency during the Revolution, Tilton revealed, had caused farm rents to be paid in produce and farms to be let "sometimes, though rarely, on shares." The chief crops for human consumption were wheat, barley, corn, buckwheat, potatoes, cabbage, various pulse crops, and other garden truck. In addition, oats and grasses, especially timothy and clover, were grown for fodder, and flax for a domestic spinning industry. Although tobacco and hemp grew very well, they were "not cultivated as articles of commerce or manufacture." [1]

These crops were grown from domestic seed. No one mode of cultivation was followed, though the "approved practice" was "to fallow up the ground" after having planted first wheat and then corn. [2] The small single plough was the usual instrument employed

---

[1] "Tilton's Notes on Agriculture," *Agricultural History*, XX (1946), 180.

[2] Eleazer McComb gives his planting schedule for six 45-acre fields in a letter to Samuel Hodgdon, Dover, May 7, 1788, Philadelphia Society for Promoting Agriculture, *Memoirs*, VI (c. 1939), 142–144. Tilton declared six fields to be the best system.

to break up the land. Wheat fields were generally tilled four to six inches deep, but it was "a growing opinion" in 1788 "that the deeper the better." Rake harrows were used to pulverize and level the fallow fields, fluke harrows to weed between rows of corn. Wheat, barley, and rye were sowed in September, and corn in May. The winter crops were harvested in June or July, bound up in sheaves, and "put into small shocks" in the field. Some days later, after drying, they were carted away and stacked out of doors. Flax, oats, and clover required more housing. Wheat and barley were trod out with horses soon after harvest, whereas oats and rye were threshed out with a flail made of wood, leather, or iron.[3]

In the colonial period there had been little need of fertilizer, dependence being placed "chiefly on the freshness & richness" of the soil, but the Confederation period brought a growing awareness of the wasteful nature of this treatment of the soil. Consequently manure was "more necessary & more used than formerly."[4] Cattle were folded in the summer and autumn, and their pens were moved every ten days to increase the fertility of the soil. "Ashes made by culinary uses" provided another source of fertilizer, but marl was not used.

The chief enemies of agricultural produce were rust and scab, cockle, cheat, wild garlic, worms, and the Hessian fly. The fly's ravages were particularly serious; it "has, of late years, done us more damage, in our crops, than all other contingencies whatsoever," asserted Dr. Tilton.[5] Dr. Charles Wharton, as befitted a clergyman, saw a silver lining to this insect cloud. The fly, he commented, would force the farmer to take great pains to save his crop; then "the predilection to large, instead of rich fields of wheat will be gradually done away—& the size of farms will be diminished, but the number of Farmers will be increased & our Country brought much Sooner into that State of cultivation from which human labour will reap the most ample fruits of its exertions."[6]

The most common trees, Tilton wrote, were oaks, hickory,

[3] "Tilton's Notes on Agriculture," 180–183.
[4] Colonel John Jones, of Sussex, made a model of a cart for scattering manure. Eleazer McComb to Samuel Hodgdon, Dover, May 7, 1788, Philadelphia Society for Promoting Agriculture, *Memoirs*, VI, 142–143.
[5] "Tilton's Notes on Agriculture," 180–184.
[6] Charles H. Wharton to Samuel Powell, Prospect Hill, June 12, 1792, Philadelphia Society for Promoting Agriculture, *Memoirs*, VI (1939), 167–169.

poplar, walnut, maple, and ash, while cedars and pines of great commercial value abounded in Sussex. An English immigrant, Dr. Bancroft, who settled in Wilmington, invested heavily in black oak bark. This bark, called quercitron, "was first sent out from Wilmington to England, . . . and after a fair investigation of the thirteen States, Delaware had the precedence." [7]

The cattle, which were small, were "bred in the greatest number on the marshes & forests of the two lower counties," then driven to New Castle County, "where the most cultivated meadows" abounded. Here they were "grazed & stall-fed for the markets of Wilmington & Philadelphia." [8] The sheep also were "chiefly of the small breed." Salt grass was cut from the marshes and stacked about four feet above the ground on horizontal poles; in the winter the sheep took shelter under this roof and ate grass from between the poles. Neither cattle nor sheep were "customarily sold under 4 years old." A few mules were bred and horses were raised "for the road & other services," but few for racing, which was discouraged by the laws.[9]

The movement for economy in land usage demonstrated by the increasing popularity of fertilizers is also evidenced by the many private acts for swamp drainage and stream embankments passed by the legislature in this period. It was necessary to secure legislative action to prevent miserly or lethargic marsh-owners from negating all attempts at land reclamation by failing to ditch or embank their own fields, thus rendering a neighbor's improvements worthless. These marshes, particularly along Duck Creek, had already become the center of a valuable muskrat-trapping business, and protests were being made against the use of iron gigs and against poaching by "loose, straggling persons without any certain Residence." [10]

[7] "Tilton's Notes on Agriculture," 185; Montgomery, *Reminiscences*, 360–361.

[8] "Tilton's Notes on Agriculture," 185. *Cf.* Major Philip Reybold, grazier, to Richard Peters, May 22, 1810, Philadelphia Society for Promoting Agriculture, *Memoirs*, II (1811), 236–237.

[9] "Tilton's Notes on Agriculture," 186. A plea for horse racing was made in a petition of twenty-eight residents of Kent. See folder, "1791, January–February, Legislature, Petitions, Misc.," Legislative Papers.

[10] *Laws*, II, "Table of Private Acts," appendix, 11–16. Petition of June, 1784, Legislative Papers.

The Penn family made an attempt after the Revolution to secure a revenue from Delaware by reviving their claims to quitrents and alienation fines, as well as to such ungranted land as remained in the state. Since quitrents had seldom been paid after 1713, this attempt at a revenue was obviously foredoomed to failure. Their claim to ungranted lands, however, stirred the legislature to action. After first warning the inhabitants against receiving deeds from the Penns, it declared, on February 2, 1793, such an act a crime punishable by a fine of one hundred dollars. On June 19 a state land office was established by statute to dispose of vacant lands at fifty cents an acre in fee simple.[11] On February 7, 1794, the land office act was amended, with the statement that "the right to the soil and lands" of Delaware had been "heretofore claimed by the crown of Great Britain" and, having been relinquished by the treaty of 1783, now belonged to the citizens of Delaware. "The claims of the late and former pretended proprietaries of this state, to the soil and lands contained within the same," it was added, "are not founded either in law or equity." [12]

Thus Delaware denied the Penns' claims without any compensation. The basis for the phrase, "pretended proprietaries," was undoubtedly the fact that William Penn's title to Delaware rested on a grant from James, Duke of York, made in August, 1682, at a time when the duke himself had no legal title from the crown to the lower counties. Although in the following spring the crown did grant this land to the duke, he made no further grant to Penn. The Quaker does seem to have had, nevertheless, a good equity claim to Delaware, although of what nature it is difficult to say. When an ejectment suit brought by Penn lawyers reached the federal court in 1804, it was nonsuited on technical grounds. The Delaware counsel were prepared to base their chief argument on the claim that Penn had received no grant to private lands in America but to a seignory on political principles and that the Revolution and Declaration of Independence "prostrated equally the

[11] *Ibid.*, II, 1077–1078, 1160–1166. A petition for the establishment of a land office in "New Sussex" had come to the legislature as early as 1783. "1783, May–June, Legislature, Petition," Legislative Papers.

[12] *Laws*, II, 1174–1175. A neighbor was given first right to vacant lands to the extent of increasing his holdings to a total of two hundred acres.

Kingly and Proprietory Powers," rights to soil and seignory being "inextricably commingled" and falling together.[13] Other ejectment suits were begun but were not prosecuted, and the Penn claims were eventually abandoned. This default was doubtless encouraged by the imminence of the War of 1812 and by the fact that the vacant lands in Delaware were of little value, while quitrents, as afore-mentioned, had generally been unpaid for decades before the Revolution.[14]

The water as well as the land proved a source of wealth. As early as 1769 protests were made that mill dams across the Brandywine obstructed the fishery.[15] Robert Honyman, in 1775, found "a great herring fishery . . . on Christeen creek, & I believe all through this country." [16] The bays of Sussex County became valuable for their shell-fisheries.[17] The legislature was asked to prohibit the exportation of oysters from Rehoboth Bay because the supply was being depleted rapidly. "Many years ago," residents of the neigh-borhood asserted, "one man in one day might have caught in Rehoboth bay Thirty Bushels of Oysters and . . . now a man is suckcessful if he can take in the Same time one Sixth part of that number." Other states had banned the exporting of oysters, "in consequence of which several vessels which were formerly en-gaged in the business of carrying oysters from New York to Phila-delphia and other Places are now Resorting to Rehobeth bay." [18] Another complaint alleged that before a ditch had been cut from Assawoman Bay to Assateague Sound this bay had been connected by an inlet to the ocean and consequently was a good port for pilot boats and "other Vessels of Trade." Then great quantities of fish,

[13] Richard S. Rodney, "The End of the Penns' Claim to Delaware, 1789–1814; Some Forgotten Lawsuits," *Pennsylvania Magazine of History and Biography*, LXI (1937), 197. This excellent treatise is the basis for the discussion in the last two paragraphs above.

[14] *Ibid.*, 200–203. In spite of the disregard of quitrents, Thomas Rodney had written as early as 1782, "The Quit-Rents which is a matter of great Consideration among the people, remain yet unsettled." To James Tilton, Wilmington, Aug. 19, 1782, Brown Collection.

[15] *House Minutes*, 1769, 185, 189–190, 198–199.

[16] *Colonial Panorama*, 73.

[17] Joseph Dyer, opening an oyster house in Frederica in 1790, advertised: "He has engaged Oysters from Rehoboth Bay, once a month, until they are out of season. Gentlemen foxhunters, will be supplied with every refreshment after a chase, at the sign of the Death of the Fox." *Delaware Gazette*, Nov. 6, 1790.

[18] Folder, "About 1796, Legislature, Petitions, Misc.," Legislative Papers.

oysters and cockels had been found in Assawoman Bay. But now the inlet was stopped, the oysters and cockels were dead, and the fishery was greatly decreased.[19] As with its land, Delaware was wasteful of its marine resources.

The interest of Delawareans in the Philadelphia Society for Promoting Agriculture, however, indicates some desire to profit from advances made in agricultural knowledge. Founded in 1785 as one of the first agricultural societies in America, within four years it claimed eight Delawareans (James Bellach, William Geddes, William Killen, Vincent Loockerman, Eleazer McComb, John Patten, James Sykes, and James Tilton) as honorary members, a designation applied to those who lived at a distance from Philadelphia.[20] In the next two decades several Delawareans addressed suggestions to this society on the improvement of agricultural methods.[21]

III. Flour-making

THE post-Revolutionary period saw manufacturing grow in New Castle County in a manner that was not so important in its extent as in its implications, for it foreshadowed the schism of modern Delaware into upstate industrial and downstate agrarian areas.

After the Revolution, as before, the most important branch of manufacturing in Delaware was flour-milling and its allied industries, such as coopering. The center of this industry was still the Brandywine, where Schoepf, travelling through this region at the close of the war, reported seeing "several mills . . . so con-

[19] Folder "1800, Legislature, Petitions, Misc.," *ibid.*

[20] Philadelphia Society for Promoting Agriculture, *Memoirs*, VI, 198–228. Among the other members with Delaware connections were John and Philemon Dickinson, Levi Hollingsworth, Thomas McKean, John Ross, Charles Thomson, Benjamin Chew, and Robert Morris.

[21] See, in addition to the items already mentioned, Charles Wharton, "Answers to Queries on Plaister of Paris," Prospect Hill, Aug. 19, 1796, *Memoirs*, II (Philadelphia, 1811), appendix, 58–61. The Society's MSS., I, refer to a communication received from William Young of Rockland on gypsum.

veniently placed on this creek that large shalops can lie close to them, and unload and load wheat and flour with great ease." "The flour trade," he wrote, "has now so increased the value of this profitable situation that an acre of land on the creek fit for a mill-site costs 100 Pd. and more Pensyl. Current." [22] Robert Hunter, who travelled through the same area about a year later, reported: "The river Brandytown [Brandywine] is famous for turning fifteen mills, which are the first in America and perhaps in the world. They were never known to cease working, summer or winter. . . . These mills belong to eleven people and bring them in an immense income. Four of them are in the possession of one person." [23] In 1786 Wilmington exported 20,783 barrels of superfine flour, 457 barrels of common flour, 256 barrels of midlings, and 346 of "ship stuff." [24]

Tilton, in 1788, asserted that "In Delaware, the manufacture of flour is supposed to be in the utmost perfection; and is much more than the produce of the state." "There are," he continued, "in one view on the brandewine, ten mills, with not less than 20 pair of stones, capable of grinding 2,000 bushels per diem." Each set of gears served two pairs of stones, one pair being dressed or cooled while the other was running so that the mill might grind "perpetually day & night." The operation was so mechanized that one man could run each mill. From the shallops or wagons the grain was put into the garners; thence by water-driven machines it was run through screws, poured into the grinding hopper, carried "from the trough aloft to the cooling floor," spread to cool, collected in the bolting hopper, and separated by the bolting cloth "from the bran, shorts &c." [25]

In 1791, according to George Bush, collector for the district, twelve mills in the Brandywine area employed only forty-five men, but many more were employed in subsidiary manufacturing. Bush's figures were as follows:

[22] Schoepf, *Travels*, I, 378.

[23] *Quebec to Carolina in 1785–1786; Being the Travel Diary and Observations of Robert Hunter, Jr., a Young Merchant of London*, Louis B. Wright and Marion Tinling, eds. (San Marino, Calif., 1943), 176.

[24] William Winterbotham, *An Historical, Geographical, and Philosophical View of the United States of America, and of the European Settlements in America and the West Indies* (New York, 1796), II, 466.

[25] "Tilton's Notes on Agriculture," 184–185.

"RETURN OF MANUFACTURERS, TRADESMEN &C IN WILMINGTON DELAWARE & ITS VICINITY INCLUDING BRANDYWINE MILLS

	No. of Mills &c	No. of Men	Remarks
Merchant Mills [flour, etc.]	12	45	
Saw Mills	6	12	
Paper Mills	1	25	*including Women*
Slitting Mills [iron]	1	16	*including Wagoners*
Barley Mills for shelling barley	1	3	
Coopers		59	
Printers & Book binders		30	
Carpenters		42	
Joiners		9	
Brick Layers		15	
Brick Makers		17	
Black Smiths		28	
Silver Smiths		7	
Taylors		36	
Weavers		22	
Wool & Cotton Card Makers		55	*includg. women*
Shoe & Boot Makers		42	*& children*
Watch & Clock Makers		5	
Spining Wheel & Chair Makers		13	
Carriage Makers		22	
Pump & Block Makers		4	
Boat Builders		3	
Ship Carpenters		6	
Comb Makers		4	
Hatt Makers		28	
Snuf Mills	1	4	
		552	*Totall employd"* [26]

In the fall of 1789 and the spring of 1790, according to Winterbotham, the Brandywine mills made fifty thousand barrels of superfine flour, 1,354 of common, four hundred of midlings, as many of ship stuff, and two thousand of corn meal. They consumed 308,000 bushels of wheat and corn, an amount equal to "the export in those articles from the port of Philadelphia for the same year." The total given employment, he judged, was two hundred; fifty to seventy of these were coopers making casks for the flour, and others formed the crews of twelve sloops, of thirty tons each, used to transport

[26] Alexander Hamilton MSS. (Library of Congress) as copied in H. Clay Reed, ed., *Readings in Delaware History, Economic Development* (mimeographed, Newark, 1939), 39.

both the grain and the flour. These sloops were unloaded very quickly; in one instance one thousand bushels were taken up four stories in four hours. A vessel bearing such a burden might arrive with the flood tide, unload, and depart on the succeeding ebb with three hundred barrels of flour aboard.[27]

La Rochefoucault compared these mills with "those at London bridge in England and those which the brothers Perrier have constructed at Paris near the Groscaillou," but he thought the mechanical process from grinding to bolting made the Brandywine mills superior. He examined particularly the mill operated in partnership by Joseph Tatnall and his son-in-law, Thomas Lea, and reported that Lea felt Europe was "in a state of decrepitude (these are his words), whilst the genius of America, full of vigour, [was] arriving at perfection." La Rochefoucault felt this to be a common opinion in America, but observed that it did not prevent Lea "from adopting all the good inventions of Europe by which he [might] improve his mill." [28]

Tatnall and Lea bought their grain in Virginia, Maryland, and New York, brought it to the Brandywine in two sloops which they owned, and in the same sloops took the manufactured flour to Philadelphia to be sold for export. They ground a hundred thousand bushels yearly; from each hundred bushels they produced nineteen barrels of fine flour, two barrels of second quality, three of third, and ninety bushels of bran, for a total produce of 5,910 pounds and a wastage of only ninety pounds. In the mill they employed but six men, who chiefly packaged the flour and were paid six to eight dollars a month, plus washing, board, and clothing. Twenty-four other men were employed on the sloops and in making the barrels. Most of the workmen were foreigners, either English or Irish, and the millers complained of their drunkenness and indolence. No Negroes were employed not only because the Quaker proprietors opposed slavery but also because they were of the opinion that Negroes were slow and did not work well with white laborers.[29]

This mill also ground large quantities of corn which was used in

[27] Winterbotham, *Historical View*, II, 466–467.
[28] The Duke de la Rochefoucault Liancourt, *Travels through the United States of North America* (London, 1800), III, 493–497.
[29] *Ibid.*, 497–499, 562, 694.

bread in parts of the United States. It was also used to fatten poultry and cattle and was exported to the West Indies. In the winter, despite Hunter's statement, river ice sometimes caused the mills to shut down for three to eight weeks. The workers were then laid off, while the millers settled their accounts, a simple process since they bought for cash and sold for sixty- or ninety-day notes. The workers were able to save enough for their support during this period, and even after a few years enough to permit the purchase of land in the West.[30]

The amazing mechanization of the Brandywine mills was largely due to the adoption of the inventions of Oliver Evans. Evans was born in or near Newport, Delaware, in 1755, son of a cordwainer turned farmer. He was early apprenticed to a wheelwright, but later joined his brothers at their mill. In 1782 he became interested in improving the elevator, the conveyor, the hopper-boy, the drill, and the kiln-drier.[31] At first the Brandywine millers were skeptical of his devices, calling them "rattle-traps," but when they observed his success in installing them elsewhere, they became more impressed. Their spokesman is reported to have told Evans, "Oliver, we have had a meeting and agreed that if thee would furnish all the materials and thy own boarding and come thyself to set up the machinery in one of our mills, thee may come and try it; and if it answers a valuable purpose, we will pay thy bill; but if it does not answer, thee must take it all out again, and leave the mill just as thee finds it, at thy own expense." [32] Testimony that they found the "rattle-traps" satisfactory can be found in a broadside recommending Evans' "improvements" which was published at Philadelphia in 1791 and signed by Joseph Tatnall, Thomas Lea, Samuel Hollingsworth, Thomas Shallcross, and Cyrus Newlin.[33] Adoption of these inventions was thereafter rapid; some patents were secured by Evans from Delaware in 1787, and others were won from Pennsylvania, Maryland, and the federal government. In 1791, Evans,

[30] La Rochefoucault, *Travels*, III, 500–501.
[31] Charles B. Kuhlmann, *The Development of the Flour-Milling Industry in the United States* (Boston, 1929), 96–98.
[32] Bishop, *History of Manufactures*, I, 145n, 146n.
[33] Greville and Dorothy Bathe, *Oliver Evans* (Philadelphia, 1935), xiii. The reputation of the Brandywine millers was such that Evans could not get widespread acceptance of his innovations until this group had accepted them. Kuhlmann, *Flour-Milling Industry*, 98.

who had moved to Philadelphia, published *The Young Mill-Wright and Millers' Guide,* and for years he labored to apply the steam engine to transportation.[34]

The methods of the Brandywine millers were not always popular.[35] Because they preferred "purchasing large Quantities of Wheat and Manufacturing the same into Flour for distant markets" (that is, merchant milling) to custom milling at a fixed toll, the legislature in 1785 ordered millers of Christina Creek and its tributaries to devote certain days each week to milling for family consumption.[36] The necessity for this law indicates that there was no great decline in the profits from merchant milling in the first years of peace. In 1789 people protested that many of the millers preferred paying a fine to obeying the law, and consequently the next legislature raised the fine.[37]

In 1796 the legislature moved to protect the reputation of Delaware flour abroad by passing legislation "to prevent the exportation of flour not merchantable." Prescriptions were established for the casks in which flour was to be shipped. The miller's brand must appear on the cask and the quantity be designated. All superfine flour and midlings were to be inspected according to designated methods before exportation. This act did not apply, however, to Kent and Sussex or to interstate commerce but only to flour being shipped to foreign countries from New Castle County.[38] The legislature also encouraged the establishment of mills and to that end frequently permitted the condemnation of necessary land throughout the state.[39] Though every stream in Delaware boasted one or more grist mills, it was, however, on the Brandywine and the adjacent Chris-

---

[34] Bathe and Bathe, *Evans,* xvii, 4; typed copy of petition in folder, "Oliver Evans," HSD; *Laws,* II, 915–917. The Delaware patent specifically permitted Marshall and Stroud of New Castle County to use machines, similar to Evans', which they had already constructed in their mill, thus indicating that the flour-milling industry of Delaware was so extensive that it fostered inventiveness.

[35] An unsuccessful attempt of the Brandywine millers to combat rising prices by a non-purchase agreement is described by a correspondent to the *Delaware Gazette,* Sept. 16, 1789, in Biblical style probably intended to ridicule the Friendly speech of the millers.

[36] Petition of January 2, 1783, Legislative Papers; Clark, *History of Manufactures,* I, 64; *Laws,* I, 326–327; II, 812–815.

[37] Petition of October 12, 1789, Legislative Papers; *Laws,* II, 967–968.

[38] *Ibid.,* 1240–1246. Such legislation was by no means peculiar to Delaware. Kuhlmann, *Flour-Milling Industry,* 35.

[39] *Laws,* II, 1027, 1085, 1202, 1320; III, 121.

tina (then spelled Christiana), that Delaware industrialization was to be born. By the last decade of the eighteenth century in the thirty to forty miles of the Brandywine's course from Pennsylvania through Delaware there were one hundred and thirty improved mill sites.[40] As an anonymous versifier sang:

> *"Nor selfish does it pass unnoticed by;*
> *Thro' wide canals it glides serene and still.*
> *The stream, conducted from its course on high,*
> *Is taught to turn full many an useful mill.*[41]

IV. Other Manufactures

THE textile industry was one of the first branches of manufacturing to follow flour-milling to the Brandywine's banks. In 1795 Robert Dawson advertised that he was making bolting cloths of American silk in Wilmington.[42] These cloths were used in the manufacture of flour and were recommended by the Brandywine millers as equal in quality to those imported from Holland.[43] The raw silk which was secured from Georgia, was apparently not very satisfactory, for in 1797 Dawson asked Congress to repeal the duties on raw silk "for his better encouragement." [44]

Fulling and dyeing mills appeared on the Brandywine as early as 1790.[45] La Rochefoucault found that one of these mills printed linens that had been imported from India and were then resold in Philadelphia.[46] Among the proprietors was Archibald Hamilton Rowan, an Anglo-Irish political refugee, who had a "Calico printing manufactory on the Brandywine" in the 1790s.[47]

[40] Winterbotham, *Historical View*, 466; *Pennsylvania Packet*, Feb. 11, 1790.
[41] "The Brandywine," *American Museum*, III (1788), 186.
[42] *Delaware Gazette*, Sept. 8, 1795.
[43] *Ibid.*, July 12, 1796; La Rochefoucault, *Travels*, III, 502–503.
[44] *American State Papers*, V, *Finance*, I, 492.
[45] *Delaware Gazette*, Oct. 2 and 9, 1790. One textile printer, John Aitkin, was said to have previously worked at his trade in Britain and in the Great Valley.
[46] La Rochefoucault, *Travels*, III, 501–502.
[47] *Delaware Gazette*, May 29, 1799; Montgomery, *Reminiscences*, 28–29. Cf. A. H. Rowan, *Autobiography* (Dublin, 1840) and Harold Nicolson, *The Desire to Please: a Story of Hamilton Rowan and the United Irishmen* (New York, 1943).

What was probably the first cotton mill in the state was established in 1795 by Jacob Broom. This wealthy Quaker was first burgess of Wilmington and had been a signer of the Constitution.[48] His factory may have been started in the Wilmington Academy building, but it was soon moved to a place on the Brandywine, near which Broom built a mansion, "spacious for that day." [49] After a visit to the mill on August 1, 1795, Thomas Rodney wrote: "This is an Improvement that exceeds any thing I have yet seen. It is without doubt very Compleat, all the carding, woofing and spinning is done by warter & machines which are excellent in their performance—very few such excellent Cotton stuffs are imported as those made here." [50] Rodney was probably viewing one of the ten oldest mills in America and seeing Arkwright's water frame in operation.[51]

On February 6, 1797, when fire destroyed the mill, only slightly more than half the loss of ten thousand dollars was covered by insurance. Broom requested the legislature to allow him to make up the loss by a lottery that he might re-establish his business, "which in its operation is so beneficial to our Country." [52] Though statutory permission was given, the mill apparently was not rebuilt.[53]

Textiles, of course, had long been commonly made in the home. "In every family," wrote Elizabeth Montgomery, "a wheel was used some part of the day, for hired girls spent their evenings in spinning." [54] The cards used in this craft were manufactured by the Mendinhalls in Wilmington and were sold by old women and children, as well as storekeepers.[55] Although Oliver Evans claimed to

---

[48] *Delaware and Eastern Shore Advertiser*, Sept. 10, 1794. A list of his properties sold at public auction is given in the (Wilmington) *American Watchman*, Nov. 7, 1810. This list shows that he owned much land in Wilmington and five hundred acres in Ohio.

[49] Montgomery, *Reminiscences*, 42–43; Bishop, *History of Manufactures*, II, 63.

[50] Rodney, Propositions and Diary, MS., collection of Mr. Charles Dorman.

[51] Clark, *History of Manufactures*, I, 535; La Rochefoucault, *Travels*, III, 502.

[52] Petition of May 31, 1797, Legislative Papers.

[53] *Laws*, II, 1366–1368; Montgomery, *Reminiscences*, 43. At the beginning of 1797 Broom had petitioned Congress for the repeal of the import duty on raw cotton and the imposition of additional duties on cotton cloth. *American State Papers*, V, *Finance*, I, 492.

[54] Montgomery, *op. cit.*, 258. An advertiser in the *Delaware Gazette*, Feb. 19, 1796, sought two girls "as apprentices to the tambour and sattin-stitch business; likewise making child-bed linen, &c."

[55] Montgomery, *loc. cit.*; *Delaware Gazette*, March 28, 1789; Arthur C. Bining, *Pennsylvania Iron Manufacture in the Eighteenth Century* (Harrisburg, 1938), 55–56.

have invented a machine which would make one thousand wool and cotton card teeth in a minute, the legislature refused to grant him a patent.[56]

The first mill on the Brandywine of another industry, papermaking, was established in 1787 by Thomas and Joshua Gilpin, English-born merchants of Philadelphia.[57] Their paper was made of rags purchased in American cities, shipped to Wilmington, and carted to the mill. The product, about one thousand reams yearly, was sent in large quantities to Philadelphia.[58] A second mill was erected a bit farther up the Brandywine at Rockland in 1793 by William Young, "a worthy Scotchman, for years in the book business in Philadelphia," [59] and La Rochefoucault on his 1797 visit found three other such mills in other parts of the state.[60]

An area of so much industry dependent largely upon marine transport was certain to encourage some endeavors in shipbuilding, an industry restored by peace and union. La Rochefoucault declared that three or four vessels were built at Wilmington every year for sale or for the trade carried on there.[61] A notable launching occurred on October 16, 1790, when the ship, *General Washington*, of 250 tons burthen, built by William Woodcock, entered the river in a ceremony conducted "with safety, elegance and true nautical propriety, amidst the largest concourse of spectators ever known to be present on a similar occasion in this place," including "a numerous and respectable assembly of the fair daughters of Columbia." [62] Shipyards also existed in lower Delaware, at least on streams leading to the Chesapeake.[63]

[56] Petitions of Jan. 16, 1786, and Jan. 3, 1787, typed copies, Oliver Evans Papers (HSD).

[57] Jeannie Riddle Field, The Story of Kentmere (typescript), Edward Gilpin Papers (HSD); Montgomery, *Reminiscences*, 32–33; Bishop, *History of Manufactures*, I, 207; II, 63. Miers Fisher of Philadelphia was at one time a partner of the Gilpins, his nephews. J. P. Brissot de Warville, *New Travels in the United States of America Performed in 1788* (Dublin, 1792), 421–422; Dard Hunter, *Papermaking in Colonial America* (Philadelphia, 1952), 82–86.

[58] La Rochefoucault, *Travels*, III, 504–508; Montgomery, *op. cit.*, 35–36.

[59] Montgomery, *op. cit.*, 50; Conrad, *History of Delaware*, II, 423. John Carnes, of Delaware, took out a patent on paper-making soon after the opening of the federal patent office. Bishop, *op. cit.*, I, 210.

[60] La Rochefoucault, *Travels*, III, 507. Samuel Meteer had a mill at Newark as did Thomas Meteer at Milford.

[61] *Ibid.*, 517. Cf. Conrad, *History of Delaware*, II, 481.

[62] *Delaware Gazette*, Oct. 23, 1790.

[63] Barkley Townsend's shipyard at Laurel is referred to in *Laws*, III, 62.

Although most of the iron goods used in Delaware were imported,[64] some branches of the iron industry, in addition to the card manufactory, were established here. Richards and Seale, for example, manufactured nails in Wilmington in 1789,[65] and Rumford Dawes, a wealthy Philadelphia merchant, had a slitting mill on the Brandywine near the factories of Broom and the Gilpins.[66] The bog iron of Kent and Sussex continued to be extracted in many furnaces.[67]

Tanning remained as important an industry of Delaware after the Revolution as before.[68] So did hat-making, which like tanning, secured part of its raw material from the live stock raised in the state.[69] The war encouraged shoemaking, as it did all the clothing manufactures.[70] A Wilmington manufacturer advertised in 1799 for six journeymen shoemakers and two apprentices.[71] "Stockings were manufactured at home, and every female taught to knit." [72] "A young lady visited here last week," Mrs. Ridgely wrote her sons from Dover in 1796, "who profess'd herself 'astonished to find your sisters at work,' and declared, in a sweet simper, that she had never [had] Sizars, thimble, needle or thread ab[ou]t her, for it was terrible in a Lady to wear a pr of Pockets—the French Ladies never did such a thing. What can such a poor vain piece of affectation and folly be worth? Nothing—and if she possess'd the wealth of The Indies and I was a man I wd scarcely even pay her the compliment of a word." [73]

There is evidence of a variety of other trades and crafts. Several silversmiths found opportunity to ply their trade in Delaware. Dun-

[64] See correspondence of Ferris and Gilpin, hardware merchants, in HSD.

[65] *Delaware Gazette*, Jan. 10, 1789.

[66] Montgomery, *Reminiscences*, 42.

[67] *Laws*, II, 1129. Lavinia Rodney wrote her father, Thomas Rodney, probably in 1793, of visiting Charles Polk's forge at Soccom, in Sussex County.

[68] *Cf.* Corbit, Higgins, Spruance Correspondence, in HSD, particularly the letters of William to Pennell Corbit. *Delaware Gazette*, Nov. 13, 1795; Montgomery, *Reminiscences*, 303; Conrad, *History of Delaware*, II, 735.

[69] *Delaware Gazette*, March 21, Aug. 8, 1789. Delaware hatters joined those of New York, Pennsylvania, and Virginia in asking Congress for help in 1794. Bishop, *History of Manufactures*, II, 54.

[70] Petition of Neal Dougherty, Oct. 28, 1782, and petition of John Freeman, June 6, 1786, Legislative Papers.

[71] *Delaware Gazette*, March 14, 1799.

[72] Montgomery, *Reminiscences*, 157.

[73] Mabel L. Ridgely, *The Ridgelys of Delaware & Their Circle, What Them Befell in Colonial & Federal Times: Letters, 1751–1890* (Portland, Me., 1949), 94.

can Beard, George Crow, and Jonas Alrichs were among the clock-makers.[74] Sampson Barnett carried on "the Twining Business" at his shop on Market Street, Wilmington, where he made "all sorts of Windsor and Rush-bottom Chairs, Settees, Bedsteads, &c. . . . at the shortest notice." [75] John Way, of Wilmington, took many apprentices to his coachmaking business.[76] Brickyards, potteries, ropewalks and breweries added to the industrial variety of Wilmington.[77] A snuff mill in New Castle County produced five hundred thousand pounds of Scotch snuff yearly.[78] About twenty bushels of salt, "of an excellent taste and flavour," were made each summer day "in a fine season" at salt works erected near Henlopen Lighthouse.[79]

The Revolution, which encouraged manufacturing in Delaware by the need for self-sufficiency, also provoked a national pride further stimulated by the adoption of the Federal Constitution. On January 9, 1788, "the principal inhabitants" of Wilmington agreed "to encourage and promote . . . the use of American manufactures, by giving them the preference to foreign articles, when there is any reasonable proportion between their prices and goodness." They also promised to kill no lamb "for sale, or for family use," for a year, in order to encourage the manufacture of woollen cloth, and to appear on January 1, 1789, "in a complete dress of the manufacture of one or most of the united states, at a general meeting to be held on that day." The "home-spun" New Year's was considered a success; a "satisfactory specimen was displayed of the abilities of this country to assert her absolute independence, respecting foreign manufactures of wearing apparel. All the dresses were warm and many elegant." A permanent organization was adopted as "the Delaware Society for the Encouragement and Promotion of the Manufactories of the United States of America." Since God has pro-

---

[74] *Delaware Gazette,* Feb. 7, 1789; Montgomery, *Reminiscences,* 258; Henry C. Conrad, *Old Delaware Clock-Makers, Papers of the HSD,* XX, (Wilmington, 1898). See advertisements in *Delaware Gazette,* May 2, Nov. 4, 1789, and *Delaware and Eastern Shore Advertiser,* June 28, 1794.

[75] *Delaware Gazette,* Oct. 3, 1789.

[76] Indentures of Isaac Shallcross, Aug. 23, 1788, and Ellis Jones, March 31, 1791, Legal Documents, HSD. See also *Delaware Gazette,* Feb. 14, 1789; May 22, 1799.

[77] Montgomery, *Reminiscences,* 231, 303, 320–321; Conrad, *History of Delaware,* II, 397; *Delaware Gazette,* April 13, 1799.

[78] Bishop, *History of Manufactures,* II, 64.

[79] *Columbian Magazine,* II (1788), 108.

vided the United States with all necessities, this society's constitution read: "it becomes the duty of the sons of America to promote the arts and sciences, to cultivate agriculture, to increase their manufactures, . . . and to live with frugality and economy." Specifically the society sought to encourage the production of wool, hemp, and flax, to prefer domestic to foreign goods, and to give premiums to promote its objects.[80]

The first year of the new constitutional government saw the advocacy of support for domestic manufacturing continued in the columns of the *Delaware Gazette*. "Cato," on January 24, 1789, called on the people to spurn foreign luxuries and gewgaws, declaring that the failure to do so immediately after the Revolution had caused all of America's woes. On January 31, "A Farmer," while opposing bounties and protective tariffs, urged merchants to stock American goods and let that fact be known to their customers. "W. M. K.," on April 11, suggested that the abundance of wild garlic should encourage the raising of sheep and the woollen manufacture. The society for promoting agriculture sent an address on the subject to President Washington later in the spring. Among the toasts offered by the Cincinnati on July 4, two were to this end: "May industry and economy finish the task which patriotism and wisdom have begun, and render us truly independent," and "May the pride of dress be most elated by decoration of American manufactures." [81]

On February 6, 1790, the *Delaware Gazette* noted with pleasure the progress of manufacturing in the state. Two paper mills had been established in three years; the manufacture of wool and cotton cards was flourishing, as was the domestic manufacture of woollen and linen cloth; the Brandywine afforded "perhaps the best situation for mills in the world." "If monied men could be persuaded to advance boldly into the manufacturing line," there was the greatest prospect of success.

[80] *American Museum*, III (1788), 103–104; V (1789), 106–107, 174–175; *Delaware Gazette*, Jan. 17, 1789.
[81] *Delaware Gazette*, May 9, July 11, 1789.

V. Transportation

THE future of manufacturing in Delaware was to some degree dependent on the development of means of transportation. The Brandywine mills owed much of their success to their water connections with the grain fields of Delaware and the Philadelphia market.

In the two decades after the Revolution, the shallop trade continued as before. A picture of one of the river shallops, a rather disreputable one, has been left us by Patrick Lyon, who voyaged from Philadelphia to Sussex County in 1798. The crew consisted of the captain and one hand. "Our schooner (alias a wood shallop)," Lyon relates, "was very leaky; the captain said he wanted to sell her, he said he was offered £50 for her sails and rigging but he thought it too little; the main sail was not without it's decorations, it was completely patched and was not confined to canvas only; but towards the lower part, were pieces of check shirts or aprons. The peak halyards had three or four knots, and it was with great difficulty some times to get the knots through the blocks either way; the foresail was passable; the gibb was a delicate piece of goods, the upper part being made fast to a woollen stocking. Who would suppose that the exalted commander of such a temporary unseamed leaky machine as this schooner or shallop should or could have the conscience to assume more dignity, more importance and more affectation than the commander of a first-rate man of war in his Britanic majesty's navy—but that was the case." [82]

If Lyon did not appreciate the shallop's importance, its captain knew that the Delaware shallopmen and their vessels carried the greatest part of their state's commerce. Wheat, corn, lumber, and hay remained the principal products exported from the creeks of lower Delaware, and their destination was usually Philadelphia or Wilmington.[83] Cider seems also to have been exported from Sussex

[82] Patrick Lyon, *The Narrative of Patrick Lyon* (Philadelphia, 1799), 11–12.
[83] Jedidiah Morse, *The American Geography; a View of the Present Situation*

County in considerable quantities.[84] The demands of the shallop trade led to legislation for the improvement of navigation on Cedar and St. Jones' creeks, and a hot quarrel grew out of a proposal to shorten the course of Duck Creek.[85]

Packet ships, carrying passengers and freight, sailed on regular schedules from the Christina River ports and New Castle to Philadelphia. Stage lines connected with Chesapeake Bay ships to Baltimore, Annapolis, and Easton.[86] During 1794, advertisements appeared in the *Delaware and Eastern Shore Advertiser* for three packet lines from Wilmington and New Castle.[87] Bond and Lees and William Clay claimed that their packets, the *Morning Star* and the *Fly*, were "built . . . purposely for this trade. . . . Their cabbins are commodious, airy, neat, and convenient; and by the addition of folding doors, a part is rendered private for Ladies, or select parties—And in every respect are considered by the best judges, the completest of their tonnage, belonging to the Union. To render the passage agreeable, the commanders are always provided with a supply of the best liquors and provisions." Passage to New Castle on such a vessel cost seventy-five cents.[88]

But before these packet ships were advertised, a new type of vessel had appeared on the Delaware. In 1787 John Dickinson recommended to the assembly a man named John Fitch, who was "endeavoring to introduce the use of steam engines in this country." Fitch came to Delaware and was interviewed by a legislative committee, of which James Tilton was a member. On February 3 he was granted "the sole and exclusive right and advantages of making,

---

of the United States of America (London, 1792), 346. Of the owners of woodlands in Sussex, La Rochefoucault wrote: "They strip their woods to supply Philadelphia; and as there are in this spot many pine-trees and cedars, they sell them at a large profit, especially as they have the advantage of conveying them by water." *Travels*, III, 522.

[84] "Cyder enables them [the people of the country adjacent to Lewes] to carry on a profitable trade with Philadelphia." *Columbian Magazine*, II (1788), 108. "The inhabitants . . . [of the Indian River region] chiefly direct their attention to the cultivation of Indian corn, and the making of cyder." *Ibid.*, 297.

[85] *Laws*, II, 1083–1085, 1166–1168; III, 370; petitions and counter-petitions of 1785 and 1786 in Legislative Papers.

[86] Easton *Maryland Herald*, Aug. 30, 1791.

[87] The operators were Thomas and Adam Mendinhall, Bond and Lees and William Clay, and Eleazer McComb and Nehemiah Tilton. *Advertiser*, June 28, Aug. 9, 1794.

[88] *Ibid.*, June 28, 1794; La Rochefoucault, *Travels*, III, 539.

constructing and employing the steam-boat, by him lately invented." [89] James Rumsey contested Fitch's patent, but the dispute was eventually referred to Congress under the new Constitution.[90] In 1790 Fitch's steamboat was launched on the Delaware, where it made at least thirty-one trips, going as far north as Trenton and as far south as Wilmington.[91] Fitch's boat was unpopular, however, and sailing ships continued to rule supreme on the Delaware for several decades.

A promising ocean trade was carried on from Wilmington, "the most interesting fact in the history of the city," according to Christopher Ward.[92] At the end of the Revolution, however, Delaware trade largely flowed through Philadelphia. The emergence of a state consciousness during the Confederation decade, and the passage in Pennsylvania of a high protective tariff in 1785, served to stir agitation in Delaware for the development of her own ports of entry.[93] Delaware had never had a state tariff law, but since most of its imports were secured via Philadelphia, Delawareans now found themselves taxed by Pennsylvania. After many citizens petitioned the legislature to "emancipate our Commerce from the . . . dependent situation in which it is at present subject to Pennsylvania, free us from the payment of heavy Duties for the support of a State in which we have no Interest and afford us a more convenient Markett for our Produce," an act was passed in 1786 to make Wilmington and New Castle free ports.[94] Later a lottery was established by legislative action to provide funds for the construction of piers at New Castle.[95]

[89] *Minutes of Council,* 1020–1021, 1027–1028, 1031–1032; *Laws,* II, 895.

[90] *Minutes of Council,* 1151, 1156, 1160–1162, 1171, 1177–1178; *Delaware Gazette,* Jan. 31, 1789.

[91] Greville Bathe, "A Digest of Fitch's Steamboats, 1786–1792," *An Engineer's Miscellany* (Philadelphia, 1938), 40; Bishop, *History of Manufactures,* II, 25; Montgomery, *Reminiscences,* 167.

[92] C. L. Ward, *Leaves from the Log-Books and Letters of James Hemphill, Mariner and Merchant of Wilmington, 1793–1797, Papers of the HSD,* LXIV (Wilmington, 1914), 5.

[93] Frank F. Stephens, *The Transitional Period, 1788–1789, in the Government of the United States* (Columbia, Mo., 1909), 85; William W. Bates, *American Navigation* (Boston, 1902), 33, 35.

[94] Three petitions in folder, "1786, January–February, Legislative, Petitions, Transportation," Legislative Papers; *Laws,* II, 831. This act was made obsolete by the adoption of the Constitution.

[95] *Laws,* II, 1189–1191; III, 81.

The developing oceanic trade of the Delaware ports found its most profitable connection to be with the West Indies, from which sugar, rum, molasses, coffee, and cocoa were secured. In 1789 eleven Wilmington vessels were engaged in this trade and six others in the trade with Ireland, from which country they brought textiles, glassware, and immigrants; [96] later, their number was increased. A few vessels brought manufactured goods from England, but most of these goods were secured from other American ports, especially Philadelphia. The coasting trade employed still more ships, which brought fish from Newfoundland, grindstones and plaster of paris from the maritime provinces, wheat from New York, coal from Virginia, and hides from New Orleans. The chief exports from Wilmington in 1788–1789 were flour and breadstuffs, corn and cornmeal, meat, potatoes, apples, flaxseed, lumber, and iron and iron goods; and the chief imports were rum, sugar, coffee, gin, molasses, wine, and salt.[97] Two years later snuff, lard, Windsor and rush chairs, peas and beans, and ground oak bark had assumed an important place in the list of exports, and in the following year the quantities of beer, cider, porter, and country-made spirits exported mounted significantly.[98] In value, the exports reached a peak of $207,985 in 1794, but soared to a new high of $418,695 and was still rising as the century closed.[99]

When yellow fever struck Philadelphia in 1793 and that city's traders sought refuge in Wilmington, trade flourished as never before; the whole town was said to be perfumed with the odor of boiling tar and pitch.[100] In 1795 increasing commerce brought a new enterprise to Wilmington when Samuel Byrnes and Isaac Hendrickson, "who buy and sell stock of the Bank of Delaware," announced the establishment of "an office for the insurance of vessels, under the FIRM of SAMUEL BYRNES and CO. Brokers." [101]

This same Hendrickson was a partner in the firm of Broom, Hen-

[96] Benjamin Ferris, A History of the Original Settlements on the Delaware . . . (Wilmington, 1846), 232.

[97] Delaware Gazette, June 27, 1789.

[98] American State Papers, VII, 148–155, 157–162.

[99] Timothy Pitkin, A Statistical View of the Commerce of the United States of America (New Haven, 1835), 50–52.

[100] Ferris, Original Settlements, 233–234.

[101] Delaware Gazette, Sept. 18, 1795.

drickson, and Summerl which, established in 1792, announced its formation as a joint partnership to the following merchants: Joseph Hallett, New York; Dominick Terry & Co., Cadiz; William Backhouse & William Laight, New York; James Dutilk, Bordeaux; Ebenezer Stevens, New York; John Kirwan & Sons, London; William & James Seton, New York; William Stevenson, St. Eustatius; Rumford & Abijah Dawes, Philadelphia; E. Dutilk, Cape François; John & Isaac Carroll, Cork; and Governeur & Rutgers, Curaçao. They proposed to Stevenson that he join them in a venture to the West Indies. The vessel would be consigned to him at St. Eustatius, famed Dutch free port of the day, to be sold there or sent further as he decided. "One of our fellow citizens," Stevenson was told, "two or three years since, formed a similar connexion with a House on your Island and thus far there has been a mutual profit derived," especially inasmuch as flour is sixpence a barrel cheaper in Wilmington than Philadelphia and, having had less handling and less exposure, is shipped cleaner from Wilmington. Furthermore, "always at the breaking up of the Winter, our vessels can depart several days sooner than from thence [Philadelphia]." [102]

Sons or relatives of the Wilmington merchants often accompanied the ships as supercargoes or with the intention of settling as merchants in a West Indian port. Many young men of Wilmington were thus able to roam the world before settling down to the more prosaic life of a Market Street storekeeper. James Hemphill and John Warner, for example, went to the West Indies; Solomon Rice went to Passamaquoddy Bay for the firm of Craig and Tinning; Jeremiah, Josiah, and John Lewden went to Haiti.[103] The merchant who remained at home studied "prices current" of the world and avidly scanned the foreign news in the gazettes, for peace and war both offered profits if one but judged correctly.[104] Then orders were drawn up for the captains and agents as, for example, these for Captain Robert Bail of the brig *Pratt:* Proceed to Cape François. Lay off shore and investigate the market (because of late disturb-

---

[102] Broom, Hendrickson, and Summerl Company Letter-Book, 1792–1794 (HSD).

[103] Ward, *Log-Books of James Hemphill*, 8 ff.; Frederick Craig to Rice, Wilmington, April 21, 1790, Stockton Papers (DSA); Lewden Papers (HSD).

[104] Ward, *Log-Books of James Hemphill*, 5.

ances) before going in. Otherwise proceed to Kingston, Jamaica, where it is said provisions are wanting, and try by fair means to be admitted. You will probably be boarded by British cruisers, which will be an opportunity to inquire about Kingston. If you think neither the Cape nor Kingston satisfactory, go to any port in Hispaniola. Keep good ballast. Be always ready to put to sea in an emergency. In case of accident, take necessary steps to enable us to recover insurance.[105]

Two vain attempts were made to build canals in Delaware in the late eighteenth century. In 1792 commissioners representing the State of Delaware and Chester County, Pennsylvania, recommended the construction of a lock canal along the Brandywine, and an act permitting the governor to incorporate a company for this purpose was passed by the Delaware General Assembly on June 17, 1793.[106] The project was lost, however, in the opposition of some Pennsylvania landholders through whose meadows it would cut and an unresolved controversy between those Delawareans who would have its mouth at the Brandywine Mills and those who preferred to have it cut overland to the Christina.[107]

Proposals for a canal between the Chesapeake and the Delaware were made before 1770,[108] and were taken up again after the war. In 1797, La Rochefoucault reported four proposed routes: (1) joining the Choptank River to St. Jones' Creek, (2) joining the Chester River to Duck Creek, (3) joining the Bohemia River to Appoquinimink Creek, and (4) joining the Elk River to the Christina. Baltimore merchants were said to oppose the canal for fear it would draw some of the Susquehanna trade out of the Chesapeake to Philadelphia, and Delaware was said to be equally opposed to all canal plans "because a great number of horses belonging to the in-

---

[105] July 10, 1793, Broom, Hendrickson, and Summerl Letter-Book.

[106] *Laws*, II, 1129; Report, Dec. 20, 1792, Legislative Papers. The commissioners for Delaware were Jacob Broom, Joseph Shallcross, Eleazer McComb, and Samuel Hollingsworth, all merchants.

[107] Petitions in folders, "1793, May–June, Legislative, Petitions, Transportation," and "1794, January–February, Legislative, Petitions, Transportation," Legislative Papers.

[108] Joshua Gilpin, *A Memoir on the Rise, Progress, and Present State of the Chesapeake and Delaware Canal* (Wilmington, 1821), 3–6. *Cf.* Hastings, *Francis Hopkinson*, 326; Tench Coxe, "Address to the Honourable the Members of the Convention of Virginia," *American Museum*, III (1788), 429.

habitants" were constantly employed "carrying corn from Elk-Town to Christiana-bridge." [109] At the end of the century, the Delaware legislature, however, had taken no action.

Roads in Delaware in the late eighteenth century led, like its river, to Philadelphia. From the southern end of the peninsula one ran north through Horn Town (Virginia), Snow Hill (Maryland), and Dagsbury, Milford, Dover, and Wilmington to Marcus Hook, Chester, and Philadelphia. Northwestward from Wilmington roads to interior Pennsylvania shortened the journey of Lancaster and Chester County products en route to Philadelphia via Christina River wharves. West from Wilmington the highway from Philadelphia continued to Newport, Christiana, and the head of Elk River in Maryland, where the traveller might choose between continuing on land to Havre de Grace and Baltimore or embarking for a sail down the Chesapeake. Southward from Wilmington to New Castle lay a much-travelled section of the road running down state past the Red Lion Tavern to Dover. Christiana Bridge, called "Christeen" by the natives, was connected at the Red Lion with both the southern highway and with New Castle. From the Red Lion another popular route led southwestward to Warwick, Maryland, and on to the Chesapeake's shore. From this Eastern Shore road and from the main road down Delaware, various other roads reached back into the interior, to Georgetown, the new seat of Sussex County, and to the coast, at Lewes, old county seat and port.[110] Thus the whole provided a network of communications

[109] *Travels*, III, 575–576, 675, 695; James W. Livingood, *The Philadelphia-Baltimore Trade Rivalry, 1780–1860* (Harrisburg, 1947), 84–86.

[110] The following maps were consulted in the map collection of the Wilmington Institute Free Library: John Churchman, *To the American Philosophical Society This Map of the Peninsula between Delaware & Chesapeak Bays* (reprint, Washington, 1937); *Delaware, engraved by A. Doolittle* (New Haven, 1798); *Delaware from the Best Authorities . . .* , *engraved for Carey's American Edition of Guthrie's Geography Improved*, W. Barker, sculp. (Philadelphia, 1795); J. Denison, *Map of the States of Maryland and Delaware* (Boston, 1796); Map of the Delaware and Chesapeak Bays with the Peninsula between them, copied by Andrew Skinner, 1780, photostat from MS. map; *Map of the State of Delaware and the Eastern Shore of Maryland . . . from Actual Survey and Soundings Made in 1799, 1800 & 1801*, Francis Shallus, eng. (Philadelphia, n.d.); Joseph Scott, "Map of Delaware River and Bay . . . 1795," from *United States Gazetteer* (Philadelphia, 1795); D. F. Sotzmann, *Maryland und Delaware* (Hamburg, 1797); "States of Maryland and Delaware from the Latest Survey," engraved for Payne's *Geography* (New York, 1799).

which the peninsula's shape tightened at the top and directed toward Philadelphia.

The Count de Ségur in the last years of the Revolution found the road from Dover to Wilmington "very wide, well marked out, and carefully kept in excellent order." [111] Fifteen years later, however, Ségur's countryman, La Rochefoucault, claimed that Delaware was "distinguished by the bad state of the roads," [112] and most contemporary evidence seems to be on the side of this latter opinion. William Cobbett, for example, said the roads were "impassable after the least rain." [113] Poor Thomas Rodney, in 1788, found "the bridge that crosses the Mill run at Duck Town . . . very Much rotten and broken" and dismounted to lead his horse over, but the beast was frightened by an "ugly hole" and jumped on Rodney's right foot.[114] "A Customer" complained in the *Delaware Gazette* for October 16, 1790, that "between Wilmington and Christiana Bridge [were] three bridges which [were] scarcely passable without endangering the life of horse and rider, by the numerous holes through the planks, filled up with pieces of rails, stones &c." In November, 1798, John Dickinson "narrowly escaped drowning in Duck Creek . . . by the horses plunging into a deep hole which the driver knew not of.—happily they did not draw the carriage in after them." [115] Contrasting this testimony with Ségur's, it appears that the road commissioners were allowing the roads to deteriorate steadily. Inhabitants of Sussex requested the assembly to build new roads to the courthouse at Georgetown, as "a great means of inducing Jurors, Witnesses and others to attend . . . , who now are in danger of life or Limb should Night at any time happen to overtake them." [116]

No extensive improvements seem to have been made in the Confederation period, but in the 1790s numerous petitions forced the legislature to take action. One new road was specifically provided

---

[111] Louis Philippe, Comte de Ségur, *Memoirs and Recollections of Count Ségur* . . . (London, 1825), 320. He said also that his journey was "through a path like a fine garden alley, shaded by the oldest and most beautiful trees in the world."

[112] *Travels*, III, 487.

[113] *The Progress of a Plough-Boy to a Seat in Parliament* . . . , William Reitzel, ed. (London, 1933), 60.

[114] T. Rodney, Diary, May 11, 1788, Rodney Collection.

[115] Deborah Ferris Bringhurst, Diary, Nov. 22, 1788 (extract in Historical Society of Delaware).

[116] Petitions of Jan. 5, 1795, Legislative Papers.

for, from Christiana through Newark to the Maryland line, where it connected with roads of Maryland and Pennsylvania tapping the Susquehanna Valley.[117] General rules were adopted for the regulation of the roads of Kent and Sussex, one of which provided that in the latter county the road tax might be discharged in labor, with a day's work valued at fifty cents.[118] Provisions were also made for the construction of a number of bridges and for the better regulation of ferries.[119]

Scheduled stage lines were well established by the 1790s. A petition of Oliver Evans for a fifteen-year monopoly "of Propelling all land Carriages by the Power of Steam and the Pressure of the Atmosphere" had been disregarded by the assembly in 1787,[120] but by 1794 Joshua Jackson ran three stages a week from Wilmington to Philadelphia and Daniel Cooke ran two each week from Wilmington to Dover, via New Castle, Appoquinimink, and Duck Creek. Each stage made the trip in one day. Another stage line made three trips a week from New Castle to Whitehall, Maryland, connecting the Philadelphia and Baltimore packets.[121] By 1796 service had improved so that the Philadelphia stage left Wilmington every morning except Sunday, and a weekly stage ran from Dover to Milford. In 1799 daily trips were being made from Dover to Wilmington, and thrice weekly from Dover to Northampton, Virginia. By this time it was possible to take a stage in Dover at 3 A.M. and arrive in Philadelphia on the same day.[122] Another stage ran to Chestertown, Maryland.[123] Alarms, breakdowns, upsets, and races added variety to the ride.[124] Mail routes ran from Wilmington through New Castle, Dover, Milford, Dagsborough, and Snow Hill, to Accomac Court House, and through Newport, Christiana, Middletown, and Warwick, to Chestertown.[125] Frederick Craig and Company, "aided by the voluntary contribution of several Public

---

[117] *Laws*, II, 1079–1081.
[118] *Laws*, II, 1263–1289, 1330–1340; III, 20–25, 60–61.
[119] *Laws*, II, 1005, 1076, 1082, 1085, 1095, 1195, 1340; III, 4, 123.
[120] Typed copy in Oliver Evans Papers (HSD).
[121] *Delaware and Eastern Shore Advertiser*, June 28, 1794.
[122] *Delaware Gazette*, Jan. 8, 1796; March 27, 1799.
[123] Wilmington *Mirror of the Times & General Advertiser*, Nov. 20, 1799.
[124] Montgomery, *Reminiscences*, 166–167.
[125] *Delaware Gazette*, Sept. 8, 1795. The post to Chestertown left three times a week, to Dover and Sussex once a week, and to Accomac biweekly.

spirited Citizens," undertook to establish a weekly post to Lewes in 1788, but neither the legislature nor the federal government offered any immediate help.[126]

Thus gradually Delaware's isolation was being pierced as the state entered into the life of the new nation. Significant of the development of commercial life in Delaware is the abandonment of the fairs. Semi-annual fairs had been intended to afford Delawareans "a Cheap and Convenient Supply of Numerous necessary Artikles which [could] not be otherwise Conveniently obtained" in a small state with no large cities.[127] However, with the abundance of useful goods and the crowds who gathered to purchase them came many undesirable concomitants: drunkenness, profane language, gambling, street fights, and fiddling and dancing night and day in the taverns.[128] It was claimed that the Dover fair, founded "principally with a view of collecting cattle from the lower counties and vending the same," had instead proved to be "a nursery of Riot, Debauchery and Vice." [129] As a result of a number of such petitions, the legislature on June 4, 1785, passed an act for their suppression, citing the fact that "the original purpose and intention of holding fairs has long since been done away by the numerous stores that are kept in every part of the country, and the ready market there is for all the produce of the state." [130] The legislature was later unsuccessfully petitioned to establish or reestablish fairs at Dover, Middletown, and Cantwell's Bridge, but it is significant in regard to the development of merchandising at Wilmington that no effort was made to resurrect the fairs in that borough. Shopkeepers' advertisements reveal the abundance of goods to be purchased there. John Orien, in 1786, offered numerous items ranging from looking glasses, tamarinds, hair powder, and anchovies to "Sugar Plumbs," English aniseed, Castile soap, and Lisbon, Port, Teneriffe, and

---

[126] Petition of Craig & Co., 1788, Legislative Papers.
[127] Petition for Dover Fair, 1784, *ibid.*
[128] Ferris, *Original Settlements*, 230, 277–279. See also Read, *Read*, 315–317.
[129] Petition of Oct. 24, 1783, Legislative Papers.
[130] *Laws*, II, 818–820. The petitions are to be found in great numbers in the Legislative Papers. The principal fairs had been held at Wilmington and Dover; there had never been any in Sussex County. The Dover fair continued to be held "half yearly . . . to the great grievance of its inhabitants and prejudice of piety and morality." Petition of Jan. 13, 1790, Legislative Papers. John Bell was indicted for holding a fair in Murderkill Hundred in October, 1788. *Delaware Gazette,* April 11, 1789.

Malaga wine. Frequently bartering arrangements were suggested, as by Harlan Cloud, of Wilmington, who offered in 1789 to exchange lime or hats for corn.[131] The sale in Wilmington shops of Irish linens, Liverpool and Turk's Island salt, Jamaica spirits, Bohea, Hyson, and Souchong tea, Holland and English gunpowder and Nankeens revealed the ramifications of eighteenth-century trade. In the semi-weekly Wilmington market, said La Rochefoucault, "every necessary is to be procured . . . , and no-where else in this part of the country."[132]

VI. Finance

AFTER the collapse of the Continental currency and concomitantly that of Delaware, this state moved to reestablish its finances on a sound basis. Allan Nevins, writing of state finances in the Confederation period, declares that those of Delaware and Connecticut were the best managed.[133] After the legal tender status of the state bills of credit was disallowed in 1781, Delaware resolutely refused to issue any more paper money. Such an issue, however, was not avoided without a bitter struggle in the depression of the mid-1780s.

A petition favoring an emission of bills of credit based on land mortgages as in the past was sent to the legislature in 1784 and recommended by a committee, but no bill was passed.[134] More petitions of the sort arrived in 1785. Forty-five citizens of Kent County, complaining of the "heavy publick Debt as well as a Multitude of Private Debts," an insufficient "Circulating Medium," and the resultant "Great and General Distress throughout the Country," asked the assembly to declare a moratorium for three years on the sale of lands for debts and also of "goods and Chattles" except at an

---

[131] *Delaware Gazette,* Jan. 18, 1786; Jan. 10, 1789.
[132] *Travels,* III, 517.
[133] *American States,* 515.
[134] Committee report in folder, "1784, May–June, Legislative, Petitions, Misc.," Legislative Papers.

appraised value.[135] At a later session that year a petition to the same purpose with 259 signatures was presented, in which reference was made to "the Voice of Lamentation which pervades" the country and to "the Cries of Women and Helpless Children . . . heard in every Neighbourhood." [136] At the same time Thomas Rodney was arguing for an emission of paper money "on the Same principles" as "before the revolution." "Is it not astonishing then," he asked, "that a people who have the Power of directing their own Measures, Shoud let themselves and their Country go to distruction, Sooner then adopt a Measure that woud afford them Immediate releaf and make them freemen instead of being slaves to a few Merciless creditors who would wish to take all they have." [137]

Indeed it does seem strange, whatever the virtues or faults of paper money issues, that Delaware, which had as a colony used paper money in spite of the mother country's displeasure, should now as a free state hesitate to employ the same device. The answer may be that, regardless of the soundness of Delaware's pre-Revolutionary bills, remembrance of the sad result of the Continental issue was still fresh in men's minds. Of course, Delaware's emissions had been soundly based on land mortgages, while the Continental money was largely unsecured. But in this very year of 1785 an action was taken to destroy the faith of the conservative members of the community in any paper issue, however soundly it might seem to be established. This was an act to redeem the state bills of credit at a ratio of seventy-five to one.[138] This partial default was excused on the basis that many of the land mortgages securing the bills had been settled in nearly worthless Continental currency, and thus the Delaware emissions remained in circulation although their security had been weakened. However, as George Read and Richard Bassett pointed out in objecting to this act, the General Assembly had not definitely ascertained the value of the mortgages still outstanding. All the money available from these mortgages, they argued, should in good faith be applied to the

[135] Folder, "1785, May–June, Legislative, Petitions," *ibid.* A moratorium on sales except at appraised values had been passed by the legislature in 1782 but had expired. *Laws,* II, 771.

[136] Folder, "1785, May–June, Legislative, Petitions," Legislative Papers.

[137] Essay in folder, "T. Rodney, Misc., I," Rodney Collection.

[138] *Laws,* II, 801–812; *Minutes of Council,* 916–918, 922–929, 936–937.

redemption of bills of credit. Some depreciation undoubtedly would be necessary, but not as much as seventy-five to one. The state was unfairly profiting at the expense of those who held its paper.[139] Such tactics did not reassure the financial interests about future paper issues, however secure they might seem originally to be.

From 1786 through 1788 many petitions were received by the legislature complaining, as phrased in one petition, of "the present Distressing Situation of a Great Majority of the Good people of the State Occationed as we apprehend by the Great Scarceity of circulating Money." The remedies suggested were of four kinds: (1) issuance of paper money, (2) suspension of forced sales except at appraised values, (3) extension of the time for the payment of debts, (4) legal tender status for "several kinds of goods . . . in payment of debts." There were 1,409 signatures to the petitions which are still extant among the Delaware Legislative Papers.[140]

Although the General Assembly remained adamant against most of these demands, it yielded to popular pressure in one very interesting case. This was the result of a demand that discrimination be shown in the support given public securities in the hands of the original holders as against those in the hands of speculators.[141] Consequently a law was passed in the fall of 1787 establishing an order for the payment of claims against the state in which pay-

[139] Read, *Read,* 387–390. *Cf.* [Tilton], *History of Dionysius,* 42–43. Tilton claimed the state bills of credit had been hoarded by the disaffected. A brief note of interest is to be found in Orin G. Libby, *Geographical Distribution of the Vote of the Thirteen States on the Federal Constitution, 1787–1788, Bulletin of the University of Wisconsin, Economics, Political Science and History Series,* I, no. 1 (Madison, 1897), 52, 61–62.

[140] Of course, many of the signatures are duplicates. *Cf. Minutes of Council,* 968–969, 974.

[141] Petitions in folders, "1787, January–February, Legislative, Petitions," and "1787, October–November, Legislative, Petitions," Legislative Papers. Among the signers of these petitions were such merchants as John Lea, James Latimer, William Hemphill, and James Brobson. A petition signed by these men spoke scathingly of speculators and "their patron Timoleon," possibly a reference to James Tilton. In reference to speculators, it is interesting to note that Hugh Thompson, of Wilmington, advertised in the *Gazette,* April 18, 1789, that he offered "the highest price . . . for Final Settlements and other Public Securities of the United States." Tilton argued years later, that "the legislature as well as private individuals employed all manner of devices for depreciating our certificates. . . . Certificates of the U.S. suffered in common with those of the State. The consequence was, they fled, in horse-loads, to other States. . . ." Tilton to Aaron Burr, Wilmington, March 13, 1802, Gratz Collection (Historical Society of Pennsylvania).

depreciation certificates remaining in the hands of the original holders and their heirs or alienated at full price were preferred to those which were transferred "for less than the principal sum specified therein." [142]

Not only the payment of obligations but also the collection of taxes posed a problem for the Delaware legislature. Protests from all sides arose against the unfair tax rates. The assessors, claimed some residents of Kent County, acted on impulse and favoritism.[143] John Dickinson and George Read in 1786 wrote each other of the inequalities of the ratings.[144] In the Confederation period, the tax collectors frequently found collecting difficult because of "the very great Scarcity of Money." [145] One collector found his fees, reduced to specie, amounted to an inadequate sum for "the Trouble, Risk, Fatigue and Expence" involved.[146] La Rochefoucault, in 1797, was told that the taxes were assessed only by a rough estimate. The income of a poor man who had many children, for instance, was always considered to be twenty dollars.[147] New Castle County was regularly assessed the highest amount and Sussex the lowest. The tax collectors were allowed a percentage of the sum they collected.

Several attempts were made to improve the system of taxation,[148] but at the end of the century complaints were still being received that the tax gatherers' "Fees sweeps off a Great part of the money that might Otherwise be placed to the use of the public" and that "great Numbers of the Honest industrious people Cannot Without the utmost difficulty . . . Discharge their public dues." [149] Taxation was so unpopular that some Delawareans proposed a union of their state with the Eastern Shore of Maryland

---

[142] *Laws,* II, 912; [Tilton], *History of Dionysius,* 62. Dickinson published "a defence of a scale of depreciation for certificates," and, according to Tilton, men became ashamed of holding certificates. *Ibid.,* 64.

[143] Folder, "1783, January–February, Legislative, Petitions," Legislative Papers.

[144] Read, *Read,* 423–424.

[145] Petition of Mark Coudrett, Jan. 23, 1785, Legislative Papers.

[146] Petition of John Wilson, Jan. 11, 1785, *ibid.* See also petition of James Delaplain, Joseph Taylor, and Jonathan Boyce in folder, "1786, January–February, Legislative, Petition, Misc.," *ibid.*

[147] *Travels,* III, 530–533.

[148] *Laws,* II, 1247, 1358; III, 26, 153.

[149] Petitions from Sussex County in folder, "1800, Legislative, Petitions, Misc.," Legislative Papers.

in order to decrease the burden of supporting a state government.[150]

The mercantile community anticipated many benefits from the establishment of the Bank of Delaware, the first private corporation established in the state. Eleazer McComb in 1785 submitted to the General Assembly, through Dr. Tilton and Governor Van Dyke, some "proposals for establishing a Bank in the Delaware State." A loan of twenty thousand pounds was to be secured from a foreign government and made the capital of a state bank at Wilmington which would issue bank notes up to the value of thirty thousand pounds. Its capital would be repaid by a land tax over a ten-year period and be guaranteed by twenty or more "Public Spirited Gentlemen" owning estates worth at least three times twenty thousand pounds. This proposition was coupled with the project to establish a free port at Wilmington, where the bank would help trade by discounting notes and bonds.[151] McComb explained in a letter to Van Dyke that "the scarcity of Money obliges us to look abroad for this loan" and recommended approaching private Dutch bankers through the delegates to Congress and the Dutch minister. The bank, he said, would "relieve those in distress, . . . avoid the depreciation of a Paper Currency, and . . . lessen the burden of taxes." [152]

No action was taken on McComb's proposals, but in 1793 a new demand was made for the incorporation of a bank. No longer did a "scarcity of money" oblige Delawareans to look abroad for bank capital. McComb was one of twenty-five men who then requested the legislature to incorporate them as "The President Directors and Company of the Bank of Delaware." They argued that banks had "been found by experience to be of general Public utility" and that "as the commercial business of Wilmington has been for sometime past encreasing, . . . it has now arrived to that degree which requires the aid of a Bank, and without which it must of necessity rather decline; as negociations of that kind are now made at Philadelphia under some material disadvantages." [153] Although the leg-

---

[150] La Rochefoucault, *Travels*, III, 533.

[151] In Delaware State Bank Papers (HSD).

[152] McComb to Van Dyke, Dover, June 25, 1785, *ibid.*

[153] Folder, "1793, January–February, Legislative, Petitions, Misc.," Legislative Papers. Among the petitioners, besides McComb, were Nicholas Way, Joseph Shall-

islature did not immediately respond, the stockholders were organized and directors chosen.[154] In 1796 petitions with 227 signatures were presented to the legislature favoring incorporation of the Bank of Delaware, the stock of which had already been subscribed to. The signers were not only the Wilmington merchants and Brandywine millers, but also such prominent residents of New Castle as George Read, Jr., William Clay, James Booth, Archibald Alexander, and Nicholas Van Dyke, and from lower Delaware, William Killen, Nathaniel Mitchell, Richard Bassett, Edward Miller, John Fisher, John Laws, and Henry Molleston.[155]

This year, on February 9, the bank was finally incorporated, with a capital permitted of not more than five hundred thousand dollars. Its capital stock was to be enlarged by fifty shares which were to be purchased by the state. The incorporation of this bank obviously was in response to a need felt for it at Wilmington, which illustrates something of the extent to which the trade and manufacturing of Delaware had grown.[156]

Even before the Revolution the development of a commercial center in northern Delaware had begun, but the separation from the British Empire and the European wars of the 1790s, as well as the security offered by the strong government under the Constitution, did much to further this growth. The first decade of the nineteenth century and especially the increasing nationalistic spirit of the era of the second war with England would do much more to establish an industrial-commercial area in what would remain for

---

cross, Jacob Broom, Isaac Hendrickson, Joseph Summerl, William Hemphill, Frederick Craig, Thomas Lea, Isaac Starr, Jr., Thomas Mendinhall, Vincent Gilpin, Joseph Capelle. All were merchants or professional men. On McComb's background, see his letter to Thomas Irons, Chestertown, Md., June 6, 1774, George V. Massey, II, ed., "Eleazer McComb Letters," *Delaware History*, II (1947), 48–53.

[154] Minutes, June 1, 1795, photostat, Banking Papers (HSD). Jacob Broom was chairman of the meeting, at which William Hemphill, Eleazer McComb, Samuel Canby, Joseph Tatnall, Isaac Hendrickson, John Ferris, Samuel Hollingsworth, Joseph Warner, and Thomas Mendinhall were elected directors. Every one of these directors was a merchant, and many were millers.

[155] "1796, January–February, Legislative, Petitions, Misc.," Legislative Papers.

[156] *Laws*, II, 1236–1239; Ferris, *Original Settlements*, 235. La Rochefoucault declared, "This bank appears to be of no real utility, at least there is no apparent necessity for it—except to the Brandywine millers." *Travels*, III, 523–524. The bank's great success proved the duke to be wrong. It should be noted that the Bank of North America received a Delaware charter in 1786, although it never established an office in this state. *Laws*, II, 838–840.

the most part an agrarian state and thus produce in this small area the anomaly of two cultures, such as is still to be found in our own times.

VII. Population

THE population of Delaware grew steadily throughout this period. The first federal census, in 1790, revealed a total population of 59,096; [157] by 1800 it had risen to 64,273 and it continued to increase in the next century.[158] It is of significance that in the decade from 1790 to 1800 the increase was concentrated almost wholly in New Castle County. The 1790 census revealed the counties to be nearly equally populated: New Castle had 19,688, Kent 18,920, and Sussex 20,488. But in 1800 New Castle County showed an increase of 5,673, whereas, in contrast, Sussex returns showed an actual decrease of 1,130. On the basis of population Sussex not only surrendered first place to New Castle but dropped to last. The reason for New Castle County's growth is doubtless to be found in the growing industrial and mercantile importance of the Wilmington area, the resultant increase in the value of near-by farms, and the arrival of immigrants from Europe and the West Indies.

Among the whites the males outnumbered the females slightly in each of the first two censuses. Slightly less than half of the whites seem to have been under sixteen years of age, and the proportion of those over that age to those under it seems to have been considerably greater in Sussex than in any other county. Sussex County also had the greatest number of slaves, though the greatest number of free Negroes and the greatest total number of Negroes, slave or free, lived in Kent, where Quaker and Methodist influence, as well as the personal efforts of Warner Mifflin, had encouraged manumissions.

[157] *Return of the Whole Number of Persons within the Several Districts of the United States* (Philadelphia, 1791), 46.

[158] *Return of the Whole-Number of Persons within the Several Districts of the United States* (Washington, 1801), lacks pagination.

The number of free Negroes rose from 3,899 in 1790 to 8,268 in 1800, but the number of slaves decreased from 8,887 to 6,153 in the same period, a trend which occurred in greater or less degree in every county. In New Castle County, however, the number of free Negroes increased most rapidly, probably because of the greater opportunities of earning a livelihood in that county as demonstrated by the total growth of its population. Manumission within this county could not by itself be responsible for this growth, since its slave population decreased only 724 while the number of its free Negroes rose by 2,115. Percentages demonstrate the changes in population clearly. From 1790 to 1800 the total population of Delaware increased by 8.76 percent, the number of whites by 7.64 percent, and the number of free Negroes by 112.05 percent; at the same time the number of slaves decreased by 30.76 percent.[159]

The most recent study of national stocks in the United States in 1790 suggests that 60 percent of the white Delawareans of that date were of English stock, 8.9 percent Swedish, 8 percent Scotch, 6.3 percent Scotch-Irish, 5.47 percent South Irish, and 4.3 percent Dutch.[160] But these figures are very inaccurate; the proportion allotted the Scotch-Irish, for example, is probably decidedly too small. The effect of the Scotch-Irish, however, was greater than their numbers suggest. Their distinct religion, their relative newness to America, their political partisanship, their industry—all these and other factors combined to make them, after the English only, the most influential group in Delaware. Through the post-Revolutionary period they continued to arrive in large numbers in New Castle County.[161] Among the Irish serving as indentured servants was the heir to the earldom of Anglesey, one James Annesley, of whose adventures Charles Reade wrote in his novel, *The Wandering Heir*.[162]

[159] *Census of 1850,* 604.

[160] American Council of Learned Societies, "Report of the Committee on Linguistic and National Stocks in the Population of the United States," *Annual Report of the American Historical Association,* 1931, pp. 122–124. The figures are estimates based on family names; in the case of Delaware, at least, the estimates are probably very poor.

[161] *Delaware Gazette,* June 26, July 24, 1790; Aug. 2, 1796; *Delaware and Eastern Shore Advertiser,* July 12, Aug. 30, 1794.

[162] Augustus H. Able, III, "Delaware Literature," H. Clay Reed, ed., *Delaware: A History of the First State* (New York, 1947), II, 942; Charles Reade, *The Wan-*

A small but influential immigrant group which added variety to the Delaware scene in the 1790s, particularly at Wilmington, were the French refugees from Haiti, whence they had been driven by uprisings of the blacks. Their property destroyed, they frequently found themselves in a new land without means of support. In New Castle a committee was formed to inquire into the need of the refugees, and La Rochefoucault reports that a subscription fund was begun to help the impoverished among the forty refugee families in Wilmington. Dickinson gave four hundred dollars to this cause, entrusting it to a noted member of the colony, Anne Louis Tousard, for distribution.[163] Tousard, who had lost an arm in the American Revolution, had also commanded troops in Haiti. He joined the United States army in 1795 and supervised the construction of forts at West Point and Newport.[164] Another important refugee was Jean-Pierre Bauduy, who later became a partner of Eleuthère Irénée du Pont in his powder business.[165] Jean Garesché du Rocher came to Delaware via France and New Jersey, being attracted to Wilmington by the large Haitian colony already formed there.[166] Pierre Chetard and Pierre Didier practiced medicine in the same city.[167]

The presence of this group attracted other Frenchmen directly from the motherland. Peter Provenchere (so Elizabeth Montgomery wrote the name), former tutor of the Duc de Berri, for example, settled in Wilmington in 1794. Another Frenchman, Dr. Joseph Capelle, remained in this country after accompanying Rochambeau here during the Revolution.[168]

---

dering Heir (London, n.d., Chatto & Windus edition de luxe), 37, 69. Annesley was here in the colonial period.

[163] George Read to George Washington, New Castle, Jan. 4, 1794, Read, *Read*, 553–554; La Rochefoucault, *Travels*, III, 518–519.

[164] Frances Sergeant Childs, *French Refugee Life in the United States, 1790–1800* (Baltimore, 1940), 41–42; Montgomery, *Reminiscences*, 66; *Delaware and Eastern Shore Advertiser*, July 23, 1794.

[165] Childs, *French Refugee Life*, 47.

[166] Walter C. Hartridge, "The St. Domingan Refugees in New Jersey," *Proceedings of the New Jersey Historical Society*, LXII (1944), 200–201; Childs, *French Refugee Life*, 49–50.

[167] Scharf, *History of Delaware*, I, 482–483; Montgomery, *Reminiscences*, 250; B. G. du Pont, ed., *Life of Eleuthère Irénée du Pont from Contemporary Correspondence* (Newark, Del., 1923–1925), XI, 232.

[168] Montgomery, *Reminiscences*, 267; Scharf, *History of Delaware*, I, 481.

The presence of this French settlement left its mark on the culture of Delaware. French became popular in the schools; frogs' legs and other new foods were introduced; the organization of a Catholic parish at Wilmington was encouraged.[169] Delaware laws forbade alien ownership of lands, but the influx of the French and other foreigners led to a movement for their repeal. The movement was unsuccessful at this time, but in 1799 all naturalized citizens who had purchased land before being naturalized were confirmed in their titles.[170]

Urban communities continued to develop in this period. Wilmington, according to La Rochefoucault, had about forty-five hundred people in 1797, exclusive of three or four hundred French settlers, and covered four square miles. The houses were "handsome, substantial brick buildings," constructed on two-acre lots which rented for four to six dollars a year. Goods were cheaper by two-fifths than at Philadelphia; a family could live on eight hundred dollars a year.[171] A new town hall, for which Bauduy drew the plans, was constructed in 1798.[172]

New Castle, having raised funds for wharves by a lottery, afforded winter shelter to vessels and seemed to be rising "from the state of decay into which it had sunk." [173] "All the houses in Dover offered a simple but elegant appearance; they were built of wood and painted with different colors. This variety in their aspect, the neatness which distinguished them, the bright and polished brass knockers of the doors, seemed all to announce the order and activity, the intelligence and prosperity of the inhabitants." [174] Lewes consisted of one street over three miles long. Many of its buildings were "in a state of decay," but the courthouse and gaol, before the county seat was moved, were "commodious structures" which gave the town "an air of importance." Part of the town was inhabited by the river pilots.[175]

---

[169] Montgomery, *Reminiscences,* 316.
[170] *Laws,* III, 64–65. The Legislative Papers contain many petitions of naturalized citizens asking confirmation of their titles to land. *Cf.* Naturalization Law of June 11, 1788, *Laws,* II, 921–923.
[171] *Travels,* III, 491–492, 519–520.
[172] Ferris, *Original Settlements,* 235; Montgomery, *Reminiscences,* 286–287.
[173] La Rochefoucault, *Travels,* III, 538.
[174] Ségur, *Memoirs and Recollections,* 319.
[175] *Columbian Magazine,* II (1788), 108.

VIII. Social Progress

ONE of the bad effects of the Revolution, or so some people felt, was the loosening of moral bonds apparent in the Confederation period. Vagabonds and thieves, who may have been the hangers-on of the Revolutionary army, overran the country. Discharged convicts from the Philadelphia prison made up one class of desperados; during their prison terms they had worked with wheelbarrows on the streets with an iron collar around their necks and heavy iron balls attached to one of their legs. This hardened and reckless band, termed "wheel-barrow men," spread terror as they roved singly or in groups. [176]

"The Licentiousness," one petition to the legislature claimed, "which originated from Idleness and the Relaxation of Civil Authority during the War, and all the Vices, and Immoralities which flow from this source can only be restrained by domestic Regulations." [177] Proclamations against vice and offers of rewards for the apprehension of criminals were issued by the governors.[178] Fairs, considered nourishers of vice, were forbidden in 1785. The promotion of "horse-racing, foot-racing, cock-fighting, shooting-matches, &c.," was outlawed, because they were "frequently made with intent to vend and sell strong liquors, to the great prejudice of religion, virtue, and industry." [179] Wilmington attempted to discourage vice by "drumming" offenders out of town. The prisoner, preceded by a constable and followed by a drummer, was paraded through the streets, while small boys pelted him with rotten eggs.[180] Gambling, however, remained popular. Of Dover in 1796, Mrs. Ann Ridgely reported: "Cock fighting, Cards, Billiards and Dice playing is as common as eating and Drinking." [181]

[176] Ferris, *Original Settlements*, 266–267.
[177] Folder, "1787, May–June, Legislative, Petitions, Misc.," Legislative Papers.
[178] *Governor's Register, State of Delaware* (Wilmington, 1926), 28; Dorothy Hawkins, A Checklist of Delaware Imprints up to and including 1800 (typescript in Wilmington Institute Free Library, 1928), 20.
[179] *Laws*, II, 866; *Minutes of Council*, 983ff.; Read, *Read*, 316–317.
[180] Ferris, *Original Settlements*, 264–265.
[181] *Calendar of Ridgely Family Letters*, I, 142.

In the wake of Pennsylvania's experiments some Delawareans concluded that criminals might be more effectively restrained by a system of confinement and labor than by the "ignominious and disgraceful punishment" then employed, such as branding, mutilation, and whipping. Petitions to the legislature and the messages of Governors Bedford and Bassett recommended such a change, committees of both houses concurred in 1797 and proposed the erection of a penitentiary, but nothing more was done.[182]

The same period saw an attempt to reform the care of the poor. A law of 1775 had provided for their care on the basis of the hundreds (subdivisions of the counties), in each of which overseers of the poor were chosen. These overseers might rent a poorhouse or provide care for the poor in their own homes, where they would be provided with "a convenient stock of hemp, flax, thread and other materials" with which to earn a part of their living.[183] In 1786 a group of prominent citizens, including John McKinly, Samuel Canby, Joseph Tatnall, and Nicholas Way, asked the assembly to establish a poorhouse for all of New Castle County because of "the increase of the Poor" in the depression then existing. Such an institution would be economical, would give opportunity for the poor to work, and would tend, by its social stigma, to decrease the number of paupers.[184] The poor relief law was redrawn in 1791 to make the county the basis of relief and to substitute in-relief, through poorhouses, for out-relief. Apparently only Christiana Hundred had established a poorhouse under the old law. Inhabitants of the poorhouses were ordered to wear a badge of red

[182] Robert G. Caldwell, *The Penitentiary Movement in Delaware, 1776 to 1829* (Wilmington [1946]), 69–72, 78–79; miscellaneous petitions in Legislative Papers for 1797 and 1798; Legislative Reports, *ibid.*, 1797. The Dover jail was described by Nathaniel Luff as "in a very miserable filthy condition," *Journal*, 57. Descriptions of the Wilmington jail may be found in Ferris, *Original Settlements*, 263, 265–266, and in a poem, "The Smoke-House, or, Wilmington Bastille," *Delaware and Eastern Shore Advertiser*, Dec. 10, 1794.

[183] *Laws*, I, 544–561. Kent desired a county poorhouse as early as 1770, but a bill to that purpose was defeated in the assembly, though supported by Read and McKean. *House Minutes*, 1770, 251–254; Caesar to Thomas Rodney, New Castle, March 14, 1770, Rodney, *Letters*, 35–36. For a discussion of this subject, see Elizabeth Howell Goggin, "Public Welfare in Delaware, 1638–1930," in *Delaware, a History of the First State*, H. Clay Reed, ed. (New York, 1947), II, 793–819.

[184] Folder "1786, May–June, Legislative, Petitions, Misc.," Legislative Papers. Half the receipts of a lecture by "Capt. John Macpherson . . . on the Divinity of our blessed Saviour" at the Wilmington Academy, November 5, 1789, were to be used to buy wood for the poor of Wilmington. *Delaware Gazette*, Nov. 4, 1789.

cloth on the left arm, with letters signifying their status.[185] The poorhouses constructed under this law soon became an object of community pride.[186] Although insolvent debtors might still be sent to jail, the government made it relatively easy for them to secure release in order that their maintenance would not be costly to the public.[187]

Laws regarding marriage were also revised in this period. A marriage regulation act was passed in 1788 in response to petitions urging that "every common Magistrate learned or unlearn'd, religious or profane," should no longer be allowed "to buckle any Sorts, in any Manner together," a "Practice . . . absurd in a Christian Country," which "must have originated among the first Planters for Want of regular Clergy." Ministers were now so plentiful that no man need travel more than half a day to reach one.[188] The new act, however, did not entirely satisfy the clergy, who objected to marriages being taxed for revenue purposes and to the heavy fine upon ministers marrying those not legally eligible to be joined.[189] A consequence was the passage in 1790 of a second act which permitted white people to be married only by a minister or a religious society and only after a license had been secured and after banns had been published for two preceding weeks.[190]

A humane attitude toward illegitimacy was revealed in 1795 when a provision of an earlier law putting out to servitude the bastard son of a white woman and "a Negro or Mulatto man" was repealed, because it was felt "unjust and inhuman to punish the child for the offence of the parent." [191] A year later a hundred-dollar fine was established for adultery, but it was declared that "no fine, forfeiture, or corporal punishment, shall be inflicted on

[185] *Laws*, II, 988–998.

[186] La Rochefoucault, *Travels*, III, 520; Luff, *Journal*, 102. *Cf.* Conrad, *History of Delaware*, II, 686; unidentified clipping in MS. book of H. B. Banning, Almshouse Papers (HSD).

[187] *Laws*, I, 444. Petitions bearing upon the problem of insolvent debtors are to be found among the Legislative Papers for 1796 and 1799.

[188] *Laws*, II, 923; petition of April 3, 1788, Legislative Papers.

[189] Petition, folder, "1789, January–February, Legislative, Petitions, Misc.," *ibid.* The Presbyterian minister, John Miller, the Episcopalian, Charles Wharton, and the Lutheran, Lawrence Girelius, were among the petitioners.

[190] *Laws*, II, 972–977. Indentured servants were forbidden to marry without their masters' consent.

[191] *Laws*, II, 1201.

any person or persons within this state for bastardy or fornication."
The mother of an illegitimate child was compelled to give security
against his becoming a public charge. If she failed to do so and also
failed to name the father, she was put in the custody of the sheriff;
if and as soon as she identified the father, he was required to pay
all expenses and the mother became free.[192]

Insofar as this act improved the status of women, it was but a
symbol of an emancipation of the sex which was now beginning,
though very slowly. Mrs. Mary Johnson of Wilmington was a
woman of property who loved litigation and became "a personage
of great notoriety . . . as the most independent woman of her
age." Wearing "a man's hat," she regularly trudged on foot to the
courts at New Castle, "entered the court-house with the confidence
of a chief justice, and pleaded her own cause." The daughter of
John Hayes, cashier of the Bank of Delaware, managed his private
affairs from the time she was thirteen.[193] Elisse Roussie, a French
Huguenot woman, built and operated a new tavern at Red Lion
after the Revolution.[194] At another tavern La Rochefoucault saw a
female apple vender who was said to support fourteen illegitimate
children without any help from the state or their fathers.[195] The
only chance of divorce lay in an appeal to the legislature, which,
though it received several petitions, granted only one divorce from
the end of the Revolution to the beginning of the new century.[196]

Little is to be found regarding the customs of courtship in Delaware, although Nathaniel Luff has recorded in great detail his
successful courtship of a widow, Lydia Boon, and her father's displeasure with his suit.[197] When Caesar A. Rodney asked his father's
"approbation of the Connection" he wished "to form" with Susan
Hunn, the magniloquent Thomas replied: "Shall I determine the
value of a Jewell I have never seen? . . . You have now arrived

---

[192] *Laws*, II, 1304–1307. *Cf. ibid.*, III, 61–62.

[193] Montgomery, *Reminiscences*, 109, 323–324.

[194] Conrad, *History of Delaware*, II, 505–506.

[195] *Travels*, III, 490.

[196] Petitions in Legislative Papers for 1786, 1788, and 1794; *Laws*, II, 944. The
divorce was granted to a man from Sussex whose wife had been unfaithful and had
declared "that She being young Airy and full of Blood that if any Person should
ask her to Commit Adultery she could not refuse." Petition of June 16, 1786, Legislative Papers.

[197] *Journal*, 82–91.

at that age which Entitles you to the free Exercise of your Own Mind, for this is the Ruler which God and Nature has placed in Your bosom to be your particular Guardian and Guide." [198] Caesar's sister Lavinia, however, slipped out and was married without telling her father.[199] A year later when Lavinia had a baby, her father went to her home "and Sat a While but did not go up to see her As it appears to Me too Vulgar & Indecent to go Into Even the Room of a daughter So Early after her delivery." [200]

Boys' pranks sometimes caused their elders concern, as when the burgesses of Wilmington protested "the frequent assemblage of boys in the night season, as well as on Sunday," for "their disorderly conduct when met together" was "too notorious not to be observed." [201] In Dover they occasionally paraded or lighted bonfires in the streets.[202]

The recreations of their fathers continued to be much as before the war, with the additional annual celebration now of the Fourth of July.[203] Particularly concerned with this celebration of American independence was the Delaware State Society of the Cincinnati, which was organized in Wilmington on July 4, 1783, with Dr. Tilton as first president, Major John Patten, vice-president, and William McKennan, secretary. The society thereafter met annually on the same day, heard a patriotic address, and dined together. From the beginning the group was distinguished by the strong support it gave to the union; for example, in 1783 the Delaware Cincinnati declared the greatest danger to the United States lay not in "usurpation," but in "discord and disunion," and that therefore the need was "to brace the bonds of our Union." After serving as president for a number of years, Tilton was succeeded by Patten, who apparently continued until the society became defunct in approximately 1800. Allen McLane, a member, claimed that its end

---

[198] March 11, 1793, Brown Collection.

[199] T. Rodney, Memorandum book, Jan. 9, 1794, *ibid.*

[200] T. Rodney, Journal, Jan. 1, 1795, *ibid.* For other courtships, see "Eleazer McComb Letters," 48–55; Ridgely, *Ridgelys of Delaware*, 137–142, 304–313; *Calendar of Ridgely Family Letters*, I, 143–145; II, 100–107.

[201] *Delaware and Eastern Shore Advertiser*, Jan. 3, 1795.

[202] T. Rodney, Journal, June 20 and 21, 1794, Brown Collection.

[203] Ferris, *Original Settlements*, 289; *Delaware Gazette*, July 18, Aug. 15, 1789; T. Rodney, Journal, July 4, 1794, Brown Collection; *Delaware and Eastern Shore Advertiser*, July 12, 16, 1794.

was caused by "death and desertion." [204] It seems likely that politics may have played a part in its demise. The three officers named above were all Presbyterians and all became partisans of Thomas Jefferson. David Hall and Joseph Haslet, the first two Republican governors of Delaware, were members of the society, as was Caleb Bennett, later a Jacksonian Democratic governor. The published toasts at the society's banquets reveal its increasing Jeffersonian sympathies. In 1796 these toasts included republicanism, extinction of monarchies, equality, knowledge, the French and Dutch republics, and "the patriots of Ireland." [205]

Anti-liquor, anti-tobacco, and Sabbatarian activity also appeared in Delaware following the Revolution. Petitions were received by the legislature in 1794 and 1795 asking that the fine for violations of the Lord's Day be increased, since stage-drivers, "Carriers, Pedlers, Waggoners, Carters, Butchers, & Drovers" were working on that day "for Emolument & Gain." [206] The desired law, raising the fine to from four to eight dollars for working, gaming, dancing, fowling, hunting, fishing, cock-fighting, or horse-racing on the Sabbath, was passed in 1795.[207]

In 1798 Luff reported that Dr. Edward Miller, of Dover, thought half the vices of mankind were due to excess of strong drink; Luff further declared that the Quakers were investigating these excesses and the improper sale of liquor by members of their society.[208] The *Gazette* in 1790 advised farmers that harvest work, as experience showed, might be better carried on without the use of rum. In the same paper's columns in 1799 "A Poor Preacher" lamented "the useless—nay the injurious increase of public-houses," and called on the people to clean their "village of the sink of moral contagion." [209] Such fear of the results of drinking had been partly responsible for the closing of the fairs in 1785 and resulted also in

---

[204] *Delaware Gazette*, June 20, July 11, 1789; Bellas, *Delaware Cincinnati*, 9, 11, 24, 29.
[205] *Delaware Gazette*, July 5, 1796. Another club organized in Delaware at this time was "The Society of Friends of Justice," of which Peter Brynberg was secretary. It met in the Town Hall quarterly in 1789, but nothing more is known of it. *Ibid.*, May 30, Aug. 5, 1789.
[206] Legislative Papers.
[207] *Laws*, II, 1209–1211.
[208] *Journal*, 80–81.
[209] *Delaware Gazette*, July 17, 1790; June 19, 1799.

the passage in 1798 of a law prohibiting the erection of booths for the sale of liquor in the county towns on election day.[210]

The anti-tobacconists had less statutory success than their fellow reformers. "Tom Whiff" in the *Gazette* for August 1, 1789, quoted James I in calling tobacco "the lively image and pattern of Hell," while "The Matrons Friend" in colorful detail proclaimed his disgust at the practice of snuff-rubbing by women. Stop it, he cried, for breeding, for teeth and gums, and for your husbands' sake.[211]

Another effect of the Revolution may be seen in the movement to limit the legal status of entails and of primogeniture. This was part of a fight waged in most of the new states against these relics of aristocracy and privilege.[212] In Delaware until 1794 the eldest son of an intestate received a double portion of any landed inheritance, but in that year he was placed on a par with the other children in matters of inheritance, the law stating "it is the duty and policy of every republican government to preserve equality amongst its citizens, by maintaining the balance of property as far as is consistent with the rights of individuals." [213] Similarly, in 1793, in another equalitarian action, the legislature permitted anyone seised of an entailed estate to convey it to another just as if it were held in fee simple.[214]

IX. Slavery

THE spirit of freedom aroused in Delaware by the Revolution did not neglect the state's lowliest inhabitant, the slave. The postwar movement to abolish slavery got under way in 1786 when a committee of the House of Assembly proposed "an Act for the gradual

[210] *Laws*, III, 7–12.
[211] *Delaware Gazette*, July 25, 1789.
[212] Nevins, *American States*, 441–443.
[213] *Laws*, I, 289, and appendix, 18; II, 1172. Read, *Read*, 13n.
[214] *Laws*, II, 1054–1055. Cf. *ibid.*, I, 331–332. It is noteworthy that some action had been taken against both entails and primogeniture more than two decades before the Revolution as the above citations show.

Abolition of Slavery." This was replaced by an act "for authorizing
the Emancipation of Slaves" which was first deferred for later consideration and then tabled.[215] Consideration of the subject at this
time was encouraged by presentation of a petition from 204 Quakers, which declared slavery a "reproachful Evil," referred to the
abolition acts passed by other states, and called on the legislature
to relieve "the oppressed Negroes" by considering "Justice, Humanity, the common natural Rights of Mankind, and above all the
Precepts and Injunctions of the christian Religion." The injustices
complained of included the hindrance to manumission afforded
by the high security required to be given against freedmen becoming public charges, the conviction of Negroes "on unequal
Laws," and the denial to them of "an open free Trial." [216]

At the same time that the Quakers were espousing the Negroes'
cause, however, fifty-nine residents of Sussex asked the legislature
to keep Negroes freed in other states from entering Delaware and
to prevent free Negroes from travelling between the counties without a permit, because, the petitioners claimed, "under the name and
Character of Free Negroes many idle and evil-disposed Slaves
throughout this County stroll thro' the same, . . . whereby their
legal Owners are for a long time deprived of their Service," and
because the freedmen from other states might become public
charges.[217]

In spite of such conservative thought, the General Assembly in
1787 passed a bill introduced by Richard Bassett "to prevent the
exportation of slaves." The preamble declared that the slave export
was "contrary to the principles of humanity and justice and derogatory to the honour of this state." Healthy slaves over eighteen and
under thirty-five years old were hereafter to be freed without
security. Manumitted slaves and their descendants were permitted
to hold property and to "obtain redress in law and equity for any
injury," but might not vote, hold office, give evidence against a
white man, or "enjoy any other rights of a freeman," except those

[215] *Votes of Assembly*, 1785–1786, pp. 41, 46, 48; Helen Black Stewart, The
Negro in Delaware to 1829 (unpublished M.A. thesis, University of Delaware),
62–63.
[216] Petition of Dec. 27, 1785, Legislative Papers.
[217] Undated petitions, folder, "1786, June, Legislature, Petitions, Negroes and
Slavery," *ibid.*

mentioned. This act did not extend to persons travelling through or moving into Delaware with their slaves.[218]

The law just mentioned was amended twice in 1789. The first amendment permitted a Delawarean who inherited slaves elsewhere to bring them into Delaware. The second forbade the equipping in Delaware of ships for the slave trade, which practice was deemed "inconsistent with that spirit of general liberty which pervades the constitution of this state." [219] The occasion was the arrival of a slave ship at Wilmington to be refitted, after having been barred from refitting in a neighboring state, of which fact the legislature was informed by petitions from the Quakers and from the newly organized "Delaware Society for the Promoting the Abolition of Slavery, and for the relief and Protection of free negroes and mulattoes unlawfully held in bondage or otherwise oppressed." [220] This society under the leadership of its president, James Gibbons, secured 223 signatures to its petition, including those of such prominent men as John Dickinson, Richard Bassett, James A. Bayard, John Lea, John McKinly, Gunning Bedford, Jr., William Killen, Jacob Broom, John Lewden, James Latimer, William McKennan, Thomas Parke, and Allen McLane. The amendment referred to also provided, at this society's request, for a strengthening of the safeguards against illegal slave exportation and for the trial by jury of slaves accused of capital offences.[221]

The law of 1787 prohibiting the exportation of slaves proved difficult to enforce. Warner Mifflin, who sent "A Serious Expostula-

---

[218] *Laws*, II, 884–888; *Minutes of Council*, 1016ff; Stewart, Negro in Delaware, 23–24, 64–65. Thomas Rodney has left notes of orations he "delivered in the Assembly 1787 against Passing any imprudent Law respecting the Negroes," when he "Contended for a gradual abolition & shew the danger of any other Conduct than Thus." On one occasion he "spoke warmly . . . & was not willing to sacrifice the happyness of the whole Community to the Immediate freedom of the Negroes. All the Assembly agreed with me Except Basset Bedford & Broom—their conduct was vile." Folder, "1779–1791, Thomas Rodney," Brown Collection.

[219] *Laws*, II, 941, 942–944; *Minutes of Council*, 1155, 1159.

[220] Folder, "1788, May–June, Legislative, Petitions, Negroes and Slavery," Legislative Papers; *Votes of Assembly*, May–June, 1788, 19; Stewart, Negro in Delaware, 66–67, 71.

[221] James Tilton, Warner Mifflin, and Fenwick Fisher appear to have been active in the society's affairs in Kent County. T. Rodney, Diary, May 1, 1788, Brown Collection; *Delaware Gazette*, Jan. 24, Aug. 29, 1789. A similar society had been formed in Philadelphia in 1775 and in New York in 1785. J. Franklin Jameson, *The American Revolution Considered as a Social Movement* (Princeton, 1940), 23–24.

tion" on slavery to the United States House of Representatives in 1793, reported to the state legislature that not only were slaves being carried out of Delaware, but also free Negroes were being taken away and sold as slaves.[222] Other petitioners declared that "evil disposed Persons on the borders have for a considerable time past made a practice of stealing . . . Free Negroe & Mulatto Persons, and the same do sell in the Southern States." [223] Consequently the assembly in 1793 passed a law against kidnapping free Negroes which carried severe penalties. A convicted kidnapper, it ordered, "shall be publicly whipped on his or her bare back with thirty-nine lashes well laid on, and shall stand in the pillory for the space of one hour, with both of his or her ears nailed thereto, and at the expiration of the hour, shall have the soft part of his or her ears cut off." [224]

Other acts regarding the Negro were passed in 1787, 1798, and 1799. The first of these required "for the security of Negro and Mulatto slaves whose masters . . . may intend to manumit them" that all manumissions should be in writing, attested by the master and one witness, and approved and recorded by a court. In 1798 Negroes, free or slave, were forbidden to be in a county town on election day unless they lived there. In 1799 free Negroes were permitted to give testimony in criminal cases when no white man was present who could testify.[225] Yet no abolition act was passed, though the General Assembly considered such legislation again in 1796 and 1797.[226]

Both religious and political thought seem to have motivated the abolitionists in their long struggle. The Quakers were the heart of this movement, but other religious groups, in part, if not in whole, participated. The Methodists had determined in 1784 to suspend all their local preachers in Delaware, Maryland, Pennsylvania, and New Jersey who had not freed their slaves.[227] A correspondent to

[222] Petition of Jan. 18, 1791, folder, "1792, January–February, Legislature, Petitions, Negroes and Slavery," Legislative Papers; American Daily Advertiser (Philadelphia), Feb. 19, 1793; Justice, Warner Mifflin, 183–197.

[223] Petitions of 1792 and 1793 in the Legislative Papers.

[224] Laws, II, 1093–1095; Stewart, Negro in Delaware, 42.

[225] Laws, II, 1321–1325; III, 7–12, 80–81. Negroes were, however, specifically forbidden to testify "against any white man" charged "with being the father . . . of any bastard child."

[226] La Rochefoucault, Travels, III, 534; Stewart, Negro in Delaware, 74–75.

[227] Minutes of Methodist Conferences, 1773–1794, 71.

the *Delaware Gazette* requested publication of an extract from the minutes of the Synod of New York and Philadelphia for 1787 and 1788 in which all Presbyterians were asked to work for the abolition of slavery.[228] Such Methodists as Richard Bassett and Allen McLane and such Presbyterians as James Tilton and John McKinly supported abolition, along with many of other faiths. One petition declared that "slavery tends to destroy that free agency necessary to render a man accountable for his actions to a Supreme Being." [229] In 1799 Bible passages were hurled back and forth by correspondents of the *Gazette* who sought thus to justify or condemn slave-holding.[230]

Abolitionists also claimed that toleration of slavery was "totally repugnant to the Spirit of the American Revolution" as proved by the equalitarian philosophy of the Declaration of Independence. They referred also to the state bills of rights and mentioned that of Delaware, which declared "that all persons professing the Christian Religion ought forever to enjoy equal rights and priviledges in this State." [231] "Philanthropos" wrote in the *Advertiser* that a real democrat must be an abolitionist, for, quoting Montesquieu, "slavery in a republic or free government is a paradox." Yet more people, he grieved, sympathize with the French revolutionists whom they have never seen than with the African slaves round about them.[232]

Both sides could play at this game. "Camillus" in defending slavery argued that the British opposed it.[233] When "Querist" asked on the eve of an election, whether slaveholders were "fit persons to represent or govern a free people," an opponent counter-questioned, "Ought men, who used all the interest they dared, to

[228] *Delaware Gazette,* Feb. 7, 1789; *cf. ibid.,* March 14, 1789.

[229] Folder, "1791, January–February, Legislative, Petitions, Negroes and Slavery," Legislative Papers. Calvinists, such as the Rev. Samuel Miller, seemed to have no objection to signing this.

[230] *Delaware Gazette,* Sept. 12, 19, 1789. The second reference claims that a Negro had been permitted to vote in Wilmington a few years earlier.

[231] Undated petition in folder, "1791, January–February, Legislative, Petitions, Negroes and Slavery," Legislative Papers. Another petition referred to the Pennsylvania abolition law. *Ibid.* For reference to the Declaration of Independence see also the 1794 and 1796 petitions. Warner Mifflin asserted that unless the new state constitution prohibited slave-holding it would be "repugnant to the pretended spirit of the Revolution." Petition of Jan. 18, 1791.

[232] Feb. 11, 1795.

[233] *Delaware Gazette,* Sept. 23, 1789.

destroy the liberties of this country, and establish tyranny, be the representatives of a free people?" [234] The point of this retort was a reflection on the attitude of the Quakers, now the foremost abolitionists, toward the Revolution. It might also have been meant to apply to the Methodists, who were second only to the Quakers in their zeal for the Negroes. Thomas Rodney would not allow Warner Mifflin to go to his grave without making a bitter diary entry: "He was opposed secretly to the American Contest for Freedom yet he Professed a great Regard for Negro Freedom & instead of Teaching Negros True Religion filled all slaves full of mischief Toward their Masters & has thereby disturbed society more than any other Person in it." [235]

Probably a moderate point of view was, characteristically, the more common one in Delaware—midway between the view of the abolitionist and that of the apologist for slave-holding. "A Plain Citizen" wrote, "I abhor the slave trade," but "I neither conceive [slaveholding] inconsistent with my Conscience, nor derogatory to the christian religion, the rights of mankind, or the different orders of subordination; yet have no objection to its gradual abolition." He did not fully agree that there was any natural inferiority of the Negroes—in which he was probably more advanced than the average Delawarean—but saw bad effects in liberation, which, he felt, must lead either to intermarriage or transportation.[236] "Humanus," who was not a slave owner and declared himself "no advocate for holding slaves," claimed that the manumitter did "an essential injury" to his neighborhood, for "it is well known that the negroes have a rooted aversion to work." Therefore, he suggested, abolition must be gradual and its method might best be decided by Congress.[237] "Test" argued that educated Negroes should be sent to Africa to reform that land and when this work was finished all the slaves could be freed with a place of freedom to turn to. Till then, they must be kept in slavery lest religion and government "partake of the negro complexion." [238]

---

[234] *Ibid.*, Sept. 5, 8, 1789.
[235] T. Rodney, Diary, Oct. 17, 1789, Brown Collection.
[236] *Delaware Gazette*, Oct. 28, 1789.
[237] *Ibid.*, Oct. 24, 1789. There was considerable discussion of slavery in the columns of the *Gazette* in 1789. Thereafter the papers seemed to steer shy of the subject.
[238] *Ibid.*, Oct. 31, 1789.

Meanwhile treatment of slaves in Delaware varied. A Philadelphia convention of abolition societies in 1794 acknowledged "the Liberality of [the Delaware] Constitution and the humanity of its Laws." [239] La Rochefoucault was persuaded that the slaves were "in every respect well treated and well fed." [240] In the writings of Thomas Rodney instances can be found of both kindly and harsh treatment. Sending a slave to his son, Rodney writes: "He must be Taugh[t] with gentleness for if he is Scolded at and threaten[ed] or abused he will be intirely frightened and foolish So that he will not know how to do anything, . . . but with gentle usage and due attention and instruction he will be very useful. . . . If he should be Sick you must See that good care is Taken of him." [241] But of another occasion Rodney related: "Jim having neglected the Kitchen & Charge I gave him last night about the Cow [which was sick] I gave him a little of the Cow Skin." [242]

That the temptations of liberty were great or the cowskin frequently applied seems indicated by the number of runaway slaves for whom advertisements were placed in the papers. La Rochefoucault declared that "the smallness of the state, its vicinity to Philadelphia, its situation on the edge of the bay or the river Delaware, affords the negroes very easy means of running away from their master; which I am told they very frequently do." [243] The newspapers frequently carried notices of slaves offered for sale; for example,

TO BE SOLD
On Easy Terms,
A STRONG, HEARTY, ACTIVE,
young Negro,
Who has been brought up on a farm.[244]

Rarely did an advertisement appear which was as heart-rending as Joseph Council's offer of "A Negro wench and two children, one a girl of 2 years old, the other a boy of 6 years old. They will be sold seperate or Together as may best suit the purchaser." [245]

---

[239] Petitions of Jan. 1, 1794, Legislative Papers.
[240] *Travels,* III, 535.
[241] Thomas to Caesar A. Rodney, Poplar Grove, Sept. 3, 1790, Rodney Collection.
[242] T. Rodney, Journal, June 6, 1794, Brown Collection.
[243] *Travels,* III, 535. See *Delaware Gazette,* June 6, 1789.
[244] *Delaware Gazette,* June 1, 1790.
[245] *Ibid.,* Oct. 30, 1795.

Neither the bans on exporting nor those on importing slaves were completely effective. Illegal means were taken to avoid the former, while the latter were evaded by statute. Eight private acts were passed by the assembly in this period to permit the importation of specific slaves into Delaware.[246] Many petitions for similar acts, however, were refused, and those that were granted often were somewhat humane in principle. McKimmey Smack, for instance, was allowed to bring in from Maryland three slaves which he had been forced by Maryland law to accept in discharge of a debt.[247] If they were not admitted to Delaware, he pleaded, he would be forced to sell them, and they might be sold into the South where the slave laws were less humane than in Delaware. When the law against importing slaves was passed, many Delawareans owned slaves which were temporarily being employed in Maryland. Sarah Frisby had left her slaves there because they had been hired out by contract. At the end of the contractual period, she found she could not bring them to Delaware, so the legislature was asked, successfully, to come to her aid.[248]

If Delawareans were reluctant to accept abolition, they nevertheless continued to free their slaves by private manumission, especially in Kent County. Here from 1787 to 1792 inclusive, sixty-five slaves were freed. The total number of slaves in the state decreased between 1790 and 1800 from 8,887 to 6,153, the decrease being proportionately the greatest in Kent County, but considerable in each of the others. At the same time the number of free Negroes increased from 3,899 to 8,268. The total number of Negroes in the state was, therefore, increasing.[249]

Many Negroes were winning good reputations in the eyes of the whites by their intelligence and achievements. Betty Jackson accumulated much property in Wilmington by keeping a very popular refreshment shop for whites. Her eldest son was one of that town's principal butchers and "died respected as an industrious, useful man." Her youngest son was a ship carpenter and master builder; he built the brig *Keziah* which was employed in the Irish

---

[246] *Laws*, II, 970, 1024, 1129, 1147, 1168, 1201, 1224, 1312.
[247] Petition of Jan. 8, 1790, Legislative Papers.
[248] Petition of Jan. 5, 1794, *ibid.*
[249] Stewart, Negro in Delaware, 22, 94.

trade.[250] Paul Cuffee, a Negro sea captain, was often in Wilmington, where he attended Quaker meeting. "Negro Tom, the famous African Calculator," was an illiterate prodigy. Brought to America at the age of fourteen, he learned to multiply and to measure time and distance, the latter "to the barley corn," and to give the diameter of the earth's orbit.[251]

The attitude of Delawareans toward slavery was indicative of their attitude toward most problems, one featured by a conservative moderation. They were loath to outlaw an established institution, even when, as the manumissions indicate, they found it of questionable merit. It matters little whether their chief objection was moral or economic, slavery was dying in Delaware, but the Delawarean hesitated to give it the death blow. Indeed this least of the slave states became, with Kentucky, the last slave state. A petition for gradual abolition, signed by 118 Delawareans, expressed the continuing attitude of the state toward more than slavery: "we wish not any sudden change in the established order of things, lest by benefitting a part, we should give a shock to the whole." [252]

X. Religion

THE nationalism resulting from the Revolution was reflected in the development of new national churches. Peace obviously did not mean that American Anglicans could reestablish their old connection with the Church of England in quite the same way in which it had existed before the war. A new organization had to be found for American Protestant Episcopalians, an obligation which bore weightily upon those of this persuasion in the Confederation period.

[250] Montgomery, *Reminiscences*, 251–252.
[251] *Delaware Gazette*, Dec. 25, 1790; Scharf, *History of Delaware*, II, 751n.
[252] Undated petition in folder, "1794, January–February, Legislative, Petitions, Negroes and Slavery," Legislative Papers.

In 1783 the Society for the Propagation of the Gospel ceased all payments to Delaware clergy. A supply of clergymen, however, was to the Episcopalians an even more serious problem than that of finances, for Philip Reading of Middletown, Sydenham Thorne of Milford, and Samuel Tingley of Lewes were the only Episcopalian clerics remaining in the state. To make matters worse, Tingley left Sussex County at the end of that year for a charge in Maryland. Gradually this situation was eased, as John Wade came to Lewes, the ex-Methodist Samuel Roe, to Dover, and the ex-Jesuit Charles Wharton, to New Castle.[253]

Delawareans took an active role in setting up the new organization. The state was represented at Episcopal conventions in 1784, 1785, and 1786. In September of the last year a state convention, presided over by Dr. Wharton, was held in Dover, and in October the General Convention was held in the Wilmington Academy. This convention sent members to England to be consecrated to the episcopacy, as Seabury had already been in Scotland, thus assuring the apostolic succession in the new church.[254] Another state convention was held in Middletown in July, 1789, to appoint delegates to represent Delaware in the General Convention held during that month in Philadelphia, where the organization of the church was completed. State conventions continued to meet through the 1790s, by which means the Episcopal Church in Delaware functioned as a diocesan unit.[255]

Although the Methodists finally seceded in this period, some additions were made to Episcopalian membership in New Castle County by the union of the Swedish Lutheran congregation at Wilmington. The last Swedish minister, Lawrence Girelius, returned to Sweden in 1791 or 1792, and after an interval during which Dr. Wharton, then principal of Wilmington Academy, may occasionally have officiated, an Episcopalian, the Rev. Joseph Clarkson, who had previously assisted the Swedish pastor in Philadelphia, was called to this charge.[256]

[253] Rightmyer, *Anglican Church in Delaware*, 27, 66, 92, 171.

[254] *Ibid.*, 179–182; George W. Doane, "Memoir of C. H. Wharton," *The Remains of the Rev. Charles Henry Wharton, D.D.* (Philadelphia, 1834), I, xxxiv; Rodney, "Immanuel Church," 24.

[255] *Delaware Gazette*, June 27, Sept. 2, 1789; Rightmyer, *op. cit.*, 182–184.

[256] *Ibid.*, 106–109; Montgomery, *Reminiscences*, 131–133; Rightmyer, "Swedish-English Relations," 13–14.

For the Methodists the period was one of organization and growth. It was in Delaware, according to Asbury, that "the design of organizing the Methodists into an Independent Episcopal Church was opened to the preachers" at Barratt's Chapel, near Frederica, Kent County, in November, 1784, by Dr. Coke, who had recently been sent to America by John Wesley. Asbury, who had previously insisted that only ordained clergy should administer communion, was "greatly surprised to see brother Whatcoat assist by taking the cup." Adjusting himself quickly to the idea of schism from the Episcopalians, Asbury made an important decision. "If the preachers unanimously choose me," he wrote, "I shall not act in the capacity I have hitherto done by Mr. Wesley's appointment." This meant the nationalization of American Methodism, and at least suggested the end of its subordination to English leadership.[257]

Before 1783 Methodism's expansion had been somewhat hampered by the war, which disrupted its connections with its English founder and caused suspicions of Toryism. Yet the progress in Delaware had been great and the coming of peace meant that the movement could continue its growth openly and unhindered. The chief circuits in Delaware were those of Milford, Dover, and Wilmington. To each of the downstate circuits, two ministers were usually appointed, while for Wilmington one sufficed.[258] The Dover circuit was the largest, with 1,239 members in 1790, while Wilmington was by far the smallest, with only 60 members in that year.[259] "Alas for poor Wilmington!" wrote Asbury, "when will this people open their eyes?"[260]

In Dover on the other hand, the success of Methodists was such that Thomas Rodney declared on a Sunday in 1800: "Great Methodist Meeting at Milford Today & no Preaching in Dover of any kind for the Methodists have so thinned the Church & Presbyterian Meeting that neither Congregation Can Support a Clergyman."[261] Duck Creek Cross Roads, in northern Kent, was also a

---

[257] Asbury, *Journal*, I, 484.
[258] *Minutes of Methodist Conferences, 1773–1794*, 113, 127, 142, 157, 174, 186, 204.
[259] *Ibid.*, 145.
[260] Asbury, *Journal*, II, 136.
[261] T. Rodney, July 20, 1800, Rodney Collection.

Methodist stronghold, and it was here that the annual meetings of the Philadelphia Conference were usually held.[262]

The "shoutings and acclamations" both by whites and blacks which featured Methodist meetings were condemned by some as interfering with other religions, and appeals were made against them to the civil authorities in Wilmington. Governor Bassett said many people shunned him after he joined the Methodists.[263] Often the Methodists were despised because of their interest in Negroes. One Negro, Black Harry, preached at Methodist meetings to white men; Benjamin Rush said that "making allowance for his illiteracy, he was the greatest orator in America." A Delaware Negro, Richard Allen, was ordained the first colored elder in America in 1799.[264] At this time the Methodists were supporters of abolition as well as of education for the poor and of plain dress.[265] However other people regarded the Methodists, their numbers gained them respect, for by 1800 it was obvious that they were a potent political force.[266]

The Presbyterians and the Baptists, having effected an independent church organization in America before the Revolution, were less disturbed by the war than were the Episcopalians and Methodists. Post-Revolutionary Delaware was divided between two presbyteries, New Castle and Lewes. The bounds of the former extended as far south as Smyrna and included all of Chester and Lancaster counties in Pennsylvania and part of Dauphin and York counties. The Lewes Presbytery included Delaware from Dover southward and some adjacent parts of Maryland.[267]

Because the Methodist movement had caused a schism in Episcopalian ranks the Presbyterians may well have been at this time the most numerous denomination in Delaware.[268] Yet their churches seldom had settled pastors. Most ministers served two or more churches and each minister spent about six Sundays a year

---

[262] *Minutes of Methodist Conferences, 1773–1794*, 132, 147, 162, 179; Asbury, *Journal*, II, 168; Boehm, *Reminiscences*, 44. Boehm tells of a revival at Duck Creek in June, 1800, at which more than 150 people were converted. One meeting lasted forty-five hours without cessation. *Ibid.*, 46–47.

[263] Luff, *Journal*, 61, 127.

[264] Buckley, *History of Methodists*, I, 288, 373–374.

[265] *Minutes of Methodist Conferences, 1773–1794*, 71, 83, 162–163.

[266] Undated note in folder, "T. Rodney, Misc., I," Rodney Collection.

[267] Vallandigham and Gayley, *Presbytery of New Castle*, 9, 18.

[268] La Rochefoucault declares them to be "the most numerous and most powerful sect in the state." *Travels*, III, 529.

supplying vacancies. Both the clergy and laity were continually gaining new members from Ireland, but both groups were also continually losing members who migrated to the West.[269] By 1800, however, many more of the churches were able to support a minister than previously.[270]

The structure of the American Presbyterian organization was largely completed with the formation of the General Assembly in 1788. The Lewes Presbytery, however, showed notable independence both of it and of the Synod of Philadelphia and New York, to which Lewes belonged. Through Mathew Wilson it expressed disagreement with the doctrine of appeals from presbyteries to synods and thence to the General Assembly as "mere human Inventions, unknown in the Word of God," and not practiced in the "first apostolic Churches for many hundred years." [271]

The Methodists and the Baptists are the only sects which seem to have grown in membership in Delaware during the Revolution. While but one or two Baptist churches existed in the state in 1776, there were eight such churches and nine ordained ministers in 1791. Five of these churches then belonged to the Philadelphia Association and three to the Salisbury Association, but in 1795 the Delaware Baptist Association was formed. The Delaware Baptists were Calvinistic in doctrine and as such were on better terms with the Presbyterians than with the other denominations, some of which attacked them bitterly.[272]

The Quakers had been unpopular during the Revolution because of their attitude toward warfare. Nevertheless their doctrines still attracted converts, and in one case they absorbed the majority of the members of another sect. This was the Nicholites, whose leader, James Harris, a man of an "innocent mind and exemplary conduct and conversation," proposed in 1797 a union with the Friends.[273]

The origins of Catholicism in Delaware were rural and culminated in the erection of a chapel at Coffee Run, New Castle County,

---

[269] Vallandigham and Gayley, *Presbytery of New Castle*, 9–10, 18; Records of the New Castle Presbytery, IV, 286, 288, 332; V, unnumbered front page.

[270] Vallandigham and Gayley, *op. cit.*, 13.

[271] Records of Lewes Presbytery, I, 134–136.

[272] Edwards, "Baptists in Delaware," 47, 212; Waterston, *Churches in Delaware*, 86; Cook, *Delaware Baptists*, 42–44, 74. The sources are not entirely in agreement in respect to organization.

[273] Luff, *Journal*, 38, 56–57.

just before the Revolution. The arrival of the French Haitian refugees at Wilmington in the 1790s stimulated the growth of Catholicism in that borough. The Rev. Etienne Faure, a Frenchman, appears to have been the first priest to make Wilmington his home. As pastor of St. Peter's he ministered to the French settlers and was succeeded at his death by the Rev. M. Cibot, who had been vice prefect apostolic and superior general of the missions of the north of Haiti.[274] In 1800 Fathers Carr and Rosseter seem to have performed all the services at St. Peter's. Irish names begin to supplant French ones in the old church's records at this time.[275]

In 1786 the General Assembly passed an act permitting the incorporation of religious societies in order that they might properly care for their property. The act followed the receipt of petitions for incorporation from two Presbyterian congregations and was recommended by a committee consisting of John Banning and James Tilton, who advised that a general incorporation law for religious societies would be more satisfactory than the passage of specific acts of incorporation. Thus, in regard to religious corporations Delaware adopted a general principle of equal treatment which it did not apply to private corporations for a century more.[276]

Unitarian and deist principles gained support in Delaware in the late eighteenth century. Thomas Rodney was expressing unitarian principles at the time of Priestley's arrival in America.[277] Dr. Theodore Wilson of Lewes and James A. Bayard were said to have been deists.[278] The most interesting example of the power of these new beliefs is to be found in the constitution of 1792. Here,

---

[274] Frances S. Childs, *French Refugee Life in the United States, 1790–1800* (Baltimore, 1940), 41; "St. Peter's Church, Wilmington, D., Notes taken from Its Register," *American Catholic Historical Researches*, XIII (Philadelphia, 1896), 65. *Cf.* Joseph Bringhurst, Diary (extract in HSD), Nov. 14, 1797.

[275] "St. Peter's Church," 65–66. For a time the Wilmington Catholics met in the Academy. Montgomery, *Reminiscences*, 296. The most famous of the early Catholic clergy was Father Patrick Kenny, who came to Delaware in 1805. Kraemer, "Catholic Church in Delaware," 682.

[276] *Laws*, II, 878–884; report in folder, "1786, May–June, Legislative, Petitions, Misc." Legislative Papers.

[277] T. Rodney, *Journal*, June 11, July 2, 1794, Brown Collection; T. Rodney to Dr. Pryor, Ionia Farm, March 27, 1793, *ibid.*; T. Rodney to unknown addressee, Dover, Oct. 24, 1791, *ibid.*; Journal of Trip to Philadelphia, Oct. 27, 1790, *ibid.*

[278] *Delaware Gazette*, April 24, July 6, 1799; Montgomery, *Reminiscences*, 102–108; John A. Munroe, ed., "William Plumer's Biographical Sketches of James A. Bayard, Caesar A. Rodney, and Samuel White," *Delaware History*, IV (1951), 367.

after guaranteeing freedom of worship and equality of religious groups before the law, Article I asserted, "No religious test shall be required as a qualification to any office, or public trust under this State." This provision directly repealed Article 22 of the constitution of 1776, which declared that every officeholder must profess faith in the Holy Trinity and "acknowledge the holy scriptures of the Old and New Testament to be given by divine inspiration."

XI. Education

EDUCATION in the post-Revolutionary period continued for the most part to follow in the path that had been made for it in colonial days. When Newark Academy reopened in 1780 after being closed for three years, it continued to provide training in "the Elements of the Latin and Greek Languages," except for the period from 1796 to 1799 when it was closed again.[279] The board of trustees gradually came to be composed largely of Delawareans, as such distinguished outsiders as Thomas McKean, John Ewing, and James Mease died or were dropped from the board for non-attendance.

The Wilmington Academy, which had also been closed for several years during the Revolution, was reopened in 1781. In 1786 James Adams published in Wilmington a *Draught of a Plan of Education for the Wilmington Academy*, which had originally been adopted by the trustees in 1768. The objects of the school, according to this plan, were the promotion of religion, morality, and literature. The officers were a principal and professors of languages, mathematics, and English, as well as an usher to assist any overburdened teacher. The professor lectured once a week to seniors on moral philosophy, consisting of ethics and natural law.

Five years were prescribed for the classical course in Latin and

---

[279] Powell, *Education in Delaware*, 77–78. The minutes for this period are extant, and a typescript of them is in the Memorial Library of the University of Delaware. *Delaware and Eastern Shore Advertiser*, Sept. 20, 1794; *Delaware Gazette*, March 14, May 11, 1799; petition in folder, "1783, May–June, Legislative, Petitions, Newark Academy," Legislative Papers.

Greek, and the books to be used for each year named, ranging from Rudiman's *Rudiments* to Demosthenes. French would be taught if parents demanded it. Of mathematics, the two highest Latin classes were to learn all the rules of arithmetic, "vulgar and decimal," algebra, Euclid, plain and spherical trigonometry, and conic sections, and the mathematics professor was also to teach geography, surveying, navigation, astronomy, and the "Newtonian System." The English class would learn to read prose and verse "with propriety and elegance," would study grammar and composition, and would each day read "some approved Essayist or Poet," while the professor strove "to inculcate a spirit of criticism." The school year began in November, following a vacation which succeeded the examinations in October. Dr. Wharton was the principal, and the standing committee of the board consisted of the Rev. Lawrence Girelius, Dr. Nicholas Way, John Dickinson, and Jacob Broom.

In 1789 the academy's Latin school was "well filled with Pupils" although the teacher was "a real Boatswain's Mate in inflicting punishment." Only after proficiency was acquired in Latin and Greek were English studies begun, "for," according to John Hamilton, "at those Classical Schools, the Professors and Teachers do not consider these of Any Importance whatever." [280]

The academy building itself proved of great benefit to the town. Here religious groups met, public functions were held, lectures were given. A group of men interested in science, including Franklin, Rittenhouse, and Rush, met there in the 1780s to make some astronomical observations. Here a convention of the Episcopal Church assembled. Here fortnightly in the winter of 1800 "a well-regulated dancing party, called a *whim*," was held. And here, before the end of the century, a factory was established, for the academy was forced to close once again in 1798 when Dr. Wharton left.[281] Wharton may have been to some degree responsible for the failure of the academy, for although a man of much learning, amiable disposition, polite manners, and sound principles, he was a poor judge of human nature and lacked the personal gravity

---

[280] Hamilton, "Reminiscences," 91.

[281] Montgomery, *Reminiscences*, 293–297; Rightmyer, *Anglican Church in Delaware*, 164–166. See especially "The Minutes of the Wilmington Academy, 1777–1802," ed. by E. Miriam Lewis, *Delaware History*, III (1949), 181–226.

which might have made his manner imposing; so Bayard described him in 1800 to Alexander Hamilton when Wharton was being considered for the presidency of Columbia.[282]

It was of one of Dr. Wharton's teachers in the Academy that Lavinia Rodney told this story: "Mr. Murdock has got very few schollars indeed he keeps the school in such order it is a pitty he has so many for some of the boys whip him every day one of [them] Whipd him the other day till he had to call out to one of the young Gentlemen for help." [283]

The Friends' academy in Wilmington continued to function, as did other schools under Quaker sponsorship elsewhere in the state.[284] John Welsh and John Dickinson donated land in the village of Brandywine for the erection by subscription of an academy building there.[285] Parson Johnson ran the "Jones's School" in Kent; the Ridgely boys were tutored in Dover by the Reverend Mr. Brush.[286] John Kennedy, "lately from Europe," taught at New Castle, where an academy was built at the end of the century; Francis Hindman kept a classical school at Lewes; William Johnson was schoolmaster at Milford; an attempt was made to incorporate the academy at Dover in 1785.[287] One country school of the time is described as without floor, chimney, or window glass. A log fire at one end hardly thawed the frozen water-soaked earth from which the pupils' feet were protected by blocks of wood.[288]

Several famous persons taught school in Wilmington: William Cobbett, the great English journalist; Lewis Cass, presidential aspirant; James Filson, the Kentucky explorer; and Joseph Ander-

[282] J. A. Bayard to A. Hamilton, Aug. 11, 1800, Elizabeth Donnan, ed. "Papers of James A. Bayard, 1796–1815," *Annual Report of the American Historical Association for the Year 1913*, II (Washington, 1915), 113. Wharton was offered the position, accepted it, but soon withdrew his acceptance.

[283] Lavinia to C. A. Rodney, Wilmington, April [1788], Rodney Collection.

[284] Dunlap, *Quaker Education*, 253–262; Ferris, *Original Settlements*, 285–287; Watkins, St. Georges and Appoquinimink, Corbit, Higgins, Spruance Papers; Conrad, *History of Delaware*, II, 470; Luff, *Journal*, 127–128. Cf. first chapter of *Friends School in Wilmington* (Wilmington, 1948).

[285] Subscription list, Feb. 20, 1797, Delaware Schools Papers (HSD); indenture, March 17, 1798, typescript, John Dickinson Papers (HSD).

[286] T. Rodney, Journal, July 23, 25, 1800, Rodney Collection; *Calendar of Ridgely Family Letters*, I, 148, 167.

[287] Powell, *Education in Delaware*, 51, 55, 58, 62; *Delaware Gazette*, Oct. 23, 1790.

[288] Watkins, St. Georges and Appoquinimink, Corbit, Higgins, Spruance Papers.

son, an early Senator from Tennessee.[289] Other teachers included Solomon Fussell, Henry Pepper, Frederick Jordan, John Thelwell, Robert Coram, and Robert McCullough.[290] The Rev. John Porter assured prospective students that he had studied at Trinity College, Dublin, taken a degree at Glasgow, and taught in Ireland. He proposed teaching English grammar, Latin and Greek classics, Euclid, arithmetic, geography, algebra, "Fluxions," surveying, navigation, "&c.," and he promised that his students might "have access occasionally to a Dublin copy of the Encyclopedia Britannica." [291] Night schools were conducted by Coram, Thelwell, and Pepper.[292] Mrs. Cooke, formerly of Queen Annes, Maryland, opened a school for "young ladies," as did a Miss Brown, who offered to teach them "the art of Drawing, Tambouring, Painting, Making of Lace, Fillegree, Artificial Flowers, &c." [293]

The arrival of the French refugees made their language especially popular. "It was so genteel," Elizabeth Montgomery explained, "to say you were learning French, if only a few monosyllables were acquired to say 'Parlez vous Français?' " J. Derpian, who had formerly taught at Dover, a M. Bergerac, onetime New Orleans merchant, and Michel Martel, instructor of Theodosia Burr, satisfied the fad for instruction in this tongue.[294] Some children continued to be sent out of state for their education, to Princeton, Philadelphia, Westtown, Chestertown, Carlisle, and Lancaster.[295]

---

[289] Montgomery, *Reminiscences*, 314–315, 323; Andrew McLaughlin, *Lewis Cass* (Boston, 1892), 39; Hamilton, "Reminiscences," 89.

[290] Lavinia to Thomas Rodney, Wilmington, Nov. 28 and Dec. 9, 1787, and Jan. 20, 1788, Rodney Collection; *Delaware and Eastern Shore Advertiser*, Jan. 28, 1795; *Delaware Gazette*, Nov. 3, 1795; Hamilton, "Reminiscences," 90–91.

[291] *Delaware Gazette*, July 5, 1796.

[292] *Ibid.*, Oct. 17, 31, 1789; Oct. 16, 1790.

[293] *Ibid.*, July 8, 1796; Aug. 14, 1799.

[294] Montgomery, *Reminiscences*, 280–282, 285, 314; Powell, *Education in Delaware*, 47–48; *Delaware and Eastern Shore Advertiser*, Oct. 25, 1794.

[295] Alexander, *Princeton in the 18th Century*, 235, 237, 240, 272, 288, 295, 300, 313; Lavinia to Thomas Rodney, Chestertown, Dec. 29, 1786, and Feb. 27 and April 21, 1787, Rodney Collection; Thomas to Caesar A. Rodney, April 27, 1790, Brown Collection; same to same, Sept. 3, Dec. 13, 1790, and several undated letters, Rodney Collection; William Corbit to Pennell Corbit, May 8, 1790, Dec. 2, 1793, and Dec. 6, 1800, Corbit, Higgins, Spruance Papers; *Delaware Gazette*, May 8, 1790; Luff, *Journal*, 126, 144; *Calendar of Ridgely Family Letters*, I, 137–138, 186, 291, 305.

The new spirit of the post-Revolutionary era manifested itself not so much through the educational media already discussed as through the few measures taken to establish a free school system. The constitution of 1792 paved the way for this movement by instructing the legislature to provide "for establishing schools and promoting arts and sciences." [296] In 1794 Robert Coram, Nicholas Van Dyke, and Caesar A. Rodney were appointed a committee of the Patriotic Society to draw up a memorial to the legislature urging the establishment of public schools "whereby the unfortunate children of indigence and neglect, may be educated and enlightened among the children of opulence and vigilance—which is an essential means of preserving that equality so necessary to the preservation of a pure Republican Government."

The memorial complained that the legislators had done nothing in respect to free schools. "There still remains in the minds of many," Coram, Rodney, and Van Dyke declared, "a torpor on this subject, as difficult to account for, as to excuse. . . . We cannot help lamenting the sad effects of such listless attention to the first principles of society. . . . We cannot avoid pressing the Legislature . . . to make some beginning in this important business." [297]

Perhaps this stimulus helped secure passage, in 1796, of an act "to create a fund sufficient to establish schools in this state," which declared that revenue from the sale of marriage and tavern licenses to the beginning of 1806 should become "the fund for establishing schools in the state of Delaware." With this money stock was to be purchased "in either the Bank of Delaware, the United States, of Pennsylvania, or of North America." The fund was eventually to be applied "to the establishment of schools" in the hundreds of Delaware, "for the purpose of instructing the children of the inhabitants thereof in the English language, arithmetic, and such other branches of knowledge as are most useful and necessary, in completing a good English education." A final provision forbade its use in "the erecting or supporting any academy, college, or university in this state," evidence of the democratic equalitarian purpose of this law. No use, however, had been made of this fund by

[296] Article VIII, Section 12.
[297] *Delaware and Eastern Shore Advertiser*, Dec. 27, 1794.

the end of the century; indeed it had been weakened by allowing the salaries of the chancellor and judges to be taken from it.[298]

One of the authors of the Patriotic Society's memorial, Robert Coram, an English-born schoolmaster, further demonstrated his devotion to the democratization of learning by his publication at Wilmington in 1791 of *Political Inquiries to Which Is Added a Plan for the General Establishment of Schools throughout the United States.*[299] Two other movements in education toward the advancement of the democratic ideal were set under way in Delaware in this period.

One was the establishment of a school for Negroes in Wilmington. In 1791 Joseph West, a Quaker, willed some money to the Wilmington Monthly Meeting to be used "toward the Schooling of Negro, Molatto, & other poor children." On February 19, 1798, an evening school for Negroes was instituted by Zachariah Jess in the Friends' schoolhouse under the direction of a committee of the meeting. The committee was well pleased with the success of this experiment, which was repeated the next winter, when about twenty or thirty Negroes attended. "Many of the Scholars," the committee reported, "have manifested much industry & attention, & made considerable advance in learning, affording ground to hope that the care of friends in promoting this School, may be very useful to them." [300]

The other movement referred to was the establishment of public libraries. A reference has been found to a "Wilmington Library" existing in 1754, but nothing more is known of this institution. In December, 1787, some citizens of Wilmington met to form a library company, which adopted articles of association the following January and elected John Hayes, cashier of the Bank of Delaware, president, and Jacob Broom, the manufacturer, treasurer.[301] A petition with forty-nine signatures, including such merchants as William Hemphill and Thomas Lea, such physicians as Nicholas Way and John McKinly, and such schoolmasters as John Thelwell and Dr.

[298] *Laws,* II, 1296–1298, 1352–1354; III, 136–139.

[299] See Charles and Mary Beard, *The American Spirit* (New York, 1942), 126–137, for a discussion of Coram's book.

[300] Dunlap, *Quaker Education,* 479–483.

[301] John P. Nields, *The Wilmington Public Library and the New Castle County Free Library; a Historical Sketch* (Wilmington, 1943), 3–4. *Cf.* Conrad, *History of Delaware,* II, 407.

Wharton, was sent to the legislature announcing the purchase of a large collection of books and the formation of the "Library Company of Wilmington" and asking for incorporation. The petition was granted, and the Wilmington Library proceeded on its long career of public usefulness.[302] A public library was also established at Dagsborough before the end of the century, and plans were afoot for the establishment of libraries at Laurel and Lewes.[303]

XII. Medical Practice

"I FLATTER myself that all things are working together for good in America," wrote Dr. James Tilton in 1785 to Dr. George Monro, then studying in Scotland. "I think we are improving both in political knowledge & public virtue. You have a right to hope for the best of your native State in particular." [304]

In the development of the culture of Delaware, physicians like Tilton and Monro made no small contribution. The only academically trained scientist of the day, the physician had an especially important role as the dispenser of knowledge to his neighbors. It was therefore of considerable importance that the assembly in 1789 provided for the incorporation of the local physicians as a Medical Society, the third such state society to be founded in America.[305]

Among the charter members were many prominent men. John McKinly had served as the state's first president and continued to distinguish himself by his interest in education and philanthropy.

[302] Folder, "1788, May–June, Legislative, Petitions, Incorporation of Wilmington Library," Legislative Papers; *Laws,* II, 931. Isaac Starr, Jr., and Robert Coram were at different times librarians. *Delaware Gazette,* March 21, Aug. 29, 1789; May 29, 1790. In 1793 this library had 891 volumes and 54 members. Nields, *loc. cit.*

[303] Outerbridge Horsey to William Hill Wells, Georgetown, July 17, 1799, Turner, *Records of Sussex County,* 300.

[304] Dover, July 8, 1785, Emmet Collection (New York Public Library), 962.

[305] Petition of Kent County physicians, folder, "1788, January–February, Legislative, Petitions," Legislative Papers; *Laws,* II, 944; Thomas C. Stellwagen, *Delaware Doctors, Papers of the Historical Society of Delaware,* XIX (Wilmington, 1897), 7; *Delaware Gazette,* April 11, June 13, 1789. James Tilton was the society's first president. *American Museum,* VI, 48–49.

Nicholas Way taught physics to many younger men, became an official of the United States mint, and won public gratitude for his service in the time of the yellow fever epidemics. George Monro, an army veteran, studied at Newark Academy and the University of Pennsylvania, and in London and Edinburgh. He was a Democratic-Republican in politics, being related by blood and marriage to David Hall and Joseph Haslet, the first two governors of that party. Henry Latimer, who also studied abroad, served in Congress as a Federalist. James Sykes, a member of the same party as Latimer, was governor of Delaware and for years president of the Senate. James Tilton and Archibald Alexander were influential Jeffersonians. Thomas McDonough was the father of the famous victor of Plattsburg. Much mention has already been made of Mathew Wilson, teacher and preacher at Lewes.[306]

Many Delawareans relied on such patent medicines as Anderson's Scots Pills, Harlem Oil, Bateman's Drops, Daffy's Elixir, Godfrey's Cordial, and Turlington's Balsam of Life. Some people employed midwives, such as Grace Milligan, who had studied with Dr. Shippen in Philadelphia.[307] Dentists were apparently itinerants like Dr. William Chandler, who advertised in 1794 that he was staying at Rumsey's in Wilmington for a few days.[308]

The problems of the physician, according to Dr. Tilton, were complicated by the fact that here "a greater variety of Soil and Climate [were] comprehended within a smaller extent of Territory than . . . anywhere else," for in Delaware, he said, were "all the varieties of Soil and Climate to be found in the middle States of America." The hilly region of the north furnished "as healthful a district of country as any in America" and "the Borough of Wilmington for health, beauty, and accommodation [was] superior to any town" he had seen "between the borders of New-England and the southern boundary of Virginia." The ocean, bay, and river shore enjoyed the healthful effects of the sea breeze; Lewes was "as healthful as Bermudas." It "furnished the longest lived in-

---

[306] Stellwagen, *op. cit.*, 8. Biographies of these men may conveniently be located through the biographical card catalogue in the Wilmington Institute Free Library. The names of the charter members of the Medical Society are listed in the Society's Minutes in the Historical Society of Delaware.

[307] *Delaware Gazette*, May 2, Oct. 14, 1789.

[308] *Delaware and Eastern Shore Advertiser*, July 9, 1794.

habitants" of Delaware, "the greatest proportion of old people and the most numerous swarms of children"; consequently it was "much resorted to by convalescents from the inland country and neighbouring states" and deserved "to be still more frequented."

Delaware was, however, very unhealthy in the "inland part, . . . where heat and stagnation occur to exalt the noxious exhalations of our low grounds." "Another fertile source of Diseases," thought Tilton, was furnished by "frequent and sudden changes in the sensible qualities of our Atmosphere." The healthiest season was through May, June, and July, with "our endemical sickness" beginning "immediately after Harvest." "Bilious, Intermitting and Remitting Fevers" were the principal fall diseases and were succeeded by "Synochous and Typhous Fever" in the winter. In Dover everyone suffered "a deminution of health during the fall season." Whereas before the Revolution fevers had been treated by repeated bleeding, little use was now made of the lancet, but Peruvian bark, or quinine, was liberally employed. "The Cholera Infantum as described by Dr. Rush [had] of late years made great devastation" among the children, especially in Dover. "Chamomile Tea," "Chicken Water," laudanum, external applications of "Bark and Camphor," and recourse to the bay shore for its sea breeze were frequently prescribed for those suffering from this disease.[309]

The most serious medical problem faced by the Delaware physicians was yellow fever. In 1793 Philadelphia was afflicted with its first great epidemic of this dread disease. Although "a Bilious Colic epidemic . . . unprecedented in the medical records or popular tradition" raged in Dover and its vicinity,[310] Delaware as a whole seems to have been spared this plague. Wilmington at first set up a quarantine enforced by guards, but this was soon abandoned and a hospital established for infected citizens of Philadelphia who were fleeing their own city. Dr. Way and Major Bush

---

[309] Letters of Tilton to Drs. Redman and Currie, 1790 and 1791, in William Currie, *An Historical Account of the Climates and Diseases of the United States* (Philadelphia, 1792), 207–221.

[310] Edward Miller to Benjamin Rush, Dover, Nov. 5, 1793, Rush, *An Account of the Bilious Remitting Yellow Fever* (Philadelphia, 1794), 149; William Currie, *A Treatise on the Synochus Icteroides, or Yellow Fever* (Philadelphia, 1794), 11. Dr. Miller and Dr. James Sykes quarreled about the nature and cause of the illness in Dover, Sykes ascribing it "to the use of Bark impregnated with lead." *Delaware and Eastern Shore Advertiser*, July 9 and 26, 1794.

were especially hospitable, opening their homes even to refugees who were unknown to them.[311] When in 1797 a second epidemic struck Philadelphia, fugitives again crowded Wilmington.[312] Although some cases appeared in Delaware, the state again largely escaped the disease.[313]

In 1798, however, the yellow fever epidemic did reach Wilmington, where it was believed to have been brought from Philadelphia. New Castle and other parts of the state were also affected.[314] A tent hospital was erected in Wilmington, but half the patients who were sent there died because, according to the opinion of Dr. Monro, the use of mercury was prohibited.[315] Before cold weather brought the epidemic to an end, 252 persons had died in Wilmington alone. Among those Delawareans fatally afflicted were Warner Mifflin, Eleazer McComb, Joseph Miller (a lawyer and brother of the physician), John Patten, and two sons of Joseph Tatnall.[316]

Communicating with Drs. Rush and Currie in Philadelphia and with Edward Miller, now in New York, Delaware physicians sought by an exchange of knowledge to prevent the recurrence of such epidemics.[317] The disease seemed to arise at the water fronts and to be traceable, often through Philadelphia, to the West Indies; Dr. John Vaughan, therefore, proposed that Wilmington should build a lazaretto "to ventilate infected goods" and that the state should

[311] A Short Account of the Yellow Fever in Philadelphia in 1793 (Philadelphia, 1794), 59. The Wilmington connection is mentioned in the excellent recent book by J. H. Powell, Bring Out Your Dead (Philadelphia, 1949).

[312] Montgomery, Reminiscences, 210; Short History of the Yellow Fever that Broke Out in . . . Philadelphia in July, 1797 (Philadelphia, 1797), 13.

[313] James Tilton to Benjamin Rush, Wilmington, Sept. 12, 1797, Rush MSS. (Ridgeway Branch, Library Company of Philadelphia), XXXVIII, 61. Delawareans contributed about six hundred dollars as well as flour, corn meal, and vegetables to the distressed of Philadelphia. Short History of Yellow Fever, 1797, 68, 71, 74, 76, and appendix.

[314] James Tilton to William Currie, Wilmington, Nov. 13, 1798, Currie, Memoirs of the Yellow Fever (Philadelphia, 1798), 138–139; John Hollingsworth to John Barry, Brandywine Bridge, Oct. 7, 1798, Brown Collection. Dover seems to have escaped. Currie, A Sketch of the Rise and Progress of the Yellow Fever . . . in Philadelphia, in the Year 1799 (Philadelphia, 1800), 56.

[315] George Monro to William Currie, Wilmington, Nov. 19, 1798, Currie, Memoirs, 139–140.

[316] Currie, Memoirs, 46, 119, 124, 129; Montgomery, Reminiscences, 211–212; T. Rodney, Diary, Sept. 24, 1794, Brown Collection. A description of Wilmington during the epidemic is to be found in Luff, Journal, 89.

[317] James Tilton to Edward Miller, Wilmington [1798], Currie, Yellow Fever, 1799, 51–52.

pass stronger health laws.[318] A quarantine law which had been passed in 1797 was strengthened in 1799, and in the latter year Wilmington escaped the dread disease.[319]

XIII. Cultural Life

THE independent American of the post-Revolutionary period sought to prepare himself for a self-reliant life. To this end he organized and joined societies for mutual improvement. A "Debating Society" was formed in Wilmington in 1790 "on the most liberal principles . . . for the discussion of different subjects of learning." At New Castle "a society of youths formed for the improvement of the mind" met in 1789. "May reason and not the sword decide all national disputes" and "may the arts and sciences and the manufacturers of our country forever flourish" they toasted as they celebrated Independence Day.[320]

More information exists about the Lyceum of Delaware, which met monthly or oftener in 1798 and 1799. At each meeting some question was discussed as, for example, "Whether there is more happiness in a Savage or a Civilized State," and an answer determined.[321] They concluded that the mental powers of the sexes were unequal; that duelling was "inconsistent with true principles of honour and courage"; that novels were "pernicious to youth"; that adversity was more "conducive to virtue" than prosperity; "that Luxury was more destructive to a republican government than war"; that private correction was preferable to public correction in answering the proper ends of punishment; that divinity was the profession with the greatest tendency to benefit mankind; that

[318] *Delaware Gazette,* June 12, 15, 26, 1799.
[319] *Laws,* II, 1354–1358; III, 47–52, 121–123; Currie, *Yellow Fever, 1799,* 21, 56.
[320] *Delaware Gazette,* July 11, 1789; May 1, 1790; *Pennsylvania Packet,* May 14, 1790.
[321] Other questions discussed included "What is the most eligible Occupation or Employment in Civilized Society?" and "Is Imprisonment for Debt consistent with Sound Policy?" *Delaware and Eastern Shore Advertiser,* Jan. 4, 11, 15, Feb. 5, May 31, 1798.

the virtues prevailing "in uncultivated States" were greater than those "in polished life"; that more misery than happiness existed "in the present state of human nature"; and that prodigality was "more injurious to society than avarice." [322]

The Lyceum's constitution stated its purposes to be (1) the improvement of morals, (2) the advancement of literature, and (3) the cultivation and diffusion of useful knowledge. The officers were drawn from the upper middle class. In 1798, Gunning Bedford, Sr., the governor, was president; a merchant, Eleazer McComb, was vice-president; a lawyer, French MacMullan, secretary; and two ministers, Joseph Clarkson and Francis Latta, an ex-Congressman, John Patten, and two physicians, James Tilton and George Monro, members of the "select committee." [323] Its discussions of weighty subjects did not always proceed smoothly; "A Spouting Member" testified to a need "to stop the current of political animosity" in order to prevent "sordid altercation and torpidity of argument." "The young men," he said, "should avoid frivolous notions and impertinent witticisms," while "the old men should restrain the natural velocity of their tongues." [324] Such difficulties, together with the growth of partisan feeling on the eve of the election of 1800, must have caused the dissolution of this interesting society.

The reading opportunities of the post-Revolutionary Delawarean were greatly enhanced by the establishment both of libraries and of bookstores. James Adams in 1789 offered for sale Burket on the New Testament, Edwards on original sin, *The History of Sir Charles Grandison, The Spectator, The Rambler, The Adventurer, The American Museum, Lord Chesterfield's Advice to His Son,* Fisher's arithmetic, "Songs, comic and satyrical, by George A. Stevens," and Brown's dictionary of the Bible.[325] Thomas Marriott's list in 1794 included *Evelina, Paradise Lost, Junius,* Young's *Night Thoughts,* Chastellux's *Travels,* Peter Pindar, Cullen's *Practice of Physic,* and *Every Man His Own Physician.*[326] John Webster, a

[322] *Delaware Gazette,* March 14, 27, April 10, May 15, June 1, 12, 26, July 10, Aug. 3, 14, 1799.
[323] *Delaware and Eastern Shore Advertiser,* Jan. 15, 1798.
[324] *Delaware Gazette,* Aug. 30, 1799.
[325] *Ibid.,* March 21, 1789.
[326] *Delaware and Eastern Shore Advertiser,* June 28, 1794.

former schoolmaster, rhymed an advertisement in which he declared,

> Among the Books you'll find there are,
> Choice Sermons wrote by Doctor Blair,
>   With Bates on Man's Redemption;
> The Voyage of Cook—when sails unfurl'd
> Had wafted him around the world—
>   Well worthy your attention.
> . . . And (if you chuse to read it)
> Paine's Age of Reason strikes your eye
> And Age of Infidelity
>   Which must of course succeed it.

Even the children

> . . . a choice may find,
> Adapted to the infant mind
>   When to the shop they skip in,
> New-England primer, A, B, C,
> The reward of integrity
>   And History of King Pippin.
> The History of Giles Gingerbread,
> With pictures and a cover red,
>   Tom Jones without a mother,
> Likewise Tom Thumb's folio,
> Who mounted on his bird could go
>   From one place to another.[327]

Marriott offered children abridged versions of *Clarissa Harlow,* *Pamela,* and *Gulliver's Travels,* as well as Mother Goose and Goody Two Shoes.[328]

The Ridgelys in Dover were reading the works of Hannah Moore, Fanny Burney's *Camilla,* Goldsmith's *Vicar of Wakefield,* Clara Reeve's *The Old English Baron,* and *Count Roderic's Castle.*[329] The irrepressible Thomas Rodney spent much time in his retirement commenting on Boileau's *Art of Poetry,* speculating on the identity of Junius, and preparing a new verse form for Macpherson's synthetic translation of Ossian.[330] He also commented

[327] *Ibid.,* Dec. 17, 1794.
[328] *Ibid.,* Dec. 24, 1794.
[329] *Calendar of Ridgely Family Letters,* I, 57, 208, 306.
[330] Folder, "Original Poems of Thomas Rodney," Rodney Collection; folder, "T. Rodney, no date, I," *ibid.;* T. Rodney, General Lee, Jan. 4, 1794, in folder "Political Writings, Legal, etc.," Brown Collection.

at length on Shakespeare, on Joel Barlow, and on Jefferson's Notes on Virginia,[331] and he considered such scientific problems as cold light, the determination of longitude, man's relation to the atmosphere, and the manufacture of dyes from sea nettles.[332]

A stimulus to the extension of learning in post-Revolutionary Delaware was the increase in the number and activity of the local printers. Proximity to Philadelphia, the lack of large urban concentrations of people in Delaware, and the difficulty of securing presses and type had been factors in limiting the pre-Revolutionary Delaware press to the establishment of James Adams. After the Revolution, however, the demands of the new state government, the growth of Wilmington, and the greater availability of presses and type, both of which were being made in Philadelphia by 1785, encouraged an expansion of the printing business.

The second press in Delaware was established at Wilmington by Jacob Killen, who founded the second newspaper in the state, the *Delaware Gazette,* a weekly, in 1785. Frederick Craig and Company took over the *Gazette* in 1786 and continued publishing it until 1790, when Peter Brynberg and Samuel Andrews, probably former associates of Craig, became its publishers. Robert Coram became publisher of the *Gazette* in 1795 as a semi-weekly; when he died in 1796 the paper was continued for several months by its printers, Bonsal and Starr. W. C. Smyth then became publisher and continued to issue the paper until 1799, when Dr. John Vaughan and Daniel Coleman succeeded him, Vincent Bonsal and Hezekiah Niles becoming the printers. The *Gazette* finally discontinued publication in 1799, when it was succeeded by the *Mirror of the Times,* edited by James Wilson, a brother-in-law of Samuel Andrews.[333]

The *Gazette's* first rival was the *Delaware Courant and Wil-*

[331] T. Rodney, Diary, May 9, 1788, Brown Collection; Rodney, On Barlow, Original Poems, Rodney Collection; Rodney to Thomas Jefferson, undated letter in folder, "T. Rodney's Political Writings, Legal, etc.," Brown Collection; T. Rodney to Lavinia Rodney, Dover, Nov. 12, 1791, Rodney Collection.

[332] T. Rodney, Propositions and Diary, Dorman Collection; T. Rodney to T. Jefferson, undated rough sketch, folder, "Misc., I," Rodney Collection; T. Rodney, Man's Relation to the Atmosphere, undated essay in Brown Collection; T. Rodney, Essay on Dyes, *ibid.*

[333] Hawkins, Delaware Imprints, ii, iv, x–xi, xvi, 73. The *Gazette* was published as a semi-weekly from September through November of 1789. It is the oldest paper of which a copy has survived and was reestablished in the nineteenth century.

mington Advertiser, published by Samuel and John Adams, sons of James Adams, in 1786 and 1787. In 1794 the Adamses, at first in partnership with W. C. Smyth, entered the newspaper field again with the *Delaware and Eastern Shore Advertiser*, which seems to have been continued until 1799. Smyth's name is also associated with two other papers, the *Wilmington Mercury*, a small sheet which he issued in 1798 during the temporary suspension of the *Gazette* due to the yellow fever epidemic, and the *Monitor, or Wilmington Weekly Repository*, which he established in 1800.[334]

The printing business expanded from Wilmington downstate. Samuel and John Adams moved their establishment to New Castle in 1796, and in 1799 William Black opened a printing office in Dover, where he hoped to profit from the state printing business. Black is believed to have begun publication of *The Friend of the People*, a newspaper, at Dover in 1799.[335] Reference has also been found to a *Dover Herald* in 1800.[336]

In addition to newspapers, Delaware printers published almanacs, government publications, religious works, schoolbooks, reprints of European publications, and occasional essays and political tracts. Many Delawareans subscribed to Philadelphia newspapers and magazines. For example, among the subscribers to the first volume of Mathew Carey's *American Museum* were fourteen Delawareans, including Richard Bassett, Jacob Broom, Gunning Bedford, Jr., Dr. Joseph Capelle, Dr. Henry Latimer, Nehemiah Tilton, Daniel Rodney, Henry Neill, and Mathew Wilson. A year later, in 1788, the number of Delaware subscribers had risen to twenty-two, and after another year the number was forty-one, all three Delaware counties being represented in each list of subscribers.

With so much reading material available as a guide and with an increased number of printing presses, it is not strange that Delawareans in the post-Revolutionary period began to write for publication more than ever before. The leading poet of Delaware at this time was Colonel John Parke, who published in 1786 a translation

---

[334] *Ibid.*, 72; Montgomery, *Reminiscences*, 313.
[335] Hawkins, Delaware Imprints, xv, xviii.
[336] Thomas Rodney to James Wilson, undated, folder, "T. Rodney, Misc., III," Rodney Collection; T. Rodney, Observations on Pompey's Pillar, for the *Herald*, folder, "Articles for Newspapers," Brown Collection.

of the *Lyrical Works of Horace* together with his and David French's original verse.[337] Many of Parke's poems appeared in the newspapers, and won favorable comments from such a literary dilettante as Thomas Rodney, who, of course, offered Parke advice:

> *Why in dull indolence, or useless lays,*
> *Spend the prime vigor of your youthful days?* . . .
> *Attack bold vice, beat her vain courage down*
> *And drive degraded folly out of Town.* . . .
> *On you the crowding multitude shall wait,*
> *And hail you Bard and Saviour of the State.*[338]

Rodney, probably with wisdom, called on Parke to describe scenes he knew rather than distant lands:

> *. . . let descriptive verse display*
> *The Italy of America.*
> *Let its fair boundaries appear*
> *The Chesipeake and Delaware.*
> *Make Kent your own fair Native place*
> *The Eden of this new-born race.*[339]

Rodney was angered by one of Parke's poems which satirized Dover and its ladies, so he warned:

> *. . . low he must be who wou'd dare*
> *To black-gard and revile the fair.*[340]

Rodney himself interminably scribbled out verse that remained unpublished. For the most part it is without merit, but occasionally it is pleasant. A few of the first lines and titles indicate his wide interests: "Pure Scorce of Wisdom Thee we praise," "On Packt Juries," "The Muses," "A Washington, A Gates, a Lee," "Two Heroes of the Rodneyan Name," "Wit is a Thing, When Times are dull," "The Naritive of Doctor Tulip," "Elegy," "Eliza bloomd with all her Charms," "Universal Paradise," and "The Song of Mirno & his Children—from Ossian." Through these poems he took out his spite on his enemies, as in a satire on a Scotch-Irishman:

> *A dreg of Europes Hostile Shore*
> *From Merlins boggs he first came o'er*
> *With wallet on his back.*

[337] Able, "Delaware Literature," 959.
[338] A printed poem by "Pericles" found in folder, "Original Poems of Thomas Rodney," Rodney Collection.
[339] "To Col. Parke," *ibid.*
[340] "To the Ladies of Dover," *ibid.*

One End a piece of Linen held
Oat Meal bread the other filld
Thus ballanc'd hung his pack.[341]

He chronicled the growing interest in literature, while deprecating the production:

I say as how
That Dover now
Is groing very Lerned
. . . now the times
Are full of rhimes
And so crowd retention.
We only say
We want a play
It comes without invention.[342]

About the year 1790 Rodney turned from rhymed to free verse, but without any improvement in quality. This deficiency, however, is not important, for it is Rodney's amazing breadth of interest which is notable. His fragments imitative of the Miltonic epic are feeble, but his plan is not.[343] His interest in history was as great as in poetry. History, he claimed, was "The most Instructive Study man can persue who Wishes To Make a figure as a Statesman," and he added, "No knowledge can be more delighting or useful." [344] He worked intermittently on an attempt to fit Greek and Roman mythology into a Biblical chronology, to "place Prometheus, Perseus, and Atlas chronologically in relation to Moses and Noah." [345] A more valuable plan was his suggestion that "a History of the Revolution of this State" be undertaken. Edward Miller urged that Rodney do it, but the latter recommended it to Philip Lewis, with no known result.[346]

[341] "Old death and Fury artful grown," *ibid.*
[342] Folder, "T. Rodney, Misc., III," Rodney Collection.
[343] "The Argument. A Transient View of Mankind from the Creation to Jacob and his Sons—Their Adventures the Chief Subject of the Poem—Jacob just before his death has a Visionary View of his posterity, and a Transient Glimps of the future ages of the world to the rise of the American Empire This Concisely described as the Ushering in of the universality of the Gospel Which Thence is to Spread over all the World and introduce the Milenium." "Original Poems," *ibid.*
[344] Folder, "Ancient History, &c.," *ibid.*
[345] Folder, "T. Rodney, 1779–1791," Brown Collection.
[346] T. Rodney, Journal, April 21, 25, 1794, *ibid.*; Edward Miller to T. Rodney [n.p.], April 21, 1794, Morse Collection (HSD), VII. See William B. Hamilton, *Thomas Rodney, Revolutionary and Builder of the West* (Durham, 1953).

The earliest attempt at dramatic writing known in Delaware is a comedy entitled "The Fortune Hunter" by Mrs. Ann Clay Booth, of New Castle, which was never intended to be performed.[347] Distinguished political essays came from the pen of John Dickinson, whose two series of letters signed Fabius, of 1787 and 1798, defended the Federal Constitution and the French Republic respectively.[348] Dickinson's argument for an alliance with the French Republic was not popular in the Federalist Delaware of 1798, but an argument tending further still to upset the characteristic Delaware pattern of thought was proffered by the schoolmaster, Robert Coram, in his *Political Inquiries*, published at Wilmington in 1791.

"Unable to discover the origin of government," Coram accepted the common belief that its object was the "public good, by which is to be understood the happiness of the community." In spite of this object, "civilized man, in every stage of his civilization, and under almost every form of government, has always been a very miserable being." [349] The reason that civilized man is less happy than the barbarian is that the former has been deprived of his "natural means of subsistence" by "the unequal distribution of property, . . . the parent of almost all the disorders of government." "Not quite so visionary as to expect that the members of any civilized community will listen to an equal distribution of lands," Coram sought "the best mode of alleviating" the injuries of civilized man "without disturbing the established rules of property."

The answer, he felt, was to provide man with new means of subsistence, "a *quid pro quo*" for the "natural liberty and common right of property" he has given up. This means of subsistence could be provided only by education, which government should provide for every child in the state, both by public schools and by binding children out to "trades or professions, that they may be en-

---

[347] It is published in Elizabeth Booth, *Reminiscences of New Castle, Delaware* (New Castle, 1884).

[348] Charles J. Stille, *The Life and Times of John Dickinson, 1732–1808, Memoirs of the Historical Society of Pennsylvania*, XIII (Philadelphia, 1891), 266–275, 295–299. The letters of Fabius are published in the second volume of *The Political Writings of John Dickinson* (Wilmington, 1801).

[349] Robert Coram, *Political Inquiries, to which is added a Plan for the General Establishment of Schools throughout the United States* (Wilmington, 1791), v, 10.

abled to support themselves." "Education should not be left to the caprice, or negligence of parents, to chance, or confined to the children of wealthy citizens." "Are ye aware, legislators," Coram asked, "that in making knowledge necessary to the subsistence of your subjects, ye are in duty bound to secure to them the means of acquiring it?" [350]

Yet, Coram quoted Noah Webster, who had lectured in Delaware five years earlier,[351] though colleges and academies were provided for the sons of people of property, "no provision is made for instructing the poorer rank of people, even in reading and writing. . . . The constitutions are republican, and the laws of education are monarchical." "Remember, my friends," Coram warned, mankind can be made better only "by incorporating education with government — — This is the rock on which you must build your political salvation!" [352]

"Education," Coram stressed, "should be brought home to every man's door." But the existing country schools were "sorry hovels," with ignorant teachers who seldom stayed in one place long, "duns the second" succeeding "duns the first." Coram proposed the establishment of tax-supported public schools "in every county of the United States" and closed his argument with an exhortation: "Let us begin by perfecting the system of education, as the proper foundation whereon to erect a temple to liberty, and to establish a wise, equitable and durable policy; that our country may become *indeed* an asylum to the distressed of every clime—the abode of liberty, peace, virtue and happiness—a land on which the Deity may deign to look down with approbation—and whose government may last till time shall be no more!" [353]

---

[350] *Ibid.*, 53–57.

[351] Harry R. Warfel, *Noah Webster, Schoolmaster to America* (New York, 1936), 135; *Votes of Assembly*, 1785–1786, p. 46. Webster was pleased with the "taste for science" he found in this area. He met John Dickinson and had a long conversation with him.

[352] Coram, *Political Inquiries*, 77–79.

[353] *Ibid.*, 93–95, 98, 107. Coram also argued for the abolition of entail and primogeniture. "To make men happy," he said, "the first step is to make them independent." And to make them independent, he agreed with Noah Webster, two things were necessary: (1) "such a distribution of lands and principles of descent and alienation as shall give every citizen a power of acquiring what his industry merits"; (2) a system of education giving every man an opportunity to acquire knowledge and fit himself for positions of trust. *Ibid.*, 104–105.

XIV. Discord

SO much attention has been given to Coram's opinions because he represents particularly well an undercurrent of dissatisfaction with the Delaware pattern of life in the period after the Revolution. The chief complaint was that the Revolution had not been complete, that Delaware had not modified itself to fit the times, to correct injustices, to make its institutions conform to the dictates of the Age of Reason.

And indeed Delaware seemed to have changed but little. The Revolution had not proceeded further in Delaware because the controlling elements of the state had no desire for it to do so. They had sought a separation from Britain not because they wanted to change their way of life but because they wanted to preserve it against the presumptuous meddling of an alien Parliament. To this extent, as McIlwain has pointed out for the colonies as a whole, the patriots of Delaware were the true conservatives, contesting for the old order against the threatened interference of the new. Gracious and hospitable Anglican landed gentry, they were for the most part satisfied with life as it was. As Thomas Rodney said, they had enough and to spare for their daily needs. They spoke as they liked; they worshiped when they could; they were free from hunger and from fear. Perhaps it was the lack of a vast, undeveloped frontier which might bring dreams of grandeur and of wealth, perhaps it was the homogeneity of their society, perhaps it was their location, apart, except for New Castle County, from the main routes of travel, with their breath of the exotic and the inspiring, that caused the general spirit of satisfaction; at any rate, they desired little that they did not have. As Howard Pyle suggested, Delaware was a "Connecticut of the South." [354]

During the critical period of the Revolution, however, the rul-

[354] Howard Pyle, "A Peninsular Canaan," *Harper's New Monthly Magazine,* LVIII (May, 1879), 803. Pyle was thinking of industrial northern Delaware in 1879, but the comparison applies to an earlier period and the whole state. See Richard Purcell, *Connecticut in Transition, 1775–1818* (Washington, 1918).

ing group in Delaware had been forced to accept some strange alliances. The newly arrived Scotch-Irish, unsurpassed in their opposition to the British crown, had proved a bulwark to Delaware's war effort and for their zeal had been granted positions of honor and of trust. New ideas had been circulated in the state; Thomas Paine and Joseph Priestley had been read; equalitarianism had reared its head beside liberty; new sects had arisen as political problems embarrassed the Anglicans.

But when the fighting ceased the old order reasserted itself. Natural allies were found among the neutrals and the moderate loyalists. Political disqualifications were removed. As a protection against the disturbing uncertainties of the future, a new union was sought and entered. Hamiltonian Federalism became the political gospel.

Yet the Revolution had not ceased with the Peace of Paris. Changes had occurred; new factors had appeared challenging the maintenance of the old order. The natural advantages of the Brandywine-Christina area of New Castle County led it to become the seat of an extensive milling industry. The manufacturers and merchants whom this industry supported and the new industrial proletariat destroyed the homogeneity of the Delaware cultural pattern. Scotch, Irish, and French immigrants added variety to the ethnical composition. Presbyterians, Methodists, and Baptists did not relinquish the advantages they had gained at the expense of the Anglicans. Rational and religious enthusiasts attacked the slave system.

Slowly retreating before these challenges, the gentry permitted certain changes. Humanitarian controls were placed around the slave trade; laws of descent were democratized; the franchise was widened; a new constitution paid tribute to public education and a fund was set up for that purpose; a bank was chartered for the manufacturing community; and Presbyterians and Methodists were even voted to the highest public offices.

Such slow hesitant steps did not satisfy Robert Coram and men like him, James Tilton and Caesar A. Rodney and the retired John Dickinson. They saw abolition defeated, penitentiary reform blocked, public education postponed. Gradually, they found their common objectives and organized to achieve them. As the eighteenth century closed, the contest was joined, and the elasticity of the old order, its ability to permit moderate reform in some particulars while adhering to the established practices in general, was tested to the full. The meaning of the Revolution to Delaware and the course of the state in the future were to be determined at the beginning of the new century.

Part III

The Old Order Triumphant

I. The Constitution and the Elections

TO meet the changed state of national affairs after 1789, Delaware's first move, as it had been in the year of independence, was to call a constitutional convention.[1] This convention began meeting in the fall of 1791 and concluded its sessions in the spring of 1792. The new constitution, which became effective without being submitted to the people, was notable for its close adherence to the Constitution of the United States and, more specifically, for its strengthening of the power of the chief executive and for the democratizing of the government. Abolition of the privy council signalized the waning of previous fears of a single powerful executive. This was not a strange development in a state which had shortly before supported the adoption of a strong national government, and particularly since two of the Delaware delegates to the Philadelphia Convention of 1787, John Dickinson and Richard Bassett, were also members of this state convention, Dickinson holding the office of president until ill health forced his resignation.[2]

A chief measure in the democratization of the government was the extension of the franchise to all taxpayers. Previously the right to vote had been limited to freeholders possessing fifty or more acres of well-settled land of which twelve acres must be cleared and improved, or to those worth forty pounds. Voting was considered not only the privilege but also the duty of those who enjoyed the right; failure to vote might, unless due to "sickness or other unavoidable accident," be punished by a fine of forty shil-

---

[1] The General Assembly explained the calling of a convention on these grounds: "it has been found, from experience, that the great and important ends of government are not effected by our present form of government, and that the general departments thereof are so blended together and improperly arranged as to prevent an impartial, beneficial and energetic operation; and . . . the burdens and expenses of government are with difficulty borne, and in some instances the present form is contradictory to the Constitution of the United States." *Minutes of Council*, 1206. The constitution of 1792 may be examined conveniently in Thorpe, *American Charters, Constitutions, and Organic Laws*, I, 568–581.

[2] Scharf, *History of Delaware*, I, 270.

lings.[3] The new constitution granted the franchise to every "white free man of the age of twenty-one years, having resided in the State two years" and "paid a State or county tax."

The chief executive, hitherto chosen by the legislature, was hereafter to be elected by the people for a term of three years. His title was changed from president to governor, and the names of the two houses of the General Assembly changed respectively from Legislative Council to Senate, and from House of Assembly to House of Representatives, a nomenclature which paralleled that of the national chambers. Representation remained as before; three delegates representing each county in the upper house and seven in the lower house. New age and residence requirements were adopted, however, and, as a counter-measure to the broadening of the franchise, it was required of each senator that he own "in the county in which he shall be chosen a freehold estate in two hundred acres of land, or an estate . . . of the value of one thousand pounds at least." [4]

The first Tuesday in October was established as the date of state and county elections. Previously elections had begun on October 1 and continued without adjournment "from day to day till the freeholders and electors then and there present" were polled.[5] Seven representatives and one senator were to be elected annually in each county, a member of the federal House of Representatives biennially, and a governor, two candidates for sheriff, and two candidates for coroner every three years. A coroner and a sheriff for each county were to be chosen by the governor from the two candidates for each office favored by the voters. Polling places for county and state elections were designated as the courthouses at New Castle, Dover, and, after 1791, Georgetown, to which place the Sussex County courthouse was transferred from

---

[3] *Laws,* I, 147.

[4] Representatives were required to be at least twenty-four years old and senators at least twenty-seven; previously twenty-five was the minimum age for members of the upper house, with no age requirement for members of the lower house. Representatives were required to be freeholders as before. All legislators were now required to be citizens and inhabitants of the state for three years prior to election and inhabitants of the county for one year. Previously there had been no such requirements.

[5] *Laws,* I, 151.

Lewes in order that it might be more centrally located.[6] On September 15 of each year the voters in each hundred separately were to choose an assessor and an inspector of elections.[7]

The sheriff was designated the presiding officer of the county election, or, in his place, the coroner, or any two overseers of the poor, or "in their absence, neglect, or refusal," any three "good and substantial freeholders of the county." [8] The inspectors of elections were to serve as election judges, each having an equal vote with the sheriff in deciding disputes; in case of a tie the sheriff would be allowed a double vote. The collector of taxes, or, in his absence, the overseers of the poor, and two freeholders named by the collector were to preside at the hundred elections. The inspector of elections for each hundred was to be furnished with "an alphabetical list of all taxables within the said hundred," so that he might better judge the qualifications of voters.[9]

Only written ballots would be considered legal. At the county polls the elector was to hand his ballot to the inspector for his hundred, who would first call out the voter's name "so as to be heard by the other judges of the said Election," and then drop the ballot into the proper box, there being one ballot box for each hundred.[10]

Competition for the county offices was very keen. A newspaper correspondent in 1790 urged the people of New Castle County to show more interest in the election of a Congressman because such an election was as important as that of a sheriff.[11] Comparatively, however, Delawareans displayed considerable interest in all elections, as is evidenced by the ratio of voters to the white population in the ten years following 1792; in spite of the difficulty involved in travelling to the county seat, this ratio was higher in Delaware than in any other state during this period.[12]

Campaigning was often extraordinarily vigorous. In 1794 a can-

[6] *Laws*, II, 1002–1005.
[7] *Laws*, I, 429–435.
[8] *Laws*, II, 665–667.
[9] *Laws*, I, 429–435.
[10] *Laws*, I, 500–504.
[11] *Delaware Gazette*, Nov. 6, 1790.
[12] George D. Luetscher, *Early Political Machinery in the United States* (Philadelphia, 1903), 25.

didate advertised that he would not "set out as an old veteran
Electioneer, nor rouse people out of bed at unusual hours, or in-
terfere with their private business," and begged to be excused from
"the custom of waiting on each one at his house." "Monitor," of
Sussex, declared sarcastically, "I intend in future to copy the example of the *great* and *honorable,* and like them traverse every
swamp in the county, till I make you all acquainted with my merit.
. . . Some people will tell you that it is not agreeable to law, to
give threats, and solicit votes." [13]

II. Federalist Rule and the Opposition

IN the 1790s the Delaware Federalists ran state affairs in their
own way. Political offices were revolved among a group of leaders.
George Read began the decade as a United States Senator and
left that position to become chief justice, after having been offered his choice of judicial posts by Governor Joshua Clayton. Until
his death in 1798, Read appears to have relinquished little of his
political leadership; Clayton consulted him regarding judicial and
senatorial appointments, and in 1796 it was Read's brother-in-law,
Gunning Bedford, Sr., who succeeded Clayton as governor.[14]
Richard Bassett also resigned from the Senate to accept a Delaware
chief justiceship, resigning this post in turn to become governor
in 1799. Dr. Joshua Clayton, last president of Delaware under the
1776 constitution and first governor under the constitution of 1792,
was elected to the Senate in 1798.

A regular practice of advancement from Representative to Senator seems to have been followed by the Delaware Federalists, for
it fell to the lot of every Federalist Representative from Delaware
in this decade—John Vining, Henry Latimer, and James A. Bayard

[13] *Delaware Gazette,* Sept. 4, 1790; Oct. 4, 1794.
[14] See Read-Clayton correspondence of July and August, 1793, and March,
1794, in Read, *Read,* 546–550, 557–561, and Richard Bassett to Read, Red Lion,
Jan. 3, 1794, *ibid.,* 557. A list of governors and Congressmen will be found in the
appendix.

—to move directly or indirectly from the lower house of Congress to the upper. In the next century promotions of such Federalists as Nicholas Van Dyke, Jr., Henry M. Ridgely, Thomas Clayton, Louis McLane, and Daniel Rodney followed the same pattern. That this became acceptable practice was probably largely due to the demonstrated wide popularity of Delaware's Representatives. Elected at large, they were as much the choice of the entire state as the governor, himself, and merited exceptional party favor when they sought entrance to the United States Senate. By reason of Delaware's equal representation in spite of its small size, a Senator occupied the most important position it was in the power of the state to grant.

Among the Delaware Federalists, and their opponents too, family connections played such an important part that the Delaware historian must be something of a genealogist. Dare he neglect, for instance, to note that Senator William Hill Wells was the son-in-law of General John Dagworthy, or that Senator John Wales had a similar relationship to Representative John Patten, and Senator James A. Bayard to Senator Richard Bassett? The number of inter-family relationships among the political leaders of Delaware is truly astonishing. There was, moreover, another type of relationship which often furnishes a better clue to an office-seeker's political alignment than any study of blood ties or attitudes toward national questions—and that is the law student–barrister relationship, for those who had read law in the office of a Bayard or a Clayton often developed and retained a greater sense of loyalty to his master than the modern law school can ever find in its alumni.

At the beginning of the 1790s party alignments were not well established. Religious affiliations and attitudes toward the Revolution were overshadowed by the more important factor of desire for office and for whatever power, prestige, and profits its attainment might make possible; it was an eternal striving of "outs" against "ins," of the "have-nots" of state jobs against the "haves." As time passed, however, the European wars and questions of national policy caused increasing discussion and resulted by the end of the century, in the gradual emergence of two contesting parties. "Let the people be no longer amused, with the idle and useless distinctions of *Whig* and *Tory, court party* and *country party, presbyterian* and *church, aristocrat* and *democrat;* they neither apply to time nor place; but let them take up the only true and useful distinction, of *federal* and *anti-federal,* of *friends* to their *country* and *enemies* to *it.*" So, in 1794, a Federalist explained party differences.[15]

A writer who called himself "Haslet" disagreed. One party, he declared, "is pursuing measures that lead to more than British corruption; the other for restoring virtue, liberty, & law. . . . It is the Lordly Few, who are wallowing in the fat of the land, and rioting upon the spoils of the People, that have reaped the sole advantage of our large taxes. . . . All the Powers of this Government, both Civil and Military, are at present, (with a very few exceptions,) in the hands of men, perfectly subservient to the will of a *Few; the Few* therefore, enact your laws; the same *Few* decide on them; and the same *Few* execute them. The Courts of justice, the Legislature, and the Executive are all composed of men in the same class. What may they not do then with impunity? . . . Let them know that the Spirit which began and accomplished the late Revolution is not yet entirely lost."[16]

A year before these diatribes were penned a quarrel had arisen over the toasts at an Independence Day celebration in Dover. Dr. Edward Miller opposed toasting Washington because "he was no more than another man," and instead proposed "equality," which others damned as French. Thomas Rodney, relating the incident, commented, "There was a strong spirit of French party and British party at the bottom."[17]

Divided opinion on Jay's negotiation of a treaty with Britain gave impetus to the development of a party which opposed the dominant faction in Delaware. In spite of the treaty's unpopularity in the state and in the nation, the General Assembly passed a resolution commending the action of the President and the Senate in approving the treaty. Disapproval of the Assembly's action was registered in the unanimous resolution of a town meeting held in

---

[15] *Delaware and Eastern Shore Advertiser,* Sept. 17, 1794.

[16] Haslet Papers (HSD). The signature "Haslet" does not necessarily indicate the author of this article, since the name was popular for its connotation of patriotic martyrdom.

[17] Rodney, note dated July 4, 1793, Brown Collection.

Wilmington at the Presbyterian church (the choice of meeting place was not without certain significance). With Dr. Tilton in the chair and Robert Coram acting as secretary, the eloquent young Democrat, Caesar A. Rodney, and John Dickinson, whom Rodney introduced as "a venerable Patriot . . . grown grey in the faithful discharge of his duties in the legislative, Judicial and Executive departments of government," spoke in opposition to the treaty. Rodney opposed any treaty with a nation as warlike as Britain, especially when it was fighting the French Republic. Dickinson spoke for two hours, "his Voice feble," until Thomas Rodney, having already heard his beloved son, "got wary and left the meeting."[18] A more riotous group assembled at Christiana Bridge, where John Jay and the Delaware Senators, John Vining and Henry Latimer, who had favored the treaty, were denounced and burned in effigy.[19]

There is evidence, from a reference made publicly, that those in Delaware directing this expression of opposition to Jay's Treaty were well acquainted with public protests against it made elsewhere in the union. Further evidence of a close relationship with national political developments is furnished by the establishment, a year before the treaty was signed, of a society apparently formed on the order of the famous Democratic Society of Philadelphia. On June 14, 1794, notice was given in a Wilmington newspaper[20] that "At a respectable Meeting of Citizens of New Castle County in the town of Newcastle, it was unanimously agreed to form themselves into a political Society." A committee was named which submitted a constitution and a declaration of principles to the next meeting of the group, henceforth to be known as the "Patriotic Society of Newcastle County, in the State of Delaware." Five principles were mentioned in the declaration: the people have a right to determine the form of their government; the federal and state constitutions, having been made by the people, should be supported by them; good citizens should consider both

---

[18] C. A. Rodney, minutes of town meeting, Aug. 4, 1795, Brown Collection; T. Rodney, notes on town meeting, *ibid.*; T. Rodney, Propositions and Diary, Aug. 4, 1795, collection of Charles Dorman. "The oldest people say they never recollect to have seen such an universal convention of the inhabitants of this place." Unsigned MS., Rodney Collection.

[19] *Delaware Gazette*, Aug. 15, 1795.

[20] *Delaware and Eastern Shore Advertiser.*

men and measures; each citizen should use his own judgment in voting; and it is the duty of the people to call attention to violations of the Constitution. The constitution of the society provided for four meetings a year in the county and as many in the hundreds as were desired.

An interesting contest arose over the adoption of the constitution and the declaration of principles. Kensey Johns, a New Castle lawyer and former law student of George Read, whom he succeeded as chief justice in 1798, demanded a record of the yeas and nays. McKennan, McCullough, Alexander, Thompson, Crow, and two Higginses—whose names indicate Scotch-Irish ancestry and therefore Democratic-Republican partisanship—voted aye. Dr. James Tilton and Robert Coram, both Democrats, had helped frame the declaration and constitution but were not at this meeting. Five members declined voting, among them Kensey Johns, John Stockton, a well-to-do merchant, and James Booth, later a Federalist candidate for governor.[21]

The group which dominated the Patriotic Society was also in control of the Society of the Cincinnati, whose chief officers in 1794 were John Patten, first Republican Congressman from Delaware, and Peter Jaquett and William McKennan, both members of the Patriotic Society. On July 4, 1794, the Cincinnati toasted the French Republic, and two years later they also drank to "the patriots of Ireland," equality, and "the extinction of Monarchy in essence as well as in name." [22] Clearly the Delaware Cincinnati were full of Republican spirit.

The growing opposition to Federal rule is also demonstrated by the organization of independent military companies in New Castle County in 1794. William McKennan was the colonel of these volunteers, who objected to Governor Clayton's appointments to offices in the militia; refusing to fight except under officers of their own choice, these men were consequently being called before a justice of the peace as "militia delinquents." [23] "A Ci-Devant Refugee," probably a Federalist in disguise, suspected that there were "emissaries among them from the Western insurgents" of the

[21] Ibid., July 2, 1794.
[22] Ibid., July 9, 1794; Delaware Gazette, July 5, 1796.
[23] Delaware and Eastern Shore Advertiser, Aug. 20, 29, Dec. 31, 1794.

Whiskey Rebellion, that their dissatisfaction with the militia law was a mere blind, and that their intent was "to effect an entire subversion of the government." [24] In August the Wilmington Independent Volunteer Company was ordered to parade in full uniform to New Castle to "join the Political Society for Constitutional Information" (*i.e.*, the Patriotic Society), a proceeding which "One of the People" condemned as an attempt to infuse the volunteers with the spirit of party. "An artificial volcano is prepared," he claimed, "composed of *political, national* and *religious principles* and *prejudices* of every kind." [25]

The reference to religious prejudice meant, of course, the rivalry between Presbyterians and Episcopalians. "Gracchus," a Republican, declared in 1794 that for nine years no Presbyterian had been sent to the legislature from Kent County, where in 1792 magistrates and judges had urged the people not to elect a Presbyterian, especially "an *Irish* presbyterian just *imported*." The "volcano" of "principles and prejudices" in dissent with the ruling faction had finally been given a name by January, 1795, when the notice of a meeting of "the Social Club" solicited "the attendance of every Democratic Republican, whose heart is susceptible of the Social Converse." [26]

III. The Rise of the Democratic-
Republican Party

WHILE the conservative faction continued to win most of the elections and therefore to dominate Delaware politics through this period of the formation of parties, its control was effectively challenged in the middle of the decade when John Patten was sent to Congress. As a matter of fact, Patten was twice the choice of a majority of Delawareans for Congress before he was permitted to

---

[24] *Ibid.*, Sept. 3, 1794.
[25] *Ibid.*, Aug. 27, Sept. 6, 1794.
[26] *Ibid.*, Sept. 3, 1794; Jan. 17, 1795. The terms Republican, Democrat, and Democratic-Republican are used hereafter interchangeably.

serve a full term. In 1792 he contested the election with Henry Latimer, a physician and member of a prominent mercantile family, and was declared elected by President Clayton. Latimer, however, protested to the House of Representatives after Patten had already been seated.

Investigating, the House discovered that a Delaware law of 1790 regulating the election of Representatives provided that each voter must "deliver in writing, on one ticket or piece of paper, the names of two persons, inhabitants of this state, one of whom at least shall not be an inhabitant of the same county with himself, to be voted for as Representative." [27] This law had confused both the voters and the election judges in October, 1792. Some of the voters had named only one man for Representative; some of those who named two chose them both from their own county. At the same time, the judges differed in interpreting the law; in Kent, tickets bearing the names of two men from New Castle County were rejected. The most serious item disputed was sixty-eight single votes for Patten, which the Sussex election officials had accepted and which were far more than enough to sway the election. [28]

It was the duty of the chief executive of Delaware to examine the returns and forward the name of the person elected. Governor Clayton had declared Patten elected by a plurality of thirty votes, but with this return he had also forwarded to Congress a protest of Latimer, the defeated candidate. Congress seated Patten but began, through its committee on elections, an investigation which lasted two months, during which time commissioners were sent to Delaware to hear the testimony of various election officials. [29]

Finally the committee reported that Latimer was the legal Representative from Delaware, this decision being based on a revision of the election returns which gave Latimer a plurality of thirty-three votes. In spite of a protest by John Page of Virginia that Patten was clearly the choice of the greatest number of Delaware voters and that the will of the majority should not be set aside because of the violation of a mere technicality in the state law,

[27] *Laws*, II, 984–986.
[28] *Annals of Congress*, 3 Cong., 1 sess., House, 442–443; *House Journal*, II, 3 Cong., 1 sess., 59.
[29] M. St. Clair Clarke and David A. Hall, comps., *Cases of Contested Elections in Congress, from the Year 1789 to 1834, Inclusive* (Washington, 1834), 69.

Patten was expelled from the House and Latimer seated.[30] In 1794, however, at the next election Patten defeated Latimer and this time was able to complete a full term in the House.

The significance of this contest is greater than it might at first glance seem. For Latimer, who supported Army and Navy appropriations and all revenue bills, was clearly a Federalist, while Patten was a leader of the country party in Kent, which, at this very time, was becoming part of the new Democratic-Republican party. "Veritas," a Federalist, declared that Patten "threw himself into the arms of the Virginia party, who seemed to wish to involve the country in a precipitate war," while Latimer "uniformly supported the federal measures, which were ultimately adopted by the majority of Congress, sanctioned by the President, and . . . approved by the cooler judgment of the people of the United States." [31]

Patten and his brothers-in-law, Joseph and Edward Miller in Kent, along with David Hall and Joseph Haslet in Sussex and Caesar A. Rodney, James Tilton, Robert Coram, and Hezekiah Niles (who was later to win fame through his weekly) in New Castle, were among the group which plotted to overthrow the political hierarchy of Delaware. Little is heard of the Patriotic Society after it published in 1795 an address, probably written by Rodney, Coram, and Tilton, defending popular societies against attack, especially on the basis of their being "self-created." [32] The *Delaware Gazette*, however, remained the organ of the new party through most of this decade.

In 1795 the Federalists sought to rescue themselves "from those factions which prevail, & which are so enemical to the peace order & dignity of government" by choosing delegates from each county to meet at Dover and nominate a candidate for governor.[33] Gunning Bedford, Sr., army veteran and brother-in-law of George Read, was their choice; Dr. Archibald Alexander, a retired army surgeon from Virginia who now lived near New Castle, was the

[30] *Annals*, 3 Cong., 1 sess., 135, 138, 140, 144, 451, 453–455; *House Journal*, II, 3 Cong., 1 sess., 9, 12, 14, 59, 63–64.

[31] *Delaware and Eastern Shore Advertiser*, Oct. 8, 1794.

[32] *Ibid.*, Dec. 17, 1794; Jan. 14, 1795. A branch of the Patriotic Society was organized in Christiana Hundred, which included Wilmington. *Delaware Gazette*, Nov. 20, 1795; March 11, 1796. *Cf.* La Rochefoucault, *Travels*, III, 518.

[33] Gunning Bedford, Jr., to William Hill Wells, Wilmington, July 27, 1795, Gunning Bedford, Jr., Papers (HSD).

candidate of the Democrats.[34] A member of the latter party declared that it opposed not the government but the men in it, that
it stood for France and republicanism, while the Federalists, the
"aristocratic party," stood for Britain and monarchy.[35]

The contest was hard fought. "Electioneering," said John Fisher,
"was probably never at such an height in the county of Kent before.
Bets run very high." "Tom Berry, one of the country candidates,
roasted a steer and an half dozen of Sheep . . . as a kind of snack
for his friends." [36] A candidate in St. Georges Hundred gave a "fish-
feast," and a "turtle-feast" was held at New Castle. At least three
vessels were available to carry the voters from Wilmington to the
county seat. "The United States are now divided into two parties,"
a Federalist handbill declared; of the local candidates, Bedford was
"an old and tried friend of his country" and a supporter of Washington, while Alexander was "a partizan of Tilton and Genet." [37] Bedford won the election, but Alexander carried New Castle, the home
county of both candidates.[38]

Federalist triumphs continued through the concluding years of
the century. Patten refused to run for reelection to Congress in 1796
and was succeeded by the Federalist, James A. Bayard, the Democratic candidate being William Peery, of Sussex.[39] In 1798 Bayard
was returned to Congress, his father-in-law, Bassett, chosen governor, and a legislature elected which completed the Federalist
triumph by sending William Hill Wells to the Senate. "The Federalists," a friend wrote Wells, are "Universally rejoicing in your
election. . . . I have often bless'd my Stars that not one d—n
democrat voted for you." [40]

The Democrats, building on the strength of the old country party,

[34] Louis C. Duncan, Medical Men in the American Revolution, 1775–1783 (Carlisle Barracks, 1931), 379; Read, Read, 35–36.
[35] Delaware Gazette, Sept. 29, 1795. The terms "Federalist" and "Democrat"
were widely used in this campaign, but so were older terms, such as "country party."
[36] John Fisher to C. A. Rodney, Dover, Sept. 30, and Oct. 4, 1795, John Fisher
Papers (HSD).
[37] Delaware Gazette, Oct. 6, Nov. 13, 1795. The new governor's cousin, Gunning Bedford, Jr., was a Republican. Calendar of Ridgely Family Letters, I, 140.
[38] Delaware Gazette, Oct. 9, 1795. That party lines were not yet well formed is
indicated by the fact that both parties supported James Stroud, one of the candidates for the legislature from New Castle County.
[39] Ibid., Aug. 23, 1796; T. Rodney, Diary, Aug. 16, 1796, Brown Collection.
[40] John W. Batson, Feb. 24, 1799, C. H. B. Turner, comp., Some Records of
Sussex County, Delaware (Philadelphia, 1909), 300.

found their greatest support in New Castle County, where the Scotch-Irish Presbyterian population was largest. "The Friends of Wilmington," Nathaniel Luff declared, were also "generally . . . ranked in the political scale as favourable to Democracy." [41] Though difficulties with France lent popularity to the Federalist cause in 1798, allowing Bassett to carry every county, the Democrats gradually won control of New Castle County.[42] Kent County, however, became definitely Federalist and "this with the ordinary superiority" of that party in Sussex counteracted "the democratical fetes of N. Castle County." [43]

In June of 1800, Justice Samuel Chase of the Supreme Court, presiding with Gunning Bedford, Jr., at a circuit court held at New Castle, was reported to have declared "that a highly seditious temper had manifested itself in the state of Delaware among a certain class of people, particularly in New-Castle county, and more especially in the town of Wilmington." [44] Chase's intention apparently was to get an indictment against James Wilson, editor of the Wilmington *Mirror of the Times,* who had printed attacks on President Adams, the Sedition Law, and the "New England Illuminati," dominated by Timothy Dwight of Yale, these articles having been reported to Chase by a Dr. McMahon, of Wilmington.[45] Bedford told Chase, in private, "I believe you do not know where you are, the people in this place are not well pleased with the sedition law."

[41] The Philadelphia Friends, on the other hand, Luff declared, were largely Federalists. Luff, *Journal,* 63–64.

[42] *Journal of the House of Representatives of the State of Delaware,* 1799, p. 23. The legislature elected in 1798 refused even to consider the Virginia and Kentucky Resolutions, although Caesar A. Rodney, Richard C. Dale, and George Gillespie, all of New Castle County, opposed the majority. *Ibid.,* 14, 26–28, 59, 102, 107.

[43] John W. Batson to [William Hill Wells?], The Grove, Sept. 23, 1798, Turner, *Records of Sussex,* 299.

[44] Charles Evans, ed., *Report of the Trial of the Hon. Samuel Chase* (Baltimore, 1805), 5.

[45] *Ibid.,* 58–60, 100. It is noteworthy that Governors Rogers, who had succeeded Gunning Bedford, Sr., when he died in office, and Bassett, as well as the General Assembly, had applauded Adams' administration. *Delaware House Journal,* 1799, 9–10, 33–34, 37, 102; *ibid.,* 1800, 10–15. Senator Bayard confided to Alexander Hamilton that he was not pleased with Adams, Aug. 11, 1800, Elizabeth Donnan, ed., "Papers of James A. Bayard, 1796–1815," *Annual Report of the American Historical Association,* 1913, II (Washington, 1915), 114–115. *Cf.* Bayard to [John Rutledge?], Wilmington, June 8, 1800, *ibid.,* 111–112. Possibly "Dr. McMahon" was William McMechen, a charter member of the Medical Society of Delaware. W. Edwin Bird, "Medicine in Delaware," H. Clay Reed, ed., *Delaware: a History of the First State* (New York, 1947), II, 739.

His opinion was substantiated by the grand jury's refusal to indict Wilson, which caused Chase to declare "that it was hard he could not get a single man indicted in Delaware, while he could in every other place."[46]

IV. Democratic Victories

IN the bitter election of 1800, the Democrats made a valiant effort to carry Delaware. John Patten was brought from political retirement to run for Congress in the hope that his Revolutionary War record would garner the necessary independent votes for his party.[47] The Jeffersonians attacked Bayard, the incumbent, and the Federalists in general for supporting the Alien and Sedition Acts, the quasi-war with France, taxes for the Army and Navy, and opposition to the Chesapeake and Delaware Canal. They sang "A New Republican Song":

> Ye Farmers, Mechanics, Republicans all,
> Who would rescue your rights from
> unjust usurpation,
> Resort to Newcastle at Liberty's call,
> And unite all your votes with the
> Voice of the Nation.[48]

The Federalists also conducted a vigorous campaign. Allen McLane, Revolutionary hero and Wilmington port collector, was reported by the *Mirror* to have been sent to Kent, where he had formerly lived, on an electioneering tour to persuade the people that the Jacobinical Democrats would if victorious "drown all the men, women, and children in Kent and Sussex." These two counties remained loyal to Bayard and his party, which was victorious in spite of the opposition in New Castle.[49]

[46] Bedford's testimony, Feb. 18, 1805, Evans, *Report of Chase Trial*, 97–98.

[47] An attempt to persuade John Dickinson to run had failed. Dickinson was now very popular among the Democrats, partially as a result of his second series of *Letters of Fabius*, 1797, supporting an alliance with France. T. Rodney, Journal, July 30, 1800, Rodney Collection.

[48] *Mirror of the Times*, Oct. 4, 1800.

[49] *Mirror of the Times*, Oct. 1, 4, 11, 1800.

The Republican tide which was sweeping the country was not, however, to be permanently checked in Delaware. In 1801 the Republicans nominated for governor David Hall of Lewes, whose attraction to the party was much the same as Patten's had been; he was a downstater and a veteran officer of the Revolution. The Cincinnati were rallied to his support and a bid was made to the downstate Methodists by putting some of them on the ticket and by claiming that Nathaniel Mitchell, the Federalist candidate, was "a professed Deist, and open scoffer at, and riviler of the Christian religion," who was especially contemptuous of Methodism. All unpopular Federalist measures from Jay's Treaty to the Sedition Law were thrown at Mitchell, and support was given to the desires of the voters to have district elections so they would not need to go to the county seat to vote.[50]

A Federalist in Kent County protested: "The Irish Jacobins are Making great Show, . . . trying Every Artifice. . . . Let No Man Stay at home thats able to ride or Walk to the Election. They have got a Jacobin President & if they git a Jacobin governor all is lost, there will be no more security for person Liberty or property in this State, Nothing but Tyrany Anarchy & confusion & distress."[51]

"You never knew the like of Handbills as have taken place here to-day," wrote John Fisher from Dover on the eve of the election.[52] Thomas Rodney noted in his diary that he was invited to John Dickinson's "To Indulge in Converse and good Wine (rather it was syder) while the younger Folks are Taking care of That Liberty we formerly contended for."[53] Perhaps because the Federalists were merely repeating the scare tactics they had used the previous year when their doleful predictions of loss of "security for person Liberty or property" in the event of Jefferson's election had not been realized, their plaints were less effective this year. Hall was

[50] *Ibid.*, Sept. 19, 26, 30, 1801. John Dickinson had been pressed by the Republicans to run for governor instead of Hall but had refused. T. Rodney, Diary, March 12, 29, 1801, Rodney Papers (Library of Congress); Thomas Mendinhall to John Mason, Wilmington, March 21, 1801, John Vaughan Papers (HSD). The listing of 111 Delaware subscribers at the back of the second volume of *The Political Writings of John Dickinson* (Wilmington, 1801) indicates the most active leaders of the Delaware Republicans.

[51] Undated, unsigned letter in folder "T. Rodney MSS. (Personal)," Rodney Collection.

[52] To C. A. Rodney, Oct. 5, 1801, John Fisher Papers.

[53] T. Rodney, Diary, Oct. 6, 1801, Brown Collection.

elected by a plurality of less than twenty votes—the Federalist majorities in Kent and Sussex being not quite large enough to overcome Hall's margin of 783 in New Castle.[54]

"Nothing can exceed the Chagrin of the feds," a Democrat exulted; "on the Tory County of Sussex rested all their hopes; & so confident were they of success that they have urge'd the republicans in some large, & numerous small bets; the consequence is that the poor federalists are strip'd. . . . This will be the first Republican Governor that Delaware has had since the Revolution, and may be considered as giving the death wound to her 'steady habits.' " He attributed the victory to "the Extraordinary exertions of the republicans of New Castle County," where Democratic strength had grown rapidly since the last gubernatorial election in 1798, when it had been carried by the Federalist, Bassett.[55]

The Federalists were reluctant to accept defeat and contested the slim Democratic margin of victory. In the nationalist spirit of 1798 a law had been passed "to prevent aliens from voting," and it was to this that the Federalists now looked, knowing that the Irish immigrants of New Castle County were Democrats.[56] The printed petitions which were circulated found more than seven hundred signers to the request that the legislature investigate the legality of the votes cast.[57] Eventually, however, the Federalists, who had, after all, retained control of the legislature, dropped the contest, and the first Republican governor of Delaware was allowed to be inaugurated in 1802.[58] The legislature attempted to provide for the prevention of voting frauds in the future by a fine of thirty dollars on every disqualified person who attempted to vote and on every

[54] *Mirror of the Times,* Oct. 10, 14, 24, 1801.

[55] Thomas Mendinhall to John Mason, Wilmington, Oct. 10, 1801, Thomas Mendinhall Papers (HSD).

[56] *Laws,* III, 12–14; William McKee to C. A. Rodney [n.p.], Dec. 24, 1801, Rodney Collection.

[57] *Cf.* folder "1802, January–February, Legislative, Petitions, Misc.," Legislative Papers; Jesse Higgins to C. A. Rodney, Jan. 3, 1802, Rodney Collection.

[58] C. A. Rodney's notes on O. Horsey's argument, Jan. 7, 1802, Brown Collection; James Madison to C. A. Rodney, Washington, Jan. 15, 1802, *ibid.;* John and William Warner to C. A. Rodney, Wilmington, Jan. 21, 1802, Rodney Collection; William Jones to C. A. Rodney, Washington, Jan. 27, 1802, *ibid.;* T. Rodney, The Returns for Governor, folder "Original Poems of T. Rodney," *ibid.;* James Tilton to Aaron Burr, Wilmington, March 13, 1802, Gratz Collection (Historical Society of Pennsylvania).

election official who accepted a vote from a person he knew to be disqualified.[59]

Having found a winning formula, the Democratic-Republicans were encouraged to employ it again in 1802 with some variations. A young Wilmington attorney was chosen without a military record or Sussex nativity but of patriot heritage and Kent rearing, with a name of great political value and with prominent relatives throughout southern Delaware—Caesar Augustus Rodney, nephew of the war governor.

Republican propagandists repeated the old themes: that Federalism was the party of "Taxation and Extravigance and for Maintaining hosts of Public officers to riot on the spoils of the People"; that the Federalist candidate had said Methodists were rather "fanatics than hypocrites"; and that Rodney's actions in Congress would reflect the will of the people.[60] "I am sure," declared John Fisher, "that so severe an electioneering contest, I have never witnessed. Carriages are going all night through Dover, insomuch, as to even prevent usual repose. Our friends are alive in every quarter, but whether we shall succeed mostly depends on our activity on the day." [61]

Success was with the Democrats. Backed by a two-to-one majority in New Castle, they again squeaked through to a bare victory (a plurality of fifteen votes) in the choice of a Representative, the one state-wide contest. When the returns were announced in Wilmington, "a multitude parade[d] the streets, firing cannon etc." The last gun was loaded with potatoes and herring and was fired in honor of Federalist ex-Senator Henry Latimer, who was reported to have said that the laboring classes in this country lived too well to be happy and should be reduced to the diet of the Irish.[62]

"Triumph is our's," announced William McKee; "on the arrival of the good news Sally Banning played on her Piano nearly half of the night. . . . All the leading Feds are like hornets." [63] "It is the

[59] *Laws*, III, 253–254. Although many accusations were made, few indictments were drawn under this law in 1802. *Mirror of the Times*, June 11, 1803.

[60] T. Rodney, article for the *Mirror*, undated, Brown Collection; *Mirror of the Times*, Sept. 29, 1802.

[61] John Fisher to C. A. Rodney, Dover, Oct. 1, 1802, John Fisher Papers.

[62] *Mirror of the Times*, Oct. 13, 1802.

[63] William McKee to C. A. Rodney, Camden, Oct. 10, 1802, Rodney Collection.

severest stroke our antagonists have ever met with," declared another Democrat.[64] Edward Livingston thought "the great political importance" of the defeated candidate, Bayard, "with his own party" made Rodney's victory especially significant. "The accession of force on the floor to the republican side," he added, "the loss of it to their adversaries and a new State added to the democratic list are subjects of sincere rejoicing." [65]

Bayard wrote that he was more disappointed for his party's sake than for himself. He was tired of public life and would not have run except to help the Federalists "resist and if possible . . . turn the encreasing torrent in the State." If he wished to remain in Congress, the Federalist "Majority in the Legislature would render a place in the Senate perfectly Secure. I think however I am done," he added, in a letter to his cousin. "I am persuaded that the people cannot be reasoned out of their folly." [66]

Senator White mourned over the imminent catastrophe: "The Democracy of Delaware has done its utmost—it has trampled on tallents and merrit and disgraced our State—Bayard is beat. . . . We are down—the irishmen of N. C. are to govern Kent & Sussex." [67]

V. The Liberal Party

THE Democratic-Republican victories in Delaware at the beginning of the nineteenth century may be explained in part by reference to the *Zeitgeist*. This was the age of revolution. Liberal, bourgeois ideas were sweeping Europe in the wake and often ahead of

[64] J. G. Brush to C. A. Rodney, Deep Creek, Oct. 11, 1802, *ibid.*

[65] Edward Livingston to C. A. Rodney, New York, Oct. 22, 1802, Rodney Correspondence (New York Public Library).

[66] J. A. Bayard to Andrew Bayard, New Castle, Nov. 8, 1802, Donnan, "Bayard Papers," 154.

[67] Samuel White to Outerbridge Horsey, Dover, Oct. 8, 1802, Turner, *Sussex Records*, 309. White was reelected to the Senate at the next legislative session. Henry C. Conrad, *Samuel White and His Father Judge Thomas White, Papers of the Historical Society of Delaware*, XL (Wilmington, 1903), 7.

the French armies. The Democratic-Republican party in Delaware represented those ideas more clearly than did the opposing party. This is demonstrated in part by the attitudes of the two parties toward foreign affairs, the Democratic party being sympathetic toward the French, the Federalist toward the English.

In Delaware, the Democratic party represented the liberal, bourgeois element of the population, whereas the Federalist was the party of the landed gentry. The Democratic stronghold was in New Castle County, and, in words attributed to Samuel Chase, "more especially in the town of Wilmington." The Federalist stronghold was in the agrarian counties of Sussex and Kent; it was doubtless this party's control of politics that moved Thomas Jefferson to characterize Delaware as "a county of England." [68] Some of the Brandywine manufacturers, as well as merchants like John Bird, Nehemiah Tilton, and the Warners, tended toward Jeffersonianism, as did the Irish immigrants who worked for them.

Able leaders also helped the Democratic party to success. Though John Dickinson, the party's elder statesman, lived in retirement in Wilmington, his letters signed "Fabius" in 1797 had advocated alliance with France, and his support was constantly given to Thomas Jefferson. Dickinson gave little time, however, to practical politics. Two men of his generation, Chancellor William Killen and Dr. James Tilton, supplied the political drive which he failed to give. Younger men who played a more active part were the attorney, Caesar A. Rodney; the editor of the *Mirror,* James Wilson; the printer, Hezekiah Niles; the teacher, Robert Coram; and Rodney's brother-in-law, John Fisher, who became Governor Hall's secretary of state.

The efforts of these men were reenforced and the spirit of the times brought to Delaware by the continued migration from Ulster. Have we not natives enough, asked Benjamin Ogle, "without importing Irishmen to fill our offices?" [69] Distinguished Frenchmen who had come to Delaware from Europe or the West Indies brought with them a breath from off the sea of world thought. Their reception, however, was never without some suspicion. "In spite of the

[68] John M. Clayton to J. A. Bayard, the younger, Washington, Jan. 28, 1830, Hilles Collection.
[69] *American Watchman* (Wilmington), Sept. 27, 1809.

equality, the rights of liberty, and the excellent government of this country," Eleuthère Irénée du Pont told his father, "we foreigners are always in a position inferior to that of citizens. . . . Worth has little to do with position; the only reputation is founded on the extent of one's credit at the bank. A foreigner counts for nothing unless he is very rich. . . . For instance, no one here knows that one of the greatest chemists of Europe [Joseph Priestley] has come to establish himself in Northumberland." [70]

Dissatisfaction with the taxes imposed by Federalist national and state administrations was another cause of adherence to the Democratic-Republican party. The Democrats regularly called for greater economy in the national government. In the state the Democratic county of New Castle, although with the smallest acreage, was regularly called on to pay a greater share of state taxes than either of the other counties. [71]

Shortly after the constitution of 1792 was adopted, many people argued that the state government established by it was too expensive for the three counties to support. [72] Thomas Rodney, writing under the name of "Minos," in 1794 proposed a peninsular union as an end to the problem of insufficient resources. The Eastern Shore counties of Virginia and Maryland, he declared, felt "all the evils of a subjected Colony," while Delaware was almost in a similar position in regard to Pennsylvania; i. e., "incapable of making any Improvement and Prosperity." If the whole Delmarva Peninsula were united as one state, a light tax would enable the waterways on either side to be joined by roads, and the increased land values would encourage swamps to be drained, waste lands to be culti-

---

[70] B. G. du Pont, ed., *Life of Eleuthère Irénée du Pont from Contemporary Correspondence* (Newark, Del., 1923–1927), VI, 252–253. The passage, in 1811, of an act allowing aliens to purchase land in Delaware revealed an improvement in the attitude toward foreigners. *Laws*, IV, 483–484. Ten years earlier E. I. du Pont had thought, "the State of Delaware has always been unfavorable for the purchase of land by foreigners and more severe against them than any other of the United States." To Peter Bauduy, New York, Nov. 30, 1801, Du Pont, *Life of E. I. du Pont*, V, 313. Peter Bauduy sought the advice of Dickinson and Rodney, Democrats, and declared Bayard "an enemy to all Frenchmen." Bauduy to E. I. du Pont, Wilmington, Oct. 16, 1801, *ibid.*, V, 300–301; to Victor du Pont, Wilmington, Dec. 13, 1804, *ibid.*, VII, 74.

[71] *Delaware Gazette*, April 6, 1815. The reason was, of course, that land values in New Castle were higher than in the other counties.

[72] *Cf.* petitions of 1794 and 1795 in the Legislative Papers; *Delaware and Eastern Shore Advertiser*, Dec. 27, 1794.

vated, and "manufacturing viliages and Trading Towns" to be established; thus "this delightful Tract of Country" would become "the garden of America." [73]

Though a constitutional convention which Rodney suggested should meet at Easton in March, 1794, apparently never was held or even seriously considered, a movement to make Delaware part of a larger state unit did receive support for a time. In 1798, more than one hundred petitioners, including William Robinson, James Latimer, Henry Geddes, Thomas Duff, Joshua Wollaston, John Flinn, David Stidham, and Solomon Hearsey, claimed that high taxes and insect pests had reduced "the value of real property so amazeingly" that at places near the northern and western boundaries it was "scarcely saleable." For relief they asked that Delaware either be divided between Pennsylvania and Maryland or that a part of the Eastern Shore be annexed "so that the number of inhabitants may bear such a proportion to the expences of government as in the neighbouring States." [74] But Delaware particularism was far too strong to permit abandonment of its identity, and the Constitution of the United States made it virtually impossible to annex neighboring territory without the consent of the neighboring state concerned.

The failure of the Federalist state government to adopt certain reforms which were being demanded in the post-Revolutionary era also brought some recruits to the Democratic party, although these reforms in some instances would have added to the expense of government. The institution of a penitentiary system and the mitigation of penalties were among those reforms most frequently pressed. After having been urged unsuccessfully in the 1790s, they were again recommended by Governor Hall in 1805, but no action was taken by the General Assembly. Although in 1807 the senate passed such a bill, it was defeated in the lower house by the Federalist representatives of the two southern counties. Governor Truitt, a Federalist, favored some reform in 1809, and consequently a com-

---

[73] To the People inhabiting the Peninsula between the Chesapeake and Delaware Bays, Jan. 15, 1794, Brown Collection.

[74] Petitions of Jan. 1, 1798, in folder, "Delaware, re Slavery, Militia, Lottery, etc.," HSD. A movement to unite Delaware with the Eastern Shore arose several times in succeeding decades. See James C. Mullikin, "The Separatist Movement and Related Problems, 1776–1851," in Charles B. Clark, *The Eastern Shore of Maryland and Virginia,* I (New York, c. 1950), 463–482.

mission was established which reported in 1810 in favor of a state penitentiary and revision of the penal laws. Opposition from Kent and Sussex, however, again defeated a penitentiary bill.

In 1812 Governor Haslet demanded reform of the criminal code and construction of a penitentiary, but a deadlock in the senate this time prevented action from being taken. In 1813 and 1814 he repeated his recommendations with substantially the same result. Governor Daniel Rodney, a Federalist, who succeeded Haslet, did not refer to the subject in his inaugural address.[75]

Failure of the Federalist government to establish public schools gave further support to the opposition. Willard Hall, who later became a prominent Democratic politician and the founder of the public school system of Delaware, was disgusted with educational conditions as he found them in 1803. "The teachers," he complained, "frequently were intemperate, whose qualification seemed to be inability to earn anything in any other way. A clergyman who had some pretensions as a scholar, but had been silenced as a preacher for incorrigible drunkenness, stood very prominent as a teacher. . . . Even in the best neighborhoods teachers of the young frequently were immoral and incapable; and in the country generally there was either a school of the worst character or none at all." [76]

Throughout this period there were no state-supported schools in Delaware. Many private academies, however, were incorporated,[77] and the act creating a public school fund was twice extended; [78] the New Castle Library Company was chartered,[79] and night schools, Sunday schools, young ladies' schools, French schools, and dancing schools flourished. Caesar A. Rodney and Gunning Bedford, Jr., joined by a Federalist, Nicholas Ridgely, asked the legislature in 1803 to reincorporate the Wilmington Academy as a college and

[75] Caldwell, *Penitentiary Movement*, 80, 82, 85, 88, 102–107, 109–116; petitions of 1808, 1810, and 1811, Legislative Papers. Such Federalists as Samuel White and Louis McLane are among the petitioners, but so are John Fisher, Willard Hall, William Killen, James Wilson, James Tilton, and many of the Quaker millers of the Brandywine.

[76] Powell, *Education in Delaware*, 142.

[77] *Laws*, III, 199–206, 300–301, 353–358; IV, 165–170, 304–308, 439–440, 484–486, 489–490, 495–497, 605–606; V, 68–70, 89–91.

[78] *Laws*, IV, 52–53, 596.

[79] *Laws*, IV, 515–516. Cf. *ibid.*, 511–514.

to grant it funds, suggesting that "the escheatable property at present throughout the State, & what may hereafter arise from that source" be appropriated, as well as profits of over ten percent on the capital stock of the Wilmington Bridge Company. Thus the legislature might evince its "just sense of the importance of education, & the diffusion of knowledge in a republican government." [80] The College of Wilmington was incorporated and permitted to establish a lottery, but no public funds were granted it,[81] which perhaps explains why the institution never set up a collegiate department.

The abolition of slavery was another reform that was sought in vain. This was by no means a partisan question, but the Federalists alone possessed legislative power to free the slaves. Though many of this party urged abolition, sponsorship of such a measure would have meant dissolution, for the greatest Federalist strength was in Sussex, where slaveholding was most popular. Realizing the political importance of downstate support, the Delaware Society for Promoting the Abolition of Slavery, whose members came from the Wilmington and Brandywine area, recommended the formation of an abolition society at Duck Creek, Dover, and Milford, chiefly of Methodists, who were "more numerous & influential than any other in Kent & Sussex," and well disposed and "eminently serviceable" to protect the colored people and to produce a change in public opinion.[82] Such a society may never have been formed, but an abolition society did appear in Sussex County in 1809 with a Federalist, Caleb Rodney, and a Democrat, Phillips Kollock, as its

[80] Folder, "1803, Legislative, Petitions, Misc.," Legislative Papers.

[81] *Laws*, III, 292–298, 377; IV, 237, 371, 465. Many trustees were appointed, including Bishop White, Dickinson, Tatnall, Broom, Bedford, Latimer, Bayard, Daniel and Caesar A. Rodney, David Hall, Tilton, Wells, Ridgely, two Leas, and Horsey. A later law provided that profits of over ten percent from the bridge should be added to the school fund. *Laws*, IV, 74.

[82] Minutes of the Abolition Society of Delaware, July 18, 1801 (Historical Society of Pennsylvania). This society was formed in December, 1800, largely of Friends, and replaced an older society previously mentioned. Among the prominent members were Cyrus Newlin, William Poole, Joseph Bringhurst, Francis Latta, John Way, Frederick Craig, James Brian, John and William Warner, John Vaughan, Edward Gilpin, George Monro, Hezekiah Niles, Caesar A. Rodney, James Wilson, Nehemiah Tilton, Jacob Alrichs, John Ferris, Allen McLane, James Gillis, Francis O'Daniel, Samuel Shipley, Thomas Mendinhall, Isaac Dixon, and John Bellach. Minutes of Abolition Society and Report of the Society, May 23, 1801, Misc. Papers, 1655–1805, Three Lower Counties Delaware (Historical Society of Pennsylvania), 303.

chief officers. It declared slavery to be "repugnant to the sacred obligations of the christian religion, the dictates of humanity, and the rights of mankind." [83]

Abolition petitions were presented to the legislature in 1801 and 1803, and in the latter year an abolition bill was presented which, supported strongly by the New Castle County Democrats, was narrowly lost.[84] The practice of manumitting Negroes remained popular through this decade, and the number of slaves decreased by over 32 percent, an even greater decrease than in the previous decade. At the same time the number of free Negroes increased by almost 59 percent.[85]

The following decade, however, revealed a startling reversal in trends. Between 1810 and 1820 the number of slaves increased by nearly 8 percent and the number of free Negroes decreased by over 1 percent, the only time either an increase of slaves or decrease of free Negroes was reported in census figures for Delaware from 1790 to the Civil War. The explanation may lie in what seems to be a reaction in the state against emancipation in the years before and after 1810.

A great and apparently increasing evil was the kidnapping of slaves and free Negroes for sale to the southward, where plantation owners offered a better price for field hands than could be had in Delaware. The Abolition Society declaimed against this practice and occasionally helped to rescue Negroes and to prosecute the kidnappers.[86] The kidnapping of Negroes, declared a magazine

[83] *American Watchman*, Nov. 15, 1809. The other officers were William Russell and Daniel Hudson. Among the members were Liston A. Houston, John and David Hazzard, Benton and Stephen Harris, John Sharp, William Derickson, Edward Dingle, Jehu Evans, Ezekiel and Samuel Williams, Jacob West, Fretwell Wright, David Wolfe, Samuel and Curtis Jacobs, William Davis, William Carlisle, Purnell Tindall, and Jehu Stockley.

[84] Legislative Papers; Stewart, Negro in Delaware, 76–77.

[85] The number of slaves in 1810 was 4,177, of whom 2,402 were in Sussex; the number of free Negroes was 13,136, of whom the greatest number, 5,616, were in Kent. The total population was 72,674. *Aggregate Amount of Each Description of Persons within the United States . . . in the Year 1810* (Washington, 1811), 52–53.

[86] Report of Abolition Society, May 23, 1801, Misc. Papers, 1655–1805, Three Lower Counties Delaware; Minutes, Abolition Society, June 19, July 17, 1802; Nov. 16, 1803; John and William Warner to C. A. Rodney, Wilmington, Jan. 21, 1802, Rodney Collection; *Governor's Register*, 51, 75, 87, 89, 101, 105, 108, 131, 134; Stewart, Negro in Delaware, 43. Among the signers from Sussex County of a petition against the slave trade were John Rodney, Rhoads Shankland, Aaron Marshall, Joshua Rowland, William Dodd, Thomas Bell, James Coulter, Mills McIlvain, Fred-

article, "has raised up a class of persons lost to all shame or religion, and familiar with the basest moral turpitude." [87] "I cannot help exclaiming," wrote Anne Steele, "Great God when will there be an end to this traffic." [88] Other exportations were allowed by special acts of the legislature.

Fear of the Negroes was increasing. Thomas Rodney reports that in 1803 the white people of Dover were summoned to the State House "to Enter into an assotiation for the defence of their lives and property." [89] Governor Mitchell warned in 1807 that Negroes should be forbidden to use firearms and to gather in large numbers on Christmas and election days. Some southern states, he said, were compelling free Negroes to migrate and they must be kept out of Delaware lest they force white farmers out.[90] The legislature responded with a law forbidding intermarriage, punishing whites who cohabited with Negroes, providing for the sale into limited servitude of certain convicted Negro criminals and making it difficult for free Negroes to enter Delaware.[91] This law was repealed in 1808, after Governor Truitt pointed out defects which allowed criminal Negroes to escape with little punishment, and a new law for the punishment of Negroes was passed in 1811.[92] "We have already too many [Negroes] for the good of society," some Delawareans argued, and in accord with their sentiment the immigration of free Negroes into Delaware was forbidden in 1811.[93]

---

erick Rowe, and William Killingsworth. Folder, "1803, Legislative, Petitions, Negroes and Slavery," Legislative Papers.

[87] "A Morning's Walk in the State of Delaware," Dover, Oct. 1, 1817, *Analectic Magazine*, X (1817), 379.

[88] Anne T. Steele to Joseph Bringhurst, New Castle, Oct. 27, 1817, Bringhurst Papers (HSD). *Cf.* Shorter, Slavery in Delaware, 33.

[89] T. Rodney, Diary, June 17, 1803, Brown Collection.

[90] *Museum of Delaware* (Wilmington), Jan. 17, 1807. John Fisher wrote Nehemiah Tilton of the industry of one Negro farmer: "A negro man named Messick Laws who is recommended by a number of respectable people as being very industrious and thrifty . . . wants your place in Littlecreek neck and from what I have heard of him will make a much better tenant than most of the white men whom you have had on your place. . . . He is one of Isaac Davis's kinsmen, and I am told is up to the system of economy, which has made Isaac so wealthy." Fisher to Tilton, Dover, Sept. 12, 1808, Brown Collection.

[91] *Laws*, IV, 108–113.

[92] *Museum*, Jan. 23, 1808; *Laws*, IV, 221, 408–409. *Cf.* Stewart, Negro in Delaware, 45–46.

[93] *Laws*, IV, 400–404; folder, "1810, Legislative, Petitions, Negroes and Slavery," Legislative Papers. Provision was also made for binding out the children of a free Negro too poor to support them. *Laws*, IV, 467–469.

At the same time that such prejudice was being displayed against the Negro, his lot in the Wilmington area was undergoing some improvement. The Abolition Society in 1802 began sponsoring a school for the blacks conducted by John Thelwell.[94] The Wilmington Association for Promoting the Education of the People of Colour was founded in about 1809 to give "that instruction which alone can qualify them for the enjoyment of liberty." [95] In 1805 an appeal had been made for funds to build a Methodist church for Negroes. Soon constructed and named Ezion, it was described by Asbury a year later as, "of stone, and equal in size to that of the whites." [96] A division occurred in 1812, and the schismatics, led by Peter Spencer, built the brick Old Union Church, "independent though Methodist," the beginning of the U. A. M. E. church movement and the first church in the United States built and governed by Negroes.[97]

VI. The Manufacturers and the Democrats

THE development of manufacturing in New Castle County added still further to the strength of the Democratic party there. According to the marshal's report, in the autumn of 1810 there were in this county two barley mills, twenty-seven grist mills, one powder mill, two rope walks, two snuff mills, four paper mills, two breweries, nineteen distilleries, ten tanneries, one nail factory, three rolling and slitting mills, six fulling mills, two woollen factories, three cot-

---

[94] Minutes, Abolition Society, Jan. 16, April 17, 1802; Report of Abolition Society, May 23, 1801, Misc. Papers, 1655–1805, Three Lower Counties, Delaware, 303.

[95] History of the Bequest of Jacob Broom, MS., African School Association Papers (HSD); *American Watchman*, Dec. 20, 1809; Stewart, Negro in Delaware, 38–39. The sponsors of this association included Eli and Samuel Hilles, Joseph Grubb, Ziba Ferris, Edward Tatnall, Edward Gilpin, Merritt Canby, and John Reynolds. *Ibid.*

[96] Asbury, *Journal*, III, 221.

[97] Buckley, *History of Methodism*, I, 421; Montgomery, *Reminiscences*, 252; Stewart, Negro in Delaware, 41.

ton factories, ten carding machines, 1,822 spindles. None of these were found in such numbers in Kent and Sussex combined, except for distilleries, of which there were twelve in Kent and twenty in Sussex, and tanneries, of which there were fourteen in the two southern counties.[98] As a matter of fact, in these two counties only fifteen grist mills, two fulling mills, and one carding machine were reported—no cotton or woollen factories, rolling or slitting mills, nail factories, breweries, paper mills, snuff mills, rope walks, powder mills, or barley mills being listed down state. On the other hand, Sussex reported five forges and seven salt works and, with Kent, much domestic manufacturing of flaxen and woollen goods. New Castle reported valuable manufactures of stockings, hats, and boots and shoes, at least a part of the industry being domestic.[99]

Of the New Castle manufactures, the product of the grist mills was most valuable, being listed at $905,000. Second was the product of the rolling and slitting mills, $156,000; third, gunpowder, $125,000; fourth, factory-made cotton and woollen goods, $91,000; and fifth, paper, $75,000.[100] One item in this list, gunpowder, had appeared there only since the turn of the century. Because of its already rapid development and because of its great importance to the future history of the Wilmington area, of Delaware, and of the nation, it deserves a further word.

On New Year's Day in the year 1800 there arrived in America Eleuthère Irénée du Pont, his brother Victor, and their father Pierre Samuel du Pont de Nemours, the *philosophe,* pupil of Quesnay, friend of Turgot, and onetime president of the Constituent Assembly and the Council of Ancients of his native France. The son, having previously worked with the famed chemist, Lavoisier, when the latter directed the manufacture of powder for the French government, determined to use his technical knowledge of this science to make his fortune in the New World. In 1802 from Jacob Broom he purchased land on the Brandywine near Wilmington, being led to choose that spot by his friendship with the French colony at Wil-

---

[98] The product of all the downstate tanneries was less than that of those in New Castle County.

[99] *American State Papers, Finance,* II, 764.

[100] *Ibid.* Isaiah Thomas, *History of Printing in America. Transactions and Collections of the American Antiquarian Society,* V (1874), 25, claims more paper mills for Delaware than the marshal reported.

mington and by the availability of water power and of transportation by water.[101]

The romance of E. I. du Pont's life thereafter revolved about his construction and management of the powder factory that bears his name. His genius was most singular in that as an inventor and technician he possessed the business acumen to exploit his technical knowledge and to retain control for himself and his heirs of the great industrial firm which he created. "My justification," he wrote in 1811, "is the result of my work. . . . I have developed a large business with a totally insufficient capital. . . . I had to struggle against internal distrusts and quarrels that for a long time threatened the destruction of the whole thing. I overcame every sort of difficulty. For nine years I gave to it all my strength—physical and moral. I was both director and head workman, and even workman —day and night. . . . The danger of teaching the men so much that they could take our knowledge to other mills forced me to do the refining myself, as well as many other tasks that filled my days with work." [102]

The success of his work was noted by Albert Gallatin, who in a section on gunpowder in his 1810 report on manufactures referred to "the manufacture of Brandywine, which employs a capital of $75,000 and 36 workmen, and is considered as the most perfect." [103] Such success merely stimulated E. I. du Pont to further effort, and soon he was planning a tannery and a textile factory on the Brandywine; thus, he advised his father, "we would have a collection of important industries which would eventually help and maintain each other by means of the good understanding of the proprietors. The country is in greater need of such enterprises than is generally supposed." [104] Four years later, in 1811, his industry partially proved his prediction, for as he was able to report: "our wool mills

---

[101] B. G. du Pont, E. I. du Pont de Nemours and Company; a History, 1802–1902 (Boston, 1920), 2–15. The Brandywine, E. I. du Pont had written in 1801, "is too appropriate for my purpose and too agreeable to me to be put aside lightly. I am more than ever decided upon it." To Peter Bauduy, New York, Oct. 7, 1801, Du Pont, Life of E. I. du Pont, V, 294.

[102] E. I. du Pont to P. S. du Pont de Nemours, May 26, 1811, ibid., VIII, 298–299.

[103] American State Papers, Finance, II, 429.

[104] June 10, 1807, Du Pont, Life of E. I. du Pont, VII, 306.

are running." [105] These woollen mills were managed by E. I. du Pont's older brother, Victor, under the firm name of Du Pont, Bauduy, and Company. "Of the first piece [of cloth] finished by those gentlemen," Hezekiah Niles reported, "the president of the United States wore a suit" on New Year's Day, 1812. "It was finished only on the 24th of December." [106]

Jefferson's embargo, of course, quickened the development of manufactures in the Wilmington area as elsewhere in the nation. "Thus do we advance to real independence," the Democratic *American Watchman* declared.[107] The same paper condemned Governor Truitt a year later for not referring to American manufacturing, "the permanent support of independence, . . . the only sure source of national prosperity and individual happiness," in his message of January 4, 1810, to the General Assembly.[108]

Only through manufacturing could this small state grow, declared a group of New Castle County manufacturers in petitioning the legislature in 1810.[109] They wanted their workers to be freed of militia duty, which often led to intemperance and kept men from work till their "money, health, strength, and credit are exhausted." Since some factories employed their labor in "a Screw, Set, or Gang of hands," all workers in the gang were made idle if any one of them was absent. The manufacturers also requested protection against those who sought to steal their techniques and their hands by plying the latter with drink and signing them to contracts.[110]

[105] To P. S. du Pont de Nemours [June? 1811], *ibid.*, VIII, 308.

[106] *Niles' Register*, Jan. 25, 1812, vol. I, 390. See also B. G. du Pont, *Lives of Victor and Josephine du Pont* (n.p., c. 1930), 176–181.

[107] Sept. 20, 1809. It was reporting the manufacture of "American Kersimere" at the "woolen establishment of Mr. McKinney & co." at Stanton, Delaware. See also Ferris, *Original Settlements*, 240.

[108] *American Watchman*, Jan. 10, 1810.

[109] Folder, "1810, January, Legislative, Petitions, Misc.," Legislative Papers. The petitioners were Rumford Dawes, rolling and slitting mill proprietor; Thomas Gilpin & Co., William Young, Horatio G. Garrett, and Thomas and Samuel Meteer, paper manufacturers; E. I. du Pont de Nemours & Co., powder makers; E. I. du Pont & P. Bauduy, woollen cloth manufacturers; Caleb Kirk, miller of pearl and shelled barley; Caleb and Samuel Kirk, woollen and cotton manufacturers; and Thomas Massey, manufacturer of cotton yarn.

[110] E. I. du Pont had been especially worried by the attempt of a Richmond firm to hire his workmen and to discover his processes. E. I. du Pont to P. S. du Pont de

They also asked that premiums be given for the importation of fine sheep, especially merinos.[111] When no action was taken on this petition, Rumford Dawes, Caleb Kirk, Thomas Massey, E. I. du Pont, and his brother, Victor du Pont, renewed it in 1811 and sent William Young to Dover to represent them. The legislature, considering "the many local advantages and facilities which many parts of this State present for the establishment of manufactories for the manufacture of articles of the first importance, . . . and the limited extent of the State, within which all agricultural pursuits are necessarily bounded," enacted most of the petitioners' requests into law. Workmen in paper, iron, powder, and textile mills were exempted from militia duty. Fines were prescribed for enticing mechanics out of state.[112]

The war with Great Britain which began in the next year further encouraged the development of manufactures.[113] A Wilmington directory of 1814 reported: "Within a few years the 'solitary desert' (figuratively speaking) has been made to 'blossom as the rose' in the adjacent country. Instead of craggy hills and dreary swamps, overgrown with 'briars and thorns,' we see villages planted near

---

Nemours, Jan. 22, 1809, Du Pont, *Life of E. I. du Pont*, VIII, 134–135, 138. Note the advertisement of John Ellis & Co. in the *Museum of Delaware* (Wilmington), Oct. 22, 1808.

[111] Many sources testify to the "merino craze" of the early nineteenth century. See the quotation from James Mease, *Archives of Useful Knowledge*, in Du Pont, *Life of E. I. du Pont*, VIII, 272–276; also E. I. du Pont to Pierre Samuel du Pont de Nemours, March 25, 1803, *ibid.*, VI, 196, as well as various other correspondence of E. I. du Pont. Woollen manufacturers had already been assisted by a law of January 27, 1809, exempting sheep for five years from assessment for taxation. *Laws*, IV, 267–268.

[112] *Laws*, IV, 397–400. Petition of Jan. 8, 1811, Hagley Works, Legislative Papers. Dawes' slitting mill was at Hagley, which soon afterwards became part of the Du Pont properties.

[113] The war was preceded, however, by a slump. The *Delaware Statesman*, a Federalist paper, declared on May 9, 1812, that thirteen mills on the Brandywine were idle, mills which would ordinarily put into circulation $32,000 a week. This cessation of milling threw about four thousand men out of work, three hundred for each mill, according to this estimate—thirty mill hands, as many on vessels owned by the miller, one hundred coopers, one hundred shallopmen employed in New Jersey and at Cantwell's Bridge, Blackbird, Smyrna, and Camden "in carrying grain, cooper's stuff, and poles" and men who prepared these goods and brought them to the shallops. In addition, the mill owners and people indirectly dependent on them were injured, and the trade of Newport and Christiana Bridge was destroyed. The Brandywine millers were said to be "unanimously opposed" to the measures of the Democratic administration, although few of them actively participated in politics.

factories, to which (factories) a numerous throng look up for support, and from which our beloved country will draw additional aid to independence." [114] The manufacturers declared that within a semicircle of twenty miles from Wilmington there were in 1815 fourteen woollen mills with over three thousand spindles and twenty-seven cotton mills with over twenty-five thousand spindles.[115]

The workers in these factories were largely Democrats and were very often of foreign birth. E. I. du Pont at first sought French and Canadian hands, but he eventually adopted the common practice of employing English and Irish immigrants.[116] In 1813 Victor du Pont's employees paraded to the polls with the workers from the factories of William Young and of Bauduy and Garesché carrying banners, "one . . . for the Weavers, one for the Spinners & one for the Shearers," which bore such mottoes as "Domestic Manufacturers—Manufacturers on the Brandywine—Bees in peace hornets in war." Federalist election handbills and papers had characterized these workers and their French employers as "Alien ennemies—Friends to Bonaparte Marat & Robespierre—Imported manufacturers—Scouring of the earth—Scrappings of Gutters." Feeling consequently was high. After several quarrels, the workers—Victor du Pont with them—were stoned on their way home; when they resisted, "a general battle ensued . . . for about ten minutes." [117]

The French manufacturers, at least, shared many of the political convictions of their Irish employees. Victor and Irénée du Pont were led to the Democratic party by their father's friendship with Jefferson and by the anti-French attitude of the Federalists. Victor du Pont eventually was elected to the legislature as a Democrat.[118]

---

[114] *A Directory and Register for the Year 1814 of the Borough of Wilmington and Brandywine* [Wilmington, 1814], 80. *Cf.* description of the Eleutherian Mills in Charles F. Parent to [Bottée] [*c.* August, 1803], Du Pont, *Life of E. I. du Pont*, VI, 265–267.

[115] Minutes of manufacturers' meeting, Wilmington, Nov. 25, 1815, Bringhurst Papers (HSD).

[116] E. I. du Pont to P. S. du Pont de Nemours, March 25, 1803, Du Pont, *Life of E. I. du Pont*, VI, 194; La Rochefoucault, *Travels*, III, 498.

[117] Affidavit of Victor du Pont, Jan. 17, 1814, Du Pont, *Life of E. I. du Pont*, IX, 156–164. *Cf. Delaware Gazette*, May 2, 1814; J. A. Bayard to C. A. Rodney, Washington, Jan. 6 [1812], Hilles Collection.

[118] *Delaware Gazette*, Oct. 12, 1815; Du Pont, *Victor and Josephine du Pont*, 187, 202–204. Dickinson was a close friend and adviser of Bauduy; Caesar A.

When British invasion threatened, the du Pont brothers were quick to organize their workers, exempt from militia duty, into independent companies, the Brandywine Rangers, which they armed and commanded. In 1814, however, a Federalist state government repealed the act to encourage manufactures and with it the workers' exemption. The du Ponts declared to their men that obviously the intent of the repeal was to disband the independent companies —"a chastisement for your patriotism." [119]

The Democratic-Republican criticism of the legislature's action was so severe that "A Citizen of Delaware," writing in a Federalist newspaper, felt called on to defend it. Exemption from the militia, he argued, had been intended only for skilled artisans but had in practice covered all workmen in the specified manufactures. Consequently many shirkers had eluded militia service by securing jobs on the Brandywine as diggers and wagoners. The independent military companies had been organized principally for the purpose of protecting private property, the Brandywine factories. They were not subject to state authority and had been arrogant in their attitude toward it. Fine plumes, terrible swords, and dread mustachios had characterized their command. [120]

The Democratic representatives left their seats and spoke angrily of the possible secession of New Castle County from Delaware and its annexation to Pennsylvania. [121] E. I. du Pont felt that the destruction of the independent companies was a Federalist act of treason. "Were the Militia of this State kept under good military regulations, well trained, well armed & well equipped," he explained, the legislature's action might be defended. Such, however, was not the case. Most of the militia neither had arms nor knew how to use them. The action of the "federal Legislature" was "truly allarming" and could "be naturally considered as part of the Massachusetts plan," showing that "there is no protection to be expected from the State of Delaware." Yet, the destruction of Wilmington and the nearby

Rodney, another Democrat, was his lawyer and "particular friend." Peter Bauduy to Victor du Pont, Wilmington, Dec. 13, 1804, Du Pont, *Life of E. I du Pont*, VII, 74; Bauduy to E. I. du Pont, Wilmington, Oct. 16, 1801, *ibid.*, V, 300–301. Cf. J. A. Bayard to C. A. Rodney, Washington, Jan. 6 [1812], Hilles Collection.

[119] *Laws*, V, 25; Address of Victor and E. I. du Pont to the Brandywine Rangers [c. January, 1814], Du Pont, *Life of E. I. du Pont*, IX, 164–167.

[120] *Delaware Gazette*, May 16, 1814.

[121] *Ibid.*, May 5, 1814.

mills would be the only incentive to bring the British up the Delaware, "for the lower part of the State is, generally speaking, inhabited by Friends of England." [122]

Shortly after this sharp attack on the Federalists, Du Pont urged reaping "the full advantage that this war may produce," the secure "establishment of american manufactories" to "make the world tributary to our industry." To this end he urged an embargo against foreign cotton and woollen goods and the naturalization of "every artist, artificer and manufacturer" after two years' residence in order to encourage skilled workers to come to America. This latter suggestion, he added, "will be the means of manufacturing a large number of republican citizens and on that point there is no doubt it will be strongly opposed by the federalists. I know that in our little state it will have the best tendency to relieve us from the federal yoke." [123]

To Du Pont's first proposal, however, manufacturers of both parties could and did subscribe. With the coming of peace the New Castle County manufacturers met together to devise means of persuading Congress that legislative encouragement must be given to American war-built industry if it was not to be crippled by an influx of cheap European goods. Petitions and representatives were sent to Washington in a united move of the manufacturers which augured their eventual political union years hence in favor of Clay's American system.[124] In 1816, however, Du Pont was strongly urging the election to Congress of Caesar A. Rodney, a Democrat, over Louis McLane, a Federalist.[125]

[122] E. I. du Pont to Callender Irvine, Feb. 7, 1814, Du Pont, *Life of E. I. du Pont*, IX, 172–173.

[123] E. I. du Pont to Robert McKim, Feb. 17, 1814, *ibid.*, 174–178. "For this reason," Du Pont continued, "I could not speak about it to our friend Young who although an excellent man in all other respects is unfortunately entirely blinded by federal prejudices."

[124] *Delaware Gazette*, Feb. 28, March 7, 1815; minutes of manufacturers' meeting, Jan. 10, 1816, Bringhurst Papers; subscription list, May 8, 1815, *ibid.*; minutes of manufacturers' meeting, Nov. 25, 1815, *ibid.* These documents reveal the interest of Irénée, Victor, and Charles du Pont, William Young, Joseph Bringhurst, Louis McLane, Jacob Alrichs, John Torbert, Caleb Kirk, Arnold Naudain, Richard C. Dale, Thomas Lea, Sr., Isaac Briggs, Raphael Duplanty, and many others in this movement.

[125] E. I. du Pont to his wife, Georgetown, D. C., Sept. 26, 1816, Du Pont, *Life of E. I. du Pont*, X, 174–175.

VII. Democratic Party Machinery

ANOTHER source of Democratic strength in Delaware lay in the party's organization and particularly in its method of making nominations. In the early 1790s the county "ticket was usually formed the day before the election by a small junto" in the county seat, "and the clerks about town would be put to writing tickets on the morning of the election, so as to supply the country people as they arrived, which was always too late to counteract this ticket, except sometimes when a sheriff was chosen." "About the time of Adams' administration the parties came nearer equal," and the New Castle County Republicans began the practice of holding mass meetings at the Red Lion Tavern to form the ticket. Soon the "Red Lion meetings became the rallying point of one party, and the object of hatred and denunciation of the other." Federalist wrath against these meetings was such that the chief justice was said to have called the attention of the grand jury to them.[126]

The Democratic-Republicans, however, proceeded to develop their machinery by appointing a committee at the county meeting to consult with similar committees from Kent and Sussex on the nomination of a governor and a Representative. County committees of correspondence and hundred committees were also chosen. When, in September, 1801, mass meetings in each county nominated David Hall for governor, the work of conferees chosen from each county was responsible for the high degree of unanimity at the county meetings.[127]

The hundred committees previously referred to were to communicate and cooperate with county committees of correspondence in affairs relating to the elections. A further refinement of the Democratic-Republican machinery was the appointment at the county mass meeting of a second group of hundred committees, smaller than those just mentioned, which were to join together to

[126] American Watchman, Sept. 20, 1809; Mirror of the Times, Sept. 19, 1801.
[127] Luetscher, Early Political Machinery, 96, 147–148.

select a county ticket. This device was adopted, probably in 1802, because a few hundreds had sought to outnumber the others in attendance at the mass meeting and so secure a ticket to their liking. By this plan the hundreds far distant from the county meeting place were assured an equal voice in nominations with those hundreds previously favored by their location.[128] It also encouraged the division of the legislative seats among the hundreds on a basis roughly proportionate to their population.[129]

Within the decade another significant change was made in the nominating procedure employed by the Democratic-Republicans. The hundred nominating committees were chosen directly by the voters at the regular September hundred elections, instead of being appointed at the county mass meeting, an arrangement that reduced the burden of attendance at meetings.[130]

Many Democrats sought a further revision of the nominating procedure; they suggested that the people of the hundreds should nominate candidates for seats in the legislature, and perhaps for other positions, at the hundred elections. In opposition to this proposal, however, other Democrats argued that it was better to choose at the hundred elections only delegates to a nominating convention. The distribution of legislative seats among the hundreds did not alter the fact that, according to the constitution, each legislator represented a whole county. The county convention method of nominating permitted the hundred delegates to have something to say about the choice of nominees from other hundreds, which was as it should be.[131]

In 1813 a compromise was reached whereby at the hundred elections nominations would be made and at the same time delegates elected to a county nominating convention. At the convention the delegates were obliged to present the names of those nominated at the hundred elections. If, however, the convention rejected these nominations, the delegates were free to make their

[128] *Ibid.*, 97; T. Rodney, Diary, March 12, 1801, Rodney Papers (Library of Congress); *Mirror of the Times*, Sept. 29, 1802; June 15, Sept. 17, 1803. The Democrats also called hundred meetings. *Mirror of the Times*, Sept. 7, 1803.

[129] *American Watchman*, Sept. 20, 1809.

[130] Luetscher, *Early Political Machinery*, 98–99. See *Mirror of the Times*, Nov. 2, 1803.

[131] *American Watchman*, Sept. 16, 23, Oct. 2, 14, 21, 1809; *Delaware Gazette*, Oct. 14, 1809.

own nominations or repeat the former nominations until the convention came to some agreement.[132]

Both the Democrats and the Federalists, in New Castle County, at least, ran stages and boats on election day to carry the voters to the polls at the county seat.[133] The Democrats, however, began to demand that more polling places be established. "A Friend of the People" urged electors to support David Hall in 1801 in order to get a district election system.[134] Many petitions urging district elections were sent to the General Assembly in 1804 and 1805, among the signers being James Wilson, George Monro, Hezekiah Niles, James Lea, John Collins, John Gibbons, and Thomas Montgomery. It was argued that party politics had reached such a height that every legal voter should be allowed to express his will, but that this was discouraged as long as some voters had to ride twenty or thirty miles "in a sickly season and sickly country." Furthermore, district elections would eliminate much of the carelessness, provoking claims of fraud, always found at the county polls, since three thousand votes were received there in six to eight hours. Finally, voters hesitated to abandon their wives and children among the slaves, "a people whose *state* and *condition* has stamped eternal enmity between them and their holders." One signer, Hezekiah Niles, was careful to dissociate himself from approval of the last statement.[135]

The Democratic-Republicans called attention to their sponsorship of measures which they claimed placed the government under the direction of the people. Their most frequent charge against the Federalist party was that it was aristocratic. "Publicola" in his pamphlet, *Features of Federalism: or a Brief History of the Principles and Views of the Federalists from the Revolution to the Present Time*,[136] urged the people of Kent and Sussex, "still the dupes of tory federal leaders," to arouse themselves against the schemes of "interested designing men," "an unprincipled faction," who would rule like lords over peasants, were they not obliged,

---

[132] Luetscher, *Early Political Machinery*, 100. Apparently this compromise had previously been employed in the selection of nominees for sheriff. *Delaware Gazette*, Oct. 14, 1809.

[133] *Mirror of the Times*, Oct. 3, 1803; *American Watchman*, Oct. 2, 1810.

[134] *Mirror of the Times*, Sept. 26, 1801.

[135] Legislative Papers; folder, "Delaware, re Slavery, Militia, Lottery, etc.," HSD.

[136] Wilmington, 1803.

since they had experienced some defeats, to affect "the most lively concern" for the common people "and the tenderest sympathy for the hardships incident to an indigent state." Only through the awakening of the people of these counties, the plea continued, "will our state be rescued from the ignominy of being governed by aristocrats and tories, the whole of our representation in Congress in future be republican, the interests of the people more faithfully attended to, and the sweetest harmony prevail between the general government and our own."

Another pamphlet, *An Address from a Late Federalist of Kent County, To his Fellow-Citizens*,[137] made similar charges, embellishing them with what is apparently fictitious autobiographical material. It claimed the leading Federalists thought the people could not be trusted and were appalled to find that "every blacksmith, taylor and shoemaker undertook to talk on politics." They felt "the most successful way to gain votes amongst the lowest class" was to distribute liquor. One Federalist was said to have asserted that "four out of five through all our back forests would think themselves so neglected if they were not treated that they would not vote for a man of us. Rum is their federalism and democracy: they care for nothing else." [138]

VIII. The Federalists Meet the Challenge

DEMOCRATIC-REPUBLICAN successes in the elections of 1801 and 1802 did not mean the end of the Federalist party. The Democrats had chosen a governor and a Representative, but the Federal-

---

[137] No place or date of publication is given; the date is probably 1804. A photostat copy is in the Memorial Library, University of Delaware.

[138] "Plain Matter of Fact," writing in the *Watchman*, Sept. 30, 1809, repeated the charge that a Federalist junto ran Kent County: "Do not offices run in the blood of families and descend from father to son? Have not most of the offices of this county for a long succession of years been confined to a few individuals? and were not the fathers, brothers, uncles, &c. of the most of the present office holders, office holders also? . . . Office creates power, and therefore ought to circulate among the people who are the proper holders of power."

ists retained control of the legislature and thereby the power to select presidential electors and Senators.

In 1803 the Federalists again won Kent and Sussex, and with them the legislature.[139] In 1804 they completely repulsed the Democratic advance and reversed the results of the gubernatorial and Congressional elections of 1801 and 1802. Victory was all the more striking in that (1) it came at the time of a presidential election in which Jefferson easily won reelection, and (2) the successful Federalist condidates, Nathaniel Mitchell and James A. Bayard, were the very men who had been defeated at the last election. Furthermore, the Democrats ran the popular incumbent, Caesar A. Rodney, for the Congressional seat. A constitutional provision against immediate reelection of a governor prevented the Democrats from renominating David Hall, so they did what seemed the next best thing: they nominated another Sussex County Democrat, Joseph Haslet, son of Delaware's foremost Revolutionary martyr, Colonel John Haslet, who had been killed at the Battle of Princeton.

Neither Bayard nor Rodney wanted to run for Congress in 1804. Both had experienced the financial sacrifice involved in abandoning a profitable career at the bar for an ill-paid, impermanent career in Washington. It was a choice between "the homely drudgery of making money and . . . the refined and elegant pursuit of attaining honor and reputation," Bayard wrote in a spirit of friendly sarcasm to Rodney, who was his close personal friend. "The course of things forced us into a competition in which the successful party was to be the loser." [140] Rodney wrote the Democratic nominating conference that he would not run again under any circumstances.[141] "My profession," he told George Read, the younger, who, unlike his father, was a Democrat, "is my sole support & my only dependence." [142] Both he and Bayard were, however, finally per-

[139] John Hamm to Thomas Rodney, Dover, Oct. 8, 1803, Rodney Collection.

[140] Wilmington, Dec. 10, 1803, Donnan, "Bayard Papers," 6–7. Bayard added: "In spite of your politicks I can't help liking you." In another testimony of his friendship, Bayard was reported to have said that "C. A. R. was as Competent To Represent the State as any Man in it and perhaps as competent as any Man in Congress." Thomas to C. A. Rodney, Washington, Mississippi Territory, Dec. 28, 1803, Rodney Papers (Library of Congress).

[141] G. Read to C. A. Rodney, New Castle, Feb. 2, 1804, Rodney Collection.

[142] C. A. Rodney to G. Read, Washington, Feb. 13, 1804, ibid.

suaded to make the contest, for the gubernatorial nominees came from Sussex, and each party needed a strong candidate from New Castle on its ticket.[143]

Had they fully understood the bitterness with which this campaign was to be waged, they might never have consented to run. Both parties established newspapers in Dover to spread their propaganda down state.[144] A correspondent who called himself "Propriety" was shocked by the personal abuse. "What," he asked, "has the religion, the amusements, the family, the connexions, or the manner of living of any man to do with the officer?"[145] After his victory, Bayard frankly admitted that he had run only "to facilitate the election of the governor." "It is important for us," he stated, "to maintain our Superiority in the State Govt. . . . I think it of no consequence considering the times [*i.e.*, the huge Democratic majority in Congress] who represents this State in the Genl. Govt."[146]

Bayard soon suited his action to his words. Before he had ever had the opportunity to enter the House, the new General Assembly elected him to the Senate to replace William Hill Wells, who had resigned to go to northern Pennsylvania.[147] James M. Broom, a New Castle County attorney and Princeton graduate, son of a signer of the Constitution, was elected by the Federalists in 1805 to replace Bayard.

These elections began a decade of unbroken Federalist successes in Congressional campaigns. In the decade from 1804 to 1814, slightly extended to include both terminal years, Delawareans were called to the polls to fill a total of ten vacancies in the House of

[143] Furthermore, the Democratic conferees had already unanimously nominated Rodney before his refusal to run was known, and on the basis of his nomination they had chosen Haslet as their gubernatorial candidate. John Fisher to C. A. Rodney, Dover, Jan. 23, 1804, Fisher Photostats (HSD); David Hall to C. A. Rodney, Dover, Jan. 23, 1804, Rodney Collection; Archibald Alexander to C. A. Rodney, New Castle, Feb. 1, 1804, Morse Collection (HSD), I; *Mirror of the Times*, Feb. 4, 1804.

[144] *Mirror of the Times*, May 23, 1804; John Fisher to C. A. Rodney, Dover, July 11, 1804, John Fisher Papers.

[145] *Mirror of the Times*, May 12, 1804.

[146] J. A. Bayard to Robert G. Harper, Wilmington, Dec. 10, 1804, Vertical File, (Maryland Historical Society, Baltimore).

[147] John Fisher to C. A. Rodney, Dover, June 18, 1804, John Fisher Papers. It had been rumored that Bayard would not serve his term. Hezekiah Niles to C. A. Rodney, Wilmington, Feb. 7, 1804, Rodney Collection.

Representatives, because twice off-year elections were required to replace men who had resigned, and because a reapportionment of House seats after the census of 1810 gave Delaware two Representatives. But the Federalists were always victorious, regardless of who was their candidate for Congress. In 1804, they ran Bayard; in 1805, Broom; in 1806, Broom; in 1807, Nicholas Van Dyke, son of a former president and Congressman; in 1808, Van Dyke again; in 1810, Henry M. Ridgely; in 1812, Ridgely and Thomas Cooper; in 1814, Cooper and Thomas Clayton, whose father had been governor and Senator.[148]

While these men were serving in the House of Representatives, Federalist legislatures—over the opposition of the Democrats from New Castle County—kept sending Federalists to the United States Senate. Senator Samuel White, son of Asbury's protector, died in 1809 [149] and was succeeded by Outerbridge Horsey, a former attorney-general who had studied law with Bayard. When Bayard resigned in 1813 to participate in writing a peace treaty, he was succeeded by William Hill Wells, who had once before been in the Senate. Only one Democratic-Republican, Caesar A. Rodney, ever served in that body from Delaware and he was not chosen for the Senate until 1822.

The governors, too, were largely Federalist. When Nathaniel Mitchell's term expired in 1808, he was succeeded by George Truitt, a farmer of southern Kent. With Nicholas Van Dyke, he defeated the strong Democratic ticket of Joseph Haslet, who was seeking the governorship a second time, and John Dickinson, who had at last been persuaded to run for the House.[150]

The year 1810, however, brought the Democrats a measure of revenge. Without scoring any unusual victories the Democrats had shown greatly increased popular support in the elections of 1809.

[148] The two off-year elections had occurred because Bayard resigned from the House to accept election to the Senate and Broom resigned to move to another state, Maryland. New accounts have recently appeared of Van Dyke and Ridgely. See John A. Munroe, "Senator Nicholas Van Dyke, of New Castle," *Delaware History*, IV (1951), 207–226; and, for Henry M. Ridgely, *Calendar of Ridgely Family Letters*, II, 87–94.

[149] Henry C. Conrad, *Samuel White and His Father Judge Thomas White, Papers of the Historical Society of Delaware*, XL (Wilmington, 1903), 3–8; J. A. Bayard to William Plumer, Wilmington, June 11, 1811, Donnan, "Bayard Papers," 184–186; Munroe, "William Plumer's Sketches of Bayard, Rodney, and White," 373–377.

[150] *Museum of Delaware*, Sept. 5, Oct. 10, 1807.

With the aid of schismatics and a "Farmers' Union Ticket" in Kent, the Federalist majority there had been reduced from 400 to 110 votes; the Democratic majority in New Castle had risen from 600 to 1300; and even in Sussex the Democrats had made inroads on the strength of their opponents.[151]

Growing difficulties with England aroused a degree of war fever and enthusiasm for the Madison administration from which local Democrats benefited. Federalist attempts to center nationalistic prejudice on Bonaparte ultimately failed, and Joseph Haslet, for a third time the Democratic candidate, was at last elected governor. Although his majority was only seventy-one votes, this was a larger majority than Hall, the only other Democratic governor, had won in 1801. Federalists still dominated the state, however, for Henry Ridgely was elected to the House of Representatives and, as usual, Kent and Sussex returned Federalist legislators.[152] When in 1813, Daniel Rodney, who had been defeated by Haslet three years earlier, was elected governor, Federalist supremacy was completely restored.[153]

IX. The Federalists Copy Democratic Methods

GEORGE D. LUETSCHER, in his monograph, *Early Political Machinery in the United States,* made the following observation: "The close relationship between the prolongation of the life of the Federal party in Delaware and party organization confirms the contention . . . that the failure of the Federal party to resuscitate in other states, after 1800, was due to its individualism, to its conservatism, which stood in the way of democratic organization."

---

[151] *Delaware Gazette,* Oct. 4, 1809; *American Watchman,* Oct. 7, 1809.

[152] *American Watchman,* Oct. 2, 10, 13, 1810; John Fisher to C. A. Rodney, Dover, Oct. 8, 1810, John Fisher Papers. The defeated Democratic candidate for Representative, Richard C. Dale of New Castle County, lost by only seven votes.

[153] Rodney had a majority of 1114 votes in Sussex and 665 in Kent to win easily. His opponent was James Riddle. Daniel Rodney, "Diary," C. H. B. Turner, comp., *Rodney's Diary and Other Delaware Records* (Philadelphia, 1911), 19.

After 1812, especially, Delaware stood out "as a lone exception" to the general abandonment of the Federalist party, because in Delaware the "party was teachable rather than self-sufficient." [154]

The Federalists in Delaware made the state government and their party organization progressively more democratic. They allowed the constitution of 1792 to provide for the popular election of the governor and for the extension of the franchise to all tax-payers, which meant the overwhelming majority of the adult white male citizenry. They permitted, in 1793, the popular election of levy court commissioners.[155] These concessions were followed by years of Federalist rule. Again in 1811 the party modified the political system of Delaware by permitting district elections,[156] long demanded by the Democrats, and again years of Federalist control followed.

The fact seems to have been that in spite of Democratic accusations of aristocracy, the Federalist party in Delaware had founded its strength on its popularity with the average voter, in the two lower counties at least. The recurrence of certain family names among the most prominent office holders was one of the facts frequently alluded to by the Democrats to prove their claims. Family connections, however, were found just about as frequently among the Democratic leaders as among the Federalist; indeed this phenomenon has been common to all major parties throughout the history of the state.[157]

Nominating conventions were used by the Federalists to choose state officers as early as 1795, but they consisted then of a few conferees not chosen by any popular method but merely by some leaders in each county.[158] By 1801, however, the Federalists were holding mass meetings in the counties to choose a county ticket. A Democratic paper declared the Federalists had once called this

---

[154] Pages 150–151.

[155] *Laws*, II, 1086–1088.

[156] A polling place was established in each hundred for the "General Elections." *Laws*, IV, 422–437.

[157] It is probably more characteristic of Kent and Sussex than of New Castle, since the latter county has experienced more immigration and therefore has a less static population.

[158] Gunning Bedford, Jr., to William Hill Wells, Wilmington, July 27, 1795, Gunning Bedford, Jr., Papers (HSD).

nominating method seditious and unconstitutional and accused them of adopting it only after the Democrats had successfully demonstrated its value. Whatever the reasoning, the fact is clear that the Federalists showed their willingness to alter their methods and popularize the control of their party in the face of growing Democratic strength.[159]

In 1810 the Kent Federalists adopted another Democratic device; their county mass meeting chose committees from each hundred, these committees to meet together to form a county ticket and to choose conferees who, with conferees from New Castle and Sussex, were to select candidates for governor, Senator, and Representative.[160] New Castle County may already have taken a further step, the selection at hundred elections, rather than at the county mass meeting, of these hundred nominating committees, for in 1811 a summons to the New Castle County Federalists to meet at Christiana Bridge explained, "A meeting by Delegation would have been preferred but the Districts [*i.e.*, hundreds], for the most part, having neglected to chuse delegates, have not now time to chuse them. Any Delegates, who have been chosen, are requested to attend." [161]

In 1812 both Sussex and New Castle Federalists were electing in the hundreds their delegates to a county convention, which chose a county ticket.[162] Delegates to the state nominating convention, however, were still chosen at county mass meetings.[163] In 1814 a further step was taken in New Castle, when a county convention made up of delegates chosen by the hundreds chose both a county ticket and conferees to a state nominating convention.[164] On the other hand, Kent County that year used the county mass meeting for both of these functions, a procedure that brought forth protests from Mispillion Hundred,[165] protests which proved to be effective,

[159] *Mirror of the Times*, Sept. 19, 1801.
[160] This was intended to be hereafter the regular method of nominating. *American Watchman*, June 16, 1810; Luetscher, *Early Political Machinery*, 100–102, 149.
[161] The hundreds of Brandywine and St. Georges, it was stated, had chosen delegates. *Delaware Statesman*, Sept. 18, 1811.
[162] *Ibid.*, Sept. 2, 5, 1812.
[163] *Ibid.*, July 11, 1812.
[164] *Delaware Gazette*, July 25, 1814.
[165] *Ibid.*, July 28, Aug. 29, 1814.

for in 1815 the county ticket was formed in Kent, and in Sussex too, and presumably in New Castle, by a county convention of hundred delegates.[166]

Apparently several years elapsed before Kent and Sussex Federalists adopted the 1814 procedure of New Castle Federalists, that is, of allowing the hundred-elected county convention to choose the delegates to the state convention.[167] The pressure of Democratic competition undoubtedly was more compelling in New Castle than downstate. Nevertheless the Federalists had brought their party organization close to the people, and the people in exercising the franchise justified the trust that the party had placed in them.

X. The Roots of Delaware Federalism

A WILLINGNESS to improve the party machinery, however, by no means entirely explains the Federalist dominance in Delaware. At best, the Federalists were merely wise enough to adopt the methods of the Democratic-Republicans to permit a broad popular participation in party organization. If success was just a matter of party machinery the Democrats should have fared better than they did; the record shows that every General Assembly in the first two decades of the nineteenth century was Federalist, that every Senator sent to Washington was Federalist, and that most of the Representatives and all but two of the governors were of the same persuasion. The true basis for this strength was not so much party organization as it was Federalist popularity in Kent and Sussex, where education, national backgrounds, religion, and economy commingled to make the people staunch supporters of the party of Hamilton and Adams and Bayard.

The lack of any system of public education assisted Federalist control in that an uneducated people tended to support the status

---

[166] *Ibid.*, May 30, June 22, 1815.
[167] Luetscher, *Early Political Machinery*, 102–103.

quo and to vote as their fathers had voted, which in the counties of Kent and Sussex was Federalist. The Delaware Federalists were, on the whole, the party of stand-pat, a doctrine subscribed to by downstaters, who faced none of the new conditions which bred radicalism on the frontier or in the city. Lacking an education, lacking a local press, except for a few spasmodic journals at Dover, the downstate farmer was stirred by few of the revolutionary doctrines stemming from Europe. With no sizable urban communities, this area did not include the bourgeois and the artisan classes from whence sprung most of the revolutionary ideas of the time. The one exception in respect to urban influences was New Castle, the one Democratic county. Here was a city, an industrial and commercial center; here was an urban life; here were people living in such proximity that printers came among them and school teachers in numbers were available to train the young.

National backgrounds also encouraged Federalist supremacy down state, in that the people were largely of English stock, inbreeding was common among them, and, with the passage of time, isolation and homogeneity bulwarked the customs and the attitudes of their forbears. The migration to northern Delaware of diverse elements, especially the Scotch-Irish, ambitious, educated, aware of the world and its fashions in thought—this migration only encouraged the people of southern Delaware to withdraw within their peninsular shell, to exalt the ancient virtues and the accustomed procedures. Whatever was Irish, they reasoned, was suspect; whatever was suspect they would eschew.

The phenomenal growth of Methodism down state was another factor in Federalist strength. The Methodists were a schismatic development from the Church of England, and they remained loyal to the politics of what had been the Church party. Since some of the Anglican clergy in Delaware had been friendly to Asbury and the early preachers, the schism had proceeded without arousing deep hatreds. Methodism had gained converts from the Anglican communion, not so much in opposition to Anglicanism as in the absence of Anglicanism resulting from the inability of the Anglican Church to minister to all of those who would have gladly accepted it had it been available. Methodism had developed most rapidly in Kent and Sussex; in Presbyterian New Castle County it had much less success. Probably its most prominent converts in Delaware were Richard Bassett, Allen McLane, Thomas White, and Philip Barratt, of whom the first two were leading Federalists, as were two sons of the others, Samuel White and Andrew Barratt.

But Methodists were not accepted in the Federalist party without some opposition. Barkley Townsend, of Laurel, threatened to split the Sussex Federalists by starting an anti-Methodist "Union Ticket" in 1798,[168] declaring that the Methodist preachers were "black dragons" as evil as "the old serpents," the "red dragons" of Presbyterianism.[169]

In spite of such fanatics as Townsend, the Federalists held the Methodist vote. Asbury was permitted to hold meetings at the State House in Dover and at the courthouse in Georgetown.[170] William Hill Wells, George Truitt, and others went to a camp meeting to electioneer in 1807.[171] In the same year the Federalists sought to weaken Haslet's support in Sussex by circulating the rumor that he played cards on Sunday and traded in slaves.[172] The Democratic Jacobins, they declared, were always attacking the Methodists, who must keep them out of office.[173]

The Democrats attempted to destroy the Methodist-Federalist alignment by accusing individual Federalists of unbelief, while at the same time they defended Jefferson's rationalism and argued that he who loved liberty was alone the true Christian.[174] "All worldly honors are but dross," the Methodists were reminded:

> Should brethren then so sharp contend
> On politics to wound their friend?

[168] Outerbridge Horsey to [W. H. Wells?], Georgetown, Sept. 9, 1799, Turner, *Records of Sussex*, 301–302.

[169] Barkley Townsend, *A Declaration of the Holy War: Shewing the Fiery Trial, the Commencement of the Millenium, and the Destruction of the Wicked* [n. p., c. 1801], 12, 22–23.

[170] Asbury, *Journal*, III, 188.

[171] John Fisher, Diary, Sept. 27, 1807, typed extracts in John Fisher Papers. The first Delaware camp meeting was held near Duck Creek Cross Roads in 1805. Boehm, *Reminiscences*, 128–132.

[172] *Museum of Delaware*, Sept. 5, 1807. Two years later, the Democratic candidate for state senator from New Castle County was attacked for taking in his hay on Sunday. *Delaware Gazette*, Sept. 30, 1809.

[173] Appeal dated Kent County, April, 1800, in folder, "Delaware, re Slavery, Militia, Lottery, etc.," (HSD).

[174] *Observations on Infidelity* (Wilmington, 1809).

Or hearken to what flatterers say,
Or politicians of the day.[175]

But the Democratic attempt to rally Methodists to Jefferson and his party ended in failure, as did all other Democratic efforts to win the downstate vote.

XI. An Economic Schism

ALTHOUGH the industrialization of New Castle County increased the strength of the Democratic party there, it also served to strengthen the Federalist hold on Kent and Sussex in that it encouraged a division of interest between New Castle County and the rest of the state. As the Democratic party became the party of the manufacturers in Delaware the Federalists became the agrarian party. And since the population of Sussex grew so rapidly at the beginning of the nineteenth century that it became the most populous part of the state, the Democrats found their popular support to be comparatively reduced.[176]

In looking after their own people, Federalist legislatures passed many bills favoring the agricultural classes, leading a Democratic journal to ridicule: "Among the most notable acts and transactions of a most notable assembly, at a late sitting of the notables, are the following very noted and notorious items, viz.

"An act to prevent swine from becoming pork—postponed for consideration till the falling of the next mast.

"An act to prevent large swine from creeping through small holes—postponed. . . .

[175] "An address to the Methodist Brethren of Sussex and particularly those of Broadkiln," Feb. 4, 1804, *Mirror of the Times*, Feb. 11, 1804.

[176] The population of Sussex grew from 19,358 in 1800 to 27,750 in 1810; that of New Castle decreased from 25,361 to 24,429. The population of Kent rose from 19,554 to 20,495 in the same period. *Return of the Whole Number of Persons within the Several Districts of the U.S., 1800; Aggregate Amount of Each Description of Persons within the U.S.A. and the Territories thereof in the Year 1810* (Washington, 1811), 52–53. Although the census figures should not be accepted as exact, the population trends which they exhibit generally seem to be correct.

"An act to prevent pigs from squealing—passed.

"An act for raising the bristles on the back of certain swine, in sufficient quantities to supply American brush manufacturers—passed, nemine contradicente. (This is patriotic.)

"An act to prevent the increase of musk-rats . . . and for other obnoxious purposes. . . .

"An act to prevent musk-rats from swimming against wind and tide, or either of them. . . ." [177]

In spite of its greater population, the taxes of Sussex County remained smaller than those set for New Castle.[178] Innumerable land drainage acts were passed.[179] The New Castle levy court was allowed to collect a fund for the destruction of crows.[180] The fishery in St. Jones' Creek was protected against "Certain individuels" whose methods threatened to destroy "those Sea rovers," which, according to a petition, "all wise Providence . . . Sends onst Every year . . . up the fresh watered Creaks and revelets to Propegate their Spaties." [181] The shell fisheries were restricted to Delawareans and to Marylanders, as long as the latter extended reciprocal rights.[182] When a storm in 1804 broke the embankments of many farmers' lands and ruined the crops, especially in Kent, the legislature gave relief by laying no property tax in the following year.[183]

In spite of their control of the legislature, the downstate farmers found their yields decreasing. "Ah, sir! our country does not yield the half now of what it used to do," they declared. Land exhaustion was the explanation. "Our farms are too large," declared one observer, "and our farmers too systematic in error." [184] Some improved methods were instituted, such as the importation of plaster for use as fertilizer, the growth of clover and timothy, the use of hitherto uncultivated land, and a vast increase in the number and quality of live stock.[185] These innovations, however, were largely

[177] *American Watchman*, Feb. 10, 1810.

[178] *Delaware Gazette*, Feb. 14, 1810; C. A. Rodney to Henry Clay, Dover, Jan. 17, 1816, draft, Brown Collection.

[179] E. g., *Laws*, III, 327–329.

[180] *Laws*, IV, 312.

[181] Petition in folder, "1802, January-February, Legislative, Petitions, Misc.," Legislative Papers; *Laws*, III, 273–274. This remarkable petition is printed in full in *William and Mary Quarterly*, 3rd series, VII (1950), 117–118.

[182] *Laws*, IV, 568–569.

[183] *Laws*, III, 375–376.

[184] "A Morning's Walk in the State of Delaware," *Analectic Magazine*, X, 375–376.

[185] Scharf, *History of Delaware*, I, 433. The experiments of Samuel H. Black

limited to New Castle County, where an Agricultural Association was formed in 1804 with the following declared purposes: "to rouse a spirit of rational enquiry; to fertilize the soil; to improve, increase, and preserve the produce of the earth and live stock . . . ; to favor . . . measures of economy . . . ; and . . . to record and make known such useful hints, accidental discoveries, and successful experiments in husbandry as may be deserving of public regard." [186]

In spite of agrarian control of the legislature, the farmers of Kent County threatened to leave the Federalist party in 1809 because they thought the taxes too high. Again it was proposed to dissolve the state government and join Delaware to the Eastern Shore of Maryland and Virginia as a new state "marked out by nature herself." [187] The Delaware house of representatives under the leadership of Wells and Ridgely, both Federalists, defeated this scheme, but Isaac Davis who had favored it led a group of Kent Federalists, including Sorden Lister, Israel Peterson, and Jacob Hazzard, to a juncture with the Democrats as the "Farmers' Union Ticket." Although the new opposition was unable to prevent the regular Federalists from carrying Kent, it was able to cut their majority by three hundred votes.[188]

The Democrats of New Castle County felt the Federalists neglected their county in its need for improved means of transportation and for new credit facilities. "The people are so virtuous and so religious," a newspaper correspondent wrote in 1794, "and their Representatives act with so much pastoral care, that they don't encourage the spirit of speculations, so dangerous to the morals of mankind—they don't improve the roads, and extend commerce, lest the vices, necessarily attendant upon them, should be intro-

---

are discussed in his commonplace book (Memorial Library, University of Delaware). Plaster was probably of no value at all as a fertilizer.

[186] *Mirror of the Times,* April 4, 1804. Active in this association were William Young, James Tilton, Jacob Broom, Archibald Alexander, John Bird, James Riddle, and Caleb Kirk, among others. *Cf.* Scharf, *loc. cit.* Thomas Rodney drew up a constitution for a state society which probably never functioned. Folder, "Misc. Writings," Rodney Collection.

[187] *American Watchman,* Sept. 30, 1809.

[188] *Ibid.,* Oct. 7, 1809; *Delaware Gazette,* Oct. 7, 1809. Isaac Davis declared he was motivated in leaving the Federalist party by his friendship for Haslet, the Democratic candidate for governor. See Davis's autobiography in the DSA.

duced." "But," he added, "they keep the State in debt, to her own people and others, that they may have a mutual interest in her support." [189]

In January, 1800, Federalist Governor Bassett called the legislature's attention to acts of Maryland and Pennsylvania for the construction of a canal between the Delaware and the Chesapeake.[190] Caesar A. Rodney, seconded by another New Castle County Democrat, urged support of this project as "an object of the first importance, which if attained, will, in time of peace, and more especially in time of war, promote the general welfare. Nicholas Ridgely, seconded by Manlove Emerson, both Kent Federalists, protested that such a canal would "be detrimental as well to the agricultural as to the commercial interest of this State," and would "affect the carrying trade of this State, and thereby injure the property of individuals, and diminish the wealth of the State." [191]

Among the more than a hundred petitioners for the canal were such Democratic stalwarts as David Hall, James Tilton, Nicholas Williamson, Isaac Starr, Hezekiah Niles, James Wilson, and Joseph Warner, along with many of the Brandywine millers.[192] The legislature's failure to act was the basis for Democratic attack on the administration in the election of 1800.[193]

Thomas Rodney was skeptical of the benefits from canals; "good Roads," he said, "are always better than Canals except in such a Country as Holland." In 1801 he reported that Dr. George Logan, Captain Hunn, who was C. A. Rodney's father-in-law, and "a back County Lawyer" came to Dover from Pennsylvania to lobby for a canal bill.[194] Their quest was successful, for in that same year the Chesapeake and Delaware Canal Company was incorporated

---

[189] *Delaware and Eastern Shore Advertiser*, Dec. 27, 1794.

[190] *Delaware House Journal*, 1800, 13.

[191] *Ibid.*, 27, 28. Ridgely later changed his mind and reported a canal bill for a committee consisting of himself, Rodney, and Henry Molleston, another Kent Federalist. Although accepted by the house it was not enacted into law at this session. *Ibid.*, 29, 40, 48.

[192] Folder, "1800, January-February, Legislative, Petitions, Transportation," Legislative Papers. John Stockton, Thomas I. Macomb, French MacMullan, Edward Gilpin, Isaac Hendrickson, Peter Bauduy, James Brobson, James Lea, Samuel Canby, and Joseph Bringhurst were other signers.

[193] *Mirror of the Times*, Oct. 1, 1800.

[194] T. Rodney, Diary, Jan. 27, 28, 1801, Rodney Papers (Library of Congress).

in Delaware, although on such terms, thought Rodney, as were unlikely to be satisfactory.[195]

His opinion foreshadowed the fact. In 1802 the Canal Act was amended to permit a lowering of the tolls by one-fourth to facilitate the company's formation.[196] Joseph Tatnall was elected president, with three directors from each of the three states concerned.[197] Politics may have entered into the determination of the route of the canal, for, according to the journalist, William Duane, the Federalists objected to the canal entrance being placed lower on the Delaware than the mouth of the Christina lest, by the weakness of the Democratic navy, the commerce be exposed to an enemy fleet. Duane immediately contradicted himself, however, by claiming that James Bayard and Kensey Johns, Federalists and directors, favored lower routes.[198] Altercations concerning the route annoyed Benjamin Latrobe, who was employed by the canal company as engineer and surveyor. "So much are our courageous stockholders swayed by public opinion, and local interests," he wrote, "that . . . I must . . . go over every range of ground proposed by every projector who has impudence or interest enough to make himself heard." [199] It seems likely that many downstate Federalists would have been of the same mind as "A Friend of the Lower Route," who argued that because land north of the canal would rise in value the canal should be put as far south as possible so that more landholders would benefit from it.[200]

The Christina River route was at last decided upon, and work

---

[195] *Ibid.*, Jan. 29, 1801; *Laws*, III, 170–188.

[196] *Laws*, III, 246–249; *Governor's Register*, 41. Caesar A. Rodney apparently had urged passage of a toll reduction act, for John Fisher wrote him: "Your Canal Law I got with much difficulty through the House . . . on account of the opposition to it in part, and in part on account of the hand-writing. . . . The Senate amended the Bill by prohibiting the Tolls being lowered more than a fourth, in which form it passed our house or it would have been totally lost." Dover, Feb. 12, 1802, John Fisher Papers. The amendment also concerned reciprocal favors Delaware had asked of Pennsylvania.

[197] Kensey Johns and James A. Bayard, New Castle County Federalists, were the other Delaware directors. It is difficult to determine Tatnall's politics. He was elected in 1798 to the lower house of the General Assembly from New Castle County, but that county's delegation was then divided and Tatnall never took his seat. *Delaware House Journal*, 1799, 4; *Mirror of the Times*, Feb. 1, 1804.

[198] *Mirror of the Times*, Feb. 1, 1804.

[199] Latrobe to John Lenthall, New Castle, Nov. 1, 1803, typescript in Historical Society of Delaware from Latrobe Papers, Library of Congress.

[200] *Mirror of the Times*, Feb. 15, 1804.

on a feeder canal begun, but insufficient funds prevented the Delaware and Chesapeake from being joined at this time, although Bayard urged the federal government to support the undertaking by granting lands in return for stock.[201] The interest of Bayard and of Kensey Johns demonstrates that the canal was not a partisan venture. The Delaware interest in it was, however, sectional; New Castle County saw many benefits to arise from the canal, but Kent and Sussex were apathetic. Since Kent and Sussex Federalists controlled the legislature, the Democrats, dominant in New Castle, were emboldened to charge their opponents with a lukewarm attitude. In seeking a revision of the Canal Act, the company showed its realization of the need to awaken downstate interest by arguing that the canal was necessary to the "preservation of the Commerce of Philadelphia on which depends the prosperity of all the Villages Towns and landing Places within the State of Delaware.[202]

Just as the General Assembly finally, in 1811, gave way to the requests of the canal company for a change in its charter of incorporation, so it generally accommodated the requests of New Castle County for legislation favorable to other internal improvements.[203] The increasing prosperity of Wilmington provided both surplus capital for investment in public improvements and at the same time a need for them.[204] The Brandywine Bridge Company was incorporated in 1806 and the Wilmington Bridge Company in 1807.[205] Successful in securing the bridge laws that they desired, the citizens of Wilmington were urged by "P," a *Museum* cor-

[201] *Museum of Delaware*, Feb. 7, 14, 21, 1807; *Delaware Gazette*, March 27, 1810; G. Read to C. A. Rodney, New Castle, Feb. 17, 1807, Rodney Collection. William Cooch, a New Castle County Democrat, had succeeded Bayard as a director by 1804. *Mirror of the Times*, June 6, 1804.

[202] Petition in folder, "1805, January, Legislative, Petitions, Transportation," Legislative Papers.

[203] *Laws*, IV, 348–349. See petition of Jan. 5, 1811, Legislative Papers. The law referred to repealed the clause in the Canal Act giving to the state all profits of the canal company over ten percent. The new law declared that whenever the profits reached fifteen percent, the tolls should be lowered so that the profits would not be greater than twelve percent, thus repealing the previous restrictions on lowering the toll rates.

[204] Ferris, *Original Settlements*, 241.

[205] *Laws*, IV, 12–23, 59–74, 158–160. Thomas Lea, William Poole, Joshua Wollaston, Moses Rea, and James Canby took subscriptions to the first company; William Collins, William Hemphill, John Warner, James Lea, and Jacob Broom, to the second. The interest of the Brandywine millers is obvious.

respondent, to back the erection of a turnpike to Lancaster in order to revive "the decaying state of" the export trade and "to reanimate . . . drooping commerce." [206] This they did, and as a consequence the Gap and Newport Turnpike Company and the Wilmington Turnpike Company were incorporated in 1808.[207]

New Castle interests sought to bring their town abreast of its larger neighbor insofar as public improvements would do so. They secured the incorporation of the New-Castle and Frenchtown Turnpike Company in 1809 and of the New-Castle Turnpike Company in 1811.[208] The incorporation in 1813 of the Newport Bridge Company gave New Castle hope that its port and market could soon be easily available to Lancaster County farmers.[209] Turnpikes became the rage; others incorporated were the Wilmington and Kennet Turnpike Company (1811), the Wilmington and Great Valley Turnpike Company (1811), the Wilmington and Philadelphia Turnpike Company (1813), the New-Castle and White-Clay-Creek Hundred Turnpike Company (1813), the Elk and Christiana Turnpike Company (1813), and the Wilmington and Christiana Turnpike Company (1815).[210]

Every one of these bridge and turnpike bills was for the benefit, primarily, of New Castle County. They were regarded as Democratic bills,[211] yet each bill was passed only through the sufferance of the downstate Federalists. At the time of this legislation, the New Castle County delegates to the General Assembly were almost all Democrats, the Kent and Sussex delegates all Federalists. This fact demonstrates the political wisdom of the Federalist party in Delaware, in that it avoided using its power to cripple the one area opposing its dominance. By so doing it kept alive a Federalist group in New Castle, who, if unable to carry the county, could

[206] *Museum of Delaware,* Feb. 7, 1807.

[207] *Laws,* IV, 176–195, 196–214. One company was to construct a road from Newport to meet the Philadelphia-Lancaster turnpike; the other was to build a road from Wilmington to Newport.

[208] *Laws,* IV, 241–258, 410–422.

[209] *Laws,* IV, 650–662. George Read, Kensey Johns, and John Crow, all of New Castle, were three of the five commissioners named in this act.

[210] *Laws,* IV, 352–370, 372–390, 492–493, 616–627, 627–645; V, 3–4, 5–8, 72–89.

[211] The Democratic delegates have been very effective, said the *Watchman,* Oct. 21, 1809, for "a road law, a bridge law, and a bank law have been carried" although only one-third of the legislature is Democrat.

limit the size of the Democrat majority there and thus aid the Federalists in winning state-wide elections for governor and Representative.

This strategy was extremely important in the maintenance of Federalist control. The Democrats were employing a variant of it by nominating either David Hall or Joseph Haslet from Sussex County for one of the important political positions at almost every state election in the hope that their candidacy would reduce the normally large Federal plurality downstate. In turn, the Federalists chose candidates from New Castle, such as James Bayard, Nicholas Van Dyke, Louis McLane, and James M. Broom, for responsible positions and carefully nursed their supporting minority in New Castle. By accepting canal bills, turnpike bills, and bridge bills, the Federalists avoided antagonizing the bulk of the upstate mercantile and industrial group, and at times they sought to win even the immigrant Irish to their cause, assuring them that in Kent and Sussex "there is no distinction in society. . . . There is nothing of the Virginia character among the people." [212]

The passage of acts to encourage manufacturing, to protect merino sheep, and to inspect exports of flour and corn meal were of a similar wise reasonableness.[213] The bank incorporation laws which the legislature was enacting in this period were less sectional in nature than most of the other corporation bills. To be sure, La Rochefoucault had reported that there was "no apparent necessity," for the Bank of Delaware "except to the Brandywine millers," but eventually a bank fever swept the state.[214] The Farmers Bank of the State of Delaware, in which the state was to have one-fifth of the shares, was incorporated in 1807, after petitions had been received from men of both parties and all counties, for example, Andrew Barratt and John Stockton, Federalists, and Archibald Alexander, John Collins, and Thomas Duff, Democrats. Its main

---

[212] *Delaware Statesman*, Sept. 28, 1811. Provision was also made for a Dover Canal Company and for a canal to connect Lewes Creek and Rehoboth Bay. *Laws*, III, 266–272; IV, 499–511.

[213] *Laws*, III, 358–361; IV, 172, 397–400, 469–471. The close connection that existed between the flour milling and coopering industries of the Wilmington area and grain farming and lumbering in Kent and Sussex respectively of course encouraged in the latter counties a sympathy for the problems faced by at least some of the manufacturers.

[214] La Rochefoucault, *Travels*, III, 523–524.

office was to be in Dover, with branches in Georgetown and New Castle, the other county seats.[215] Henry M. Ridgely, a Kent Federalist, was its president for its first forty years.

In 1810 Wilmington capital organized the Bank of Wilmington and Brandywine; "no sooner were the subscription books opened at the Town-Hall . . . than the people tumbled in helter skelter, head over heels like potatoes out of a half bushel, to pay the money to get their names entered on the list." [216] "Whether a Charter will be granted for the institution," wrote Nicholas Williamson, who was beginning to be recognized as Democratic leader in the county,[217] "is a matter which I fear but few amongst us have sufficiently thought of—on this subject however with the Legislature, I fear there will be insuperable difficulties." [218] There were. From Dover came a protest that a national bank was about to be established in which Delaware could participate, that a branch of the Farmers Bank could be put in Wilmington if another bank was needed there, and that the merchants and millers now had enough capital for their needs [219]—which objections, in view of the rapid subscription, seem to have partaken of an agrarian prejudice against urban capitalism. The new bank, however, did not let the lack of a charter prevent it from operating.[220] After five months the stock had risen 20 percent, and a third Wilmington bank was being planned.[221]

At its next session the General Assembly forbade individuals thereafter to associate themselves to perform banking functions without a charter, but immediately protests arose that Smyrna and Milford, which had no chartered banks, were being treated un-

[215] Petitions in folder, "1807 January, Legislative, Petitions, Misc.," Legislative Papers; *Laws*, IV, 87–103. This bank was permitted to sell insurance in 1810. *Laws*, IV, 325–327. A Wilmington branch was authorized in 1813. *Laws*, IV, 594–595.

[216] *American Watchman*, April 4, 1810. See also issues of March 3, 14, 17, 31, April 7, 1810.

[217] "I now consider N. Williamson at the head of the state politics in the County of NCastle." Nehemiah Tilton to C. A. Rodney, Washington, Mississippi, June 17, 1811, Rodney Collection.

[218] N. G. Williamson to C. A. Rodney, Wilmington, March 21, 1810, *ibid.*

[219] *American Watchman*, March 31, 1810. Cf. *ibid.*, March 7, April 4, 21, 1810.

[220] *Ibid.*, June 23, 1810. William Poole had been elected its president. At least one of the directors, John Way, was a Democrat. *Delaware Gazette*, April 18, 1810.

[221] The Bank of Delaware was paying 12 percent dividends. *American Watchman*, Nov. 21, 1810.

fairly.[222] Other petitions were soon circulating for banks at Lewes and Laurel. An anti-bank correspondent from Milford protested that if these were granted Delaware would have nine banks for a population, not counting women, children, and Negroes, of only five thousand, of whom but less than one-fifth would become borrowers. James Bayard was warning a Federalist candidate for the state senate: "The Banks will give you some trouble. I care about none of them, but the old Mother Bank of the State. I always thought she had every claim to a continuance of her charter." [223]

The Federalist legislature proved again, however, to be sympathetic to the desires of commerce and capital, despite an obvious reluctance among many members of the party. The high dividends paid by the banks probably made the monied men of all parties desire opportunity to share in such an investment as banks seemed to offer.[224] The charter of the "Mother Bank," the Bank of Delaware, in which such prominent Federalists as Bayard, Outerbridge Horsey, James M. Broom, William Young, and Louis McLane held stock, was extended for ten years in 1812.[225] In the same year three other banks were chartered: the Bank of Wilmington and Brandywine; the Accommodation Bank of Delaware, the name of which was soon changed to Farmers' and Mechanics' Bank, at Laurel; and the Commercial Bank of Delaware, at Smyrna and Milford.[226]

[222] Federalists such as James Clayton and Peter Robinson, Jr., were among the petitioners. Folder, "1811, January, Legislature, Petitions, Misc.," Legislative Papers. *Laws*, IV, 473–475.

[223] *Delaware Statesman*, Jan. 8, 1812; Bayard to William Hill Wells, Washington, Jan. 12, 1812, Donnan, "Bayard Papers," 188.

[224] *Delaware Statesman*, Jan. 8, 1812. James A. Bayard warned Caesar A. Rodney to be wary about investing in the new banks; the money market of Philadelphia was already saturated by Jersey bank stock, and without Philadephia aid the stock of the new Delaware banks would not be subscribed. Bayard to Rodney, Washington, Feb. 27, 1812, Hilles Collection.

[225] *Laws*, IV, 524–527; stockholders' petition, folder, "1811, January, Legislative, Petitions, Misc.," Legislative Papers.

[226] *Laws*, IV, 528–534, 536–547, 548–561. Isaac Davis, a Democrat convert from Federalism, was a manager of subscriptions for the Commercial Bank. John Collins and Manaen Bull, Democrats, and Jesse Green and William B. Cooper, Federalists, were among the managers for the Laurel bank. The Democratic governor, Joseph Haslet, was elected a director of the Milford bank. *Delaware Statesman*, May 9, 1812.

XII. The Aid of Circumstance

THE Federalists of Delaware, their strength based solidly on their popularity among the agrarian element and bulwarked by a wise coalition with some influential minority leaders in New Castle, found events of the early nineteenth century playing into their hands, even as their party, on a national scale, was gradually disappearing.

The rivalry in New Castle County between New Castle, the ancient county seat, and Wilmington, the new industrial-commercial center, caused a schism in the ranks of the dominant county party, the Democratic-Republicans, which aided the Federalists. In 1801 the people of Wilmington began petitioning the legislature to incorporate a company to erect "a substantial Draw-Bridge" across the Christina. Such a bridge, they claimed, would facilitate trade between the downstate areas and Wilmington, render access to the courts at New Castle easier than by the ferry, which could not be used at some seasons, and encourage the use of the marshy meadows below the Christina for raising crops, which development would also improve the health of Wilmington.[227]

Opposition arose immediately. Merchants of Newport, Stanton, and Christiana Bridge saw a threat to their business. One of them protested that the port of Philadelphia received one-third of its flour, about 140,000 barrels annually, besides scantling, iron, flaxseed, and other commodities, from the upper Christina. "It is the highway," he declared, "for a large Proportion of the produce of Lancaster Chester & York Counties in Pennsylvania, ⅗ths of Cecil & Harford Counties in Maryland & a large Portion of New Castle County. Wilmington in concert with New Jersey, might with equal Propriety stop the Navigation of the Delaware so as to prohibit all produce & Shipping from Passing higher up than their Borough for their exclusive Benefit." [228]

[227] Petitions in folder, "1801, January-February, Legislative, Petitions, Transportation," Legislative Papers.
[228] Levi Hollingsworth to C. A. Rodney, Philadelphia, Jan. 17, 1801; same to same, Philadelphia, Jan. 23, 1802, Brown Collection.

Supporters of the Wilmington bridge declared that the people of New Castle were encouraging opposition to it purely out of jealousy of Wilmington. At the Red Lion Democratic mass meeting in 1801, "New Castle poured forth more votes than has perhaps attended all the meetings of republicans held at the Red Lion in the aggregate," with the object of making John Bird, an enemy of the bridge, state senator, and of depriving Christiana Hundred, which included Wilmington and had a quarter of the county's population, of its customary two seats in the lower house. They succeeded, but Wilmington had supported the ticket in order not to imperil David Hall's chance of becoming governor. New Castle was still conspiring against Wilmington in 1802, argued a group of Wilmingtonians—James Lea, James Brobson, John Warner, William Warner, John Way, Joseph Hoopes, and Hezekiah Niles—so the issue should be decided openly in the General Assembly. "If we loose it, we shall as good Democrats submit; but like as in our opposition to federalism itself we shall pursue it even when there is little or no probability of success." [229]

Wilmington continued to flood the General Assembly with petitions for the bridge. In 1803 the lower house passed a bridge bill, but the senate, receiving it near the end of the session, postponed action.[230] The question continued to be agitated for three years, to the detriment of Democratic unity. In 1806 John Fisher reported that the bridge issue had "brought down all Newcastle county to Dover," and was "like to do away all other distinctions." "I see men," he wrote to his brother-in-law, Rodney, " 'pigging together in the same truckle-bed,' who have been heretofore at dagger's draw. . . . J. Warner & G. Read have had a quarrel—John Way & George Truitt ditto—The feds laugh at all this." This year the bill did pass the senate, but was held up in the house, which appointed

[229] Lea, Brobson, *et al.* to C. A. Rodney, Wilmington, Jan. 26, 1802, Rodney Collection. This letter proves that James Lea, a member of the distinguished Quaker milling family, considered himself a Democrat. He later became first president of the Wilmington Bridge Company. The letter also indicates that the Democratic-Republican party was the urban, bourgeois party in Delaware. In another letter, Lea, Niles, and John Warner declared that the New Castle merchants had persuaded Secretary of the Treasury Gallatin to believe "that *sink of iniquity* to have much more trade than this borough." To C. A. Rodney, Wilmington, July 9, 1802, *ibid.*

[230] Petitions in folder, "1806, January, Legislative, Petitions, Transportation," Legislative Papers. See also petitions of 1802 and 1803 and counter-petitions of 1806 against the bill.

a committee to report at the next session on the proper site for the bridge.[231]

In the election of 1806 "the old Parties" in New Castle County were "swallowed up in the new divisions" over the bridge. Broom, Federalist candidate for Representative, "was not opposed and *we* of Wiln. supported Warners Bridge ticket," Bayard declared. "We beat the Anti-Bridgemen 200 votes—more or less." [232]

At the next session of the house, it heard a report from its committee on the bridge—Thomas Clayton, Thomas Cooper, William Warner, and William Hughlett. These men reported the best site to be the south end of Market Street. They found a large trade with Philadelphia from the upper Christina "in flour, wheat, iron, plaister of Paris, etc." The existing ferry brought the county much revenue, but passage by it was often dangerous. A drawbridge would not ordinarily hinder navigation, but at some seasons—for example, the breaking up of ice—it would. On the main question, the committee hedged, declaring it did not attempt to judge whether the usefulness of a bridge would counterbalance its disadvantages. Thus the downstate Federalist members avoided taking sides in a New Castle County dispute.[233]

The success of the Bridge party in the election of 1806 had, however, decided the matter. Supported by the knowledge that such influential New Castle County Federalists as James Bayard and Jacob Broom favored the bill, the Kent and Sussex legislators "behaved well" and permitted the "Bridgemen" of New Castle County to enact their bill.[234]

Soon after the Wilmington Bridge Company was incorporated, the antagonism between Wilmington and New Castle broke forth again, to the advantage of the Federalists, over another issue in which the downstate delegates had little interest. New Castle pro-

[231] Fisher to C. A. Rodney, Dover, Jan. 25, 1806, John Fisher Papers; *Museum of Delaware*, Jan. 17, 1807.

[232] J. A. Bayard to C. A. Rodney, Wilmington, Oct. 2, 1806; same to same, Oct. 9, 1806, Hilles Collection.

[233] *Museum of Delaware*, Jan. 17, 1807.

[234] A New Castle County legislator wrote that the downstaters had been told a majority of the people in New Castle opposed the bridge, and therefore they had voted for postponement in order to get correct information. "The late election has put that in their power, and they have, honorably, acted accordingly." *Ibid.*, Jan. 24, 1807. See *Laws*, IV, 59–74, 158–160. Accounts of the bridge movement appear in Montgomery, *Reminiscences*, 272–273, and Ferris, *Original Settlements*, 240–241.

posed to compete with Wilmington for the trade with the back country of Pennsylvania by bridging the Christina at Newport, where a ferry already met a road to New Castle.

Wilmington immediately opposed the project. The ferry at Newport, Wilmingtonians claimed, was well conducted but little used. A Newport bridge was "calculated only to militate against" the interests of the Wilmington Bridge Company and "advance the interests of a few marsh and land-holders" of Newport and New Castle. It would present an "insuperable barrier" to navigation of the Christina, which was only ninety feet wide at Newport, whereas at Wilmington the river was six hundred feet wide and yet navigation had been somewhat impeded.[235]

Christiana Village merchants also took alarm at this second threat to their trade. George Massey paid a messenger five dollars to ride through the night and inform them that a bipartisan group of New Castle men were lobbying for the bridge in Dover, some staying at the Democrat inn and others at the "Federal House" "doing everything to influence the members." To oppose them, more signatures were gathered against the bill and depositions of shallopmen were introduced testifying to the hindrance which the Wilmington bridge already offered to Christina River trade, as well as the importance of that trade.[236] This opposition was successful in securing defeat of the bridge bill in 1810, but New Castle eventually won, the Newport Bridge Company being incorporated in 1813.[237]

Still another local quarrel occurred to disturb the Democrats of New Castle County, when a movement arose in 1809 to move the courts from New Castle to a more central location, such as Chris-

---

[235] Federalists like Jacob Broom and John McKinly joined Democrats such as Joseph England and James Wilson in this petition, which had 322 signers. Folder, "1808, January, Legislative, Petitions, Transportation," Legislative Papers. Petitions of 1809 in favor of the Newport bridge had 235 signers, including James Booth and John Stockton, Federalists, and George Read, Senior and Junior, Archibald Alexander, and James Riddle, Democrats.

[236] Massey to Jeremiah Lewden, David Nivin, Sylvester Welsh, or James Price [Dover], Jan. 22 [1810], Lewden Family Papers (HSD); depositions of Daniel Smith and Daniel Holmes, copies, Legal Documents (HSD). For other statements of opposition see the American Watchman, Aug. 26, Oct. 16, 1809; Delaware Gazette, Jan. 13, 1810; petition of Jeremiah Lewden, Dover, Jan. 29, 1811, Legislative Papers.

[237] Delaware Gazette, Jan. 31, 1810; Laws, IV, 650–662.

tiana Bridge, Red Lion, Stanton, or the Bear.[238] The Democratic mass meeting at the Red Lion in June, 1809, appointed a committee, of which John Way of Wilmington was chairman, and Jeremiah Lewden of Christiana secretary, to draft a petition to the legislature for this purpose. William Cooch, Andrew Reynolds, and Enoch Thomas prepared the petition, which declared as reasons for moving the courts that (1) New Castle was remote from the population and geographical center of the county and difficult of access, and that (2) "in the present piratical state of the world" New Castle's exposed position made the court records unsafe there. It was further observed that most of the counties in adjoining states, as well as the county of Sussex, had recently moved their courts.[239] In rebuttal, it was pointed out that there was no adequate building to house the courts outside of New Castle except in Wilmington, where the Town Hall was rumored to have been planned secretly for this purpose. Wilmington, however, was not a more central location than New Castle.[240]

This plan, which was soon dropped, might well have been merely a political counterattack on New Castle intended to prevent obstruction of the Christina by the Newport bridge. Its chief motivation came not from Wilmington, although Way was active in the movement, but from the Christina valley above Newport. A correspondent signing himself "Cid Hamet Benengeli" declared that the real leaders were Hall, a Federalist, and George Massey, an active opponent of the Newport Bridge.[241] Before the adoption of district elections in 1811, the location of the one county polling place was of obvious political importance.

All this Democratic dissension was valued by the Federalists. "Marcus" declared in the Democrat journal, the *Watchman*,[242] that it had cost the Democrats the loss of a state election. Another correspondent warned that as New Castle County was "undoubtedly the stronghold of democracy in Delaware," the Democrats of

[238] *Delaware Gazette*, July 22, 1809.
[239] *American Watchman*, Sept. 2, 1809; undated petitions in folder, "1810, January, Legislative, Petitions, Misc.," Legislative Papers. See also *American Watchman*, Aug. 16, 1809.
[240] *Delaware Gazette*, July 29, 1809.
[241] *American Watchman*, Aug. 5, 1809.
[242] Aug. 2, 1809. Cf. *Delaware Gazette*, July 29, 1809.

the county must avoid quarrels; they could learn the value of unity and discipline from the Federalists.[243]

Not only local events, but also the progress of international affairs brought aid to the Federalists of Delaware. At the beginning of the century, the Louisiana Purchase had quite an opposite effect. Although Senators White and Wells opposed it, E. I. du Pont declared that "it had a great effect on public opinion and gave Jefferson the position that his talents and his patriotism deserve." "The Federals," he added, "are ashamed of their blustering of last year and are obliged to admit that Jefferson's methods are better, safer, and cheaper than would have been a war with France and Spain." [244] A *Mirror* correspondent called the attention of Christians, especially Quakers and Methodists, to the fact that this was a "peaceful annexation." [245]

The *Leopard-Chesapeake* affair of 1807 also stirred up anti-British sentiment in Delaware, and such sentiment was always of value to the Democrats. A public meeting of protest against this British attack on an American vessel was held in Wilmington. Even James Bayard declared "we must go to war" unless substantial reparations were given. "To be an American," he wrote Rodney, "and not to feel upon the occasion would be impossible." [246] Both parties joined in a protest meeting at Georgetown.[247]

As this crisis passed by peacefully, native prejudices and opinions began to assert themselves and conservative, moderate Delaware abandoned its momentary support of national policies. Wilmington Democrats staged a great town meeting, preceded by a parade, to encourage support of the embargo. A letter of encouragement was sent to the President, but the true state of opinion was indicated by the fact that it was considered necessary to deprecate a petition being circulated against the embargo.[248]

The Federalists of New Castle County had already declared it

[243] *Delaware Gazette,* July 22, 1809.
[244] To P. S. du Pont de Nemours, July 16, 1803, Du Pont, *Life of E. I. du Pont,* VI, 250–251.
[245] *Mirror of the Times,* May 5, 1804. A celebration of the event was held in Mill Creek Hundred. *Ibid.,* May 23, 1804.
[246] Bayard to Rodney, Wilmington, July 24, 1807, Hilles Collection.
[247] *Museum of Delaware,* Aug. 1, 1807. David Hall, Democrat, presided, and Peter Robinson, Federalist, was secretary.
[248] *Ibid.,* Feb. 4, 1809.

"a measure impolitic, totally inadequate to the objects for which it was *said* to be intended, highly oppressive and ruinous to the Citizens of the United States, and to their national prosperity"—a feeling they would hardly have expressed openly had they not felt it would find a sympathetic reception even in the most anti-British county of Delaware.[249] In Kent, John Fisher, a Democrat, testified to the unpopularity of the embargo by noting, in 1808, that the Democrats had a strong ticket there which "might be carried except for the embargo." [250]

As the war fever mounted, the Democrats temporarily gained strength. At a July Fourth celebration in Wilmington in 1810 they toasted "Connecticut and Delaware—Again sole companions in affliction, and the only props of federalism," and the chairman invoked the prevailing expansionist spirit by offering a volunteer toast: "The introduction of Canada, Nova Scotia, and the Floridas into the Union, and the right hand of fellowship to S. America." [251] Such feeling helped Haslet win the governorship in that year, but when war became an actuality the popularity of the Democrats declined.

In the Senate Bayard had cynically observed the activities of the War Hawks. "We are going on in a strange temper," he told Rodney, "all talking about war which no one seems to expect." [252] A month later he wrote: "A great many gentlemen express themselves anxious for war, but they don't know how to get at it. . . . There was no sensation while the question was about raising men, but the taxes are the rub with your popularity-men." [253] Just before the war declaration, he notified Rodney: "You have thought the thing all along a jest and I have no doubt in the commencement it was so but jests sometimes become serious and end in earnest." [254]

[249] Resolutions adopted at Federal Republican meeting, Christiana Bridge, Sept. 17, 1808, Collection of Broadsides on Various Subjects relating to Delaware (Wilmington Institute Free Library).

[250] John Fisher to Nehemiah Tilton, Dover, Sept. 12, 1808, Brown Collection.

[251] *American Watchman*, July 7, 1810.

[252] Bayard to Rodney, Washington, Dec. 22, 1811, Hilles Collection. Rodney had recently resigned the attorney-generalship and returned to private practice, because he felt insulted when President Madison passed over him in filling a vacancy in the Supreme Court. C. A. Rodney to Albert Gallatin, Wilmington, Nov. 25, 1811, Brown Collection.

[253] Bayard to Rodney, Washington, Jan. 26, 1812, Hilles Collection.

[254] Bayard to Rodney, Senate Chamber, June 11, 1812, *ibid.*

Bayard sought at first to prevent war and, when that hope was gone, to postpone its outbreak till the fall of 1812 so that the nation might better prepare itself. But when war was finally declared, he loyally supported all defense measures, advising Rodney, "as we are now at war we must defend ourselves, and I think you had better bestir yourself in organizing a military force." [255]

Bayard's attitude probably represented the feeling of a majority of his constituents, for throughout the war members of his party were annually returned to all elective positions, except in New Castle County. The dangerous, exposed position of Delaware, and the dependence of its farmers and traders upon the war-depressed Philadelphia market were probably responsible for this attitude.

The British blockaded the entrance to Delaware Bay, preyed upon the shallop trade of Kent and Sussex County, and occasionally sent armed bands ashore for supplies.[256] The entire state of Delaware lay so close to the water that it could be raided almost at will by a naval power. Commodore Beresford, commanding the British squadron at the Delaware capes, demanded twenty live bullocks and a proportionate quantity of vegetables and hay from the town of Lewes, which he threatened to destroy if his request was refused. Since no supplies were given him, Beresford began the promised bombardment on April 6, 1813, and continued it on the next day, but although some of the houses were damaged, no lives were lost.[257]

This bombardment and the continued presence of British ships, along with British raids on the Chesapeake shores which threatened Delaware with invasion from the west, further discountenanced to the Delawareans the national government's conduct of the war. In January, 1814, Daniel Rodney, of Lewes, a Federalist, succeeded Haslet as governor. Rodney, who had witnessed the Lewes bom-

---

[255] Bayard to Rodney, Senate Chamber, June 20, 1812, *ibid.*

[256] Daniel Rodney, "Diary," Turner, *Rodney's Diary and Other Delaware Records*, 4, 27. Enemy barges, *Niles' Register* reported on June 5, 1813, "have lately been as high up as Duck Creek; near which they burnt some small vessels." Vol. IV, 228.

[257] *Ibid.*, 5, 7–8; "A Brief Sketch of the Military Operations on the Delaware during the War of 1812," C. L. Reese, Jr., ed., *Delaware History*, III (1948), 80–82. The defense was directed by Colonel Samuel Davis, a native of Lewes. See also *Niles' Register*, March 27, 1813, Vol. IV, 69, for a copy of Beresford's letter. There is a discrepancy in the number of animals demanded.

bardment, almost immediately appealed to the federal authorities for the use of a gunboat flotilla to protect river and bay trade and for troops to defend the coast, "Exposed and defenseless," he declared, "every point of which from the Ocean to New Castle . . . is assailable by the Maritime forces of the enemy, by which the last season from the 14 March till the 28th Novr we were very much harassed." [258]

As the war continued, the Delaware Federalists avoided the pitfalls that lured their New England brethren to destruction. Governor Rodney, in his address to the legislature in January, 1815, lamented the growing spirit of sectionalism manifested by the Hartford Convention.[259] Consequently, when peace was shortly proclaimed, the local Federalist party was free of the stigma of treason which helped to destroy its national organization. Indeed, through the fact that Bayard had been a leading member of the American commission at Ghent, it could even claim a share in the popularity of the peace, just as it also rejoiced at the exploits of the navy, "the Herculean child of Federal policy," and of such native heroes of its service as Jacob Jones, commander of the *Wasp,* and Thomas Macdonough, the victor of Lake Champlain.[260]

Thus the Peace of Ghent found the Federalist party triumphant. In the elections of the fall of 1815, they again swept all state and all Kent and Sussex offices. Even Democratic New Castle was invaded by the Federalist tide, which carried its candidate, Nicholas Van Dyke, into the state senate.[261] By rooting itself in the dominant agrarian culture of Delaware, by following a policy of moderation which suited the prevalent conservatism, by wisely restraining its overly zealous partisans, by yielding on a bank bill, a canal bill, a road bill to encourage its minority following in New Castle, by shrewd leadership which correctly gauged and represented the Delaware climate of opinion, Federalism had not only entrenched itself in Delaware's past history, but was prepared to direct the state's destinies for another decade and more.

[258] Turner, *Rodney's Diary,* 20–21.
[259] *Delaware Gazette,* Jan. 10, 1815.
[260] *Ibid.,* Feb. 28, 1815.
[261] *Ibid.,* Oct. 12, 1815.

"In Medio Tutissimus"

IN the process of developing from a colony to a state, the three counties on the Delaware had changed very little. Their patterns for the most part had already been set. Their bounds had been filled out; the lands largely taken up. The limited area hardly permitted any physical or encouraged any philosophical expansion. The lack of western lands, of great undeveloped natural resources, and of good harbors opening a vista of a world beyond, discouraged the people from entertaining any very positive belief in a theory of progress and from considering the changes and undertaking the reforms necessary to the introduction of a new order.

La Rochefoucault was shocked to find William Hill Wells boasting of an income of $5,400 a year from his twenty thousand acres of Sussex County woodland, half in cedars. "I demonstrated to him," wrote the Frenchman, "that allowing all this profit to arise entirely from the ten thousand acres of cedars, even in that case, each acre is worth only half a dollar a year. . . . He was struck with the calculation, which he could not contradict; but as his neighbours do not draw so much wealth from their woods as he does from his, he is satisfied with that difference." [1]

The most striking development in the cultural life of Kent and Sussex in this period was the rapid spread of Methodism. Asbury found his work welcomed by the men of the Delaware backwoods. For a time Methodism gave promise of occasioning many changes in the state. It emphasized plain living and good conduct; it gave hope and fervor to life; it condemned drunkenness and slaveholding. But as Methodism gradually gained the respectability that came with widespread acceptance, its evangelistic ardor was stilled, its cries for social reform became less shrill. It brought spiritual joy and solace to its congregations; it raised them to a level beyond the drab monotony of animal existence, but it urged them to contentment with their lot in this life in the expectation, a great con-

[1] La Rochefoucault, *Travels,* III, 522–523.

tribution to the individual, of a better life in the world to come. Methodism thus reformed the man but not the system.

New Castle County was the Rhode Island of Delaware—the county that was otherwise. Its people were of more heterogeneous backgrounds and cultures than were those of Kent and Sussex. Delaware was agricultural, except New Castle; Delaware had no cities, except in New Castle; Delaware welcomed Methodism, except in New Castle; Delaware was conservative, except New Castle; Delaware had no ports, except in New Castle; Delawareans were of English stock, except in New Castle. To almost any statement that could be made of Delaware, New Castle was thus the exception.

The continuing migration of non-Englishmen to New Castle County produced a culture there which shocked the other regions. Its resources of water power encouraged du Ponts and Bauduys, Gilpins and Leas, Shipleys and Kirks to believe in an improving universe, in an age of progress, in a pre-Darwinian kind of evolution. They wished to better the materials they found in the world; a stand-pat attitude was alien to them; they were not to be satisfied with fifty cents an acre.

As their water power offered the people of New Castle County an opportunity for the development of a milling industry, so they hoped to increase the value of their lands from their fortunate situation between sources of raw materials and consuming centers. Their harbors at Wilmington and New Castle, especially, put in their grasp the resources of the American seaboard, of the West Indies, of Newfoundland and Nova Scotia, of Europe, the Atlantic islands and Asia. With the commodities that they imported came ideas, new modes of thought challenging the old patterns. Roads and rivers furnished outlets for their goods, their capital, their imaginations. Their world was an expanding one, moving out from the locality in the wake of geographical discovery and economic enterprise.

Consequently a schism developed in Delaware, a division between the expanding world of the Christina and the Brandywine and the conservative rural life of Kent and Sussex. On occasion the times united them, as when the Constitution offered protection to the future hopes of the New Castle merchant and miller and security to the established modes of the downstate farmers.

The spirit of the Revolution, borne home by the soldiers who fought in New York and the Carolinas, supported by the Philadelphia connections common to the artisans and the landholders alike and by the moderate social upheaval which temporarily dissevered loyalist gentry from politics, brought a democratization of government that was expressed in taxpayer voting and in popular election of the governor and the levy court commissioners.

The growing schism between New Castle and the southern counties and the political parties which arose from it set up a rivalry which encouraged some further progress. Polling places were opened in the hundreds and a voice in party nominations was granted to the people. But movements for reform of the penal system and the criminal code, for public schools, and for abolition were waning as this period closed.

The three most significant changes occurring in Delaware from the beginning of the first war with Britain to the end of the second were (1) the rise of Methodism, (2) the growth of the Brandywine manufactories, and (3) the development of self-government. The first two accentuated the differences, colonial, indeed geographical, in origin, between the north and the south of Delaware. The third permitted the agrarians to retain control of the state government against an opposition which aroused the dominant group to a display of political ingenuity and even of wisdom but which was unable, by the democratic principles it acclaimed, to carry the day.

A conservative, moderate policy prevailed in Delaware politics not against the wishes of the people but by the demand of the people. The conservative particularism of Delaware caused it to sever its connections with Britain when it suspected the Crown of changing its attitude toward the relations between them. The same conservatism drew it to quick acceptance of a Constitution which promised protection for the established order against the anarchy and chaos, the upheaval that threatened. The same conservatism led Delaware to support Washington and Hamilton, to oppose the program of Jefferson and his combination of frontiersmen and Jacobins.

The Delaware of 1815 clearly foreshadowed the Delaware of

the next century. Whenever abrupt changes were proposed in the established order, Delaware, dominated by her two contained, agrarian seaboard counties, would be found on the conservative side. So this little state clung more loyally to Federalism than any capitalist mercantile stronghold. When Jacksonian democracy ushered in the reform era of the 1830s, Delaware became a stronghold of Whiggism. When, in the 1850s, the Democrats became the champions of the established order as the Whig ship split on the rocks of abolitionism, prohibitionism, and nativism, Delaware swung to the Democrat column and after the war sent a Bayard to lead the fight for the established principles against the parvenus and the profiteers and the profligate dispensers of American resources. Finally, when Democracy found a spokesman on the Platte for a popular rebellion, Delaware stood back, resurveyed the scene, and threw its strength to what seemed now the Grand Old Party.

"In medio tutissimus," wrote a despondent Clayton. With him Delaware sang: "Moderacy is safest."

Appendix

Presidents of the Delaware State

John McKinly, 1777
° Thomas McKean, 1777
° George Read, 1777–1778
Caesar Rodney, 1778–1782
John Dickinson, 1782–1783

° John Cook, 1783
Nicholas Van Dyke, 1783–1786
Thomas Collins, 1786–1789
° Jehu Davis, 1789
Joshua Clayton, 1789–1793

Governors of Delaware

Joshua Clayton (*Fed.*), 1793–1796
Gunning Bedford, Sr. (*Fed.*), 1796–1797
° Daniel Rogers (*Fed.*), 1797–1799
Richard Bassett (*Fed.*), 1799–1801
° James Sykes (*Fed.*), 1801–1802

David Hall (*Rep.*), 1802–1805
Nathaniel Mitchell (*Fed.*), 1805–1808
George Truitt (*Fed.*), 1808–1811
Joseph Haslet (*Rep.*), 1811–1814
Daniel Rodney (*Fed.*), 1814–1817

° Not elected but served because of death, resignation, or incapacity of elected official.

Delegates from Delaware to the Continental Congress

	DATE OF ELECTION
Thomas McKean George Read Caesar Rodney	August 2, 1774
Thomas McKean George Read Caesar Rodney	March 16, 1775
Thomas McKean George Read Caesar Rodney	October 21, 1775
† John Dickinson † John Evans George Read	November 7, 1776

James Sykes
Nicholas Van Dyke
    (*Replaced Dickinson
    and Evans who
    declined to serve*)
	February 22, 1777

Thomas McKean † Caesar Rodney Nicholas Van Dyke	December 17, 1777
John Dickinson Thomas McKean Nicholas Van Dyke	January 18, 1779
† John Dickinson † George Read Nicholas Van Dyke	December 22, 1779

Thomas McKean
    (*Replaced Read,
    who declined
    to serve*)
	December 24, 1779

Thomas McKean Thomas Rodney Nicholas Van Dyke	February 10, 1781
Philemon Dickinson Thomas McKean † Caesar Rodney Samuel Wharton	February 2, 1782

† Men who never attended Congress under appointment noted; election was usually for one year.

DATE OF ELECTION

Gunning Bedford, Jr.	February 1, 1783
Eleazer McComb	
† Caesar Rodney	
James Tilton	
† Henry Latimer	April 8, 1784
† John McKinly	
† Thomas Rodney	
† John Vining	
Gunning Bedford, Jr.	October 26, 1784
† Samuel Patterson	
† James Tilton	
John Vining	
† Gunning Bedford, Jr.	November 4, 1785
John Patten	
William Peery	
Thomas Rodney	
John Vining	
† Gunning Bedford, Sr.	October 27, 1786
Nathaniel Mitchell	
† Thomas Rodney	
Dyre Kearny	February 3, 1787
(*Replaced Bedford who declined*)	
† Isaac Grantham	November 10, 1787
Dyre Kearny	
Nathaniel Mitchell	

Members of the Senate of the United States

Note: A vacancy existed from George Read's resignation on September 18, 1793, until 1795. When the legislature neglected to fill Read's place, Governor Clayton appointed Kensey Johns, Sr., to it, but the Senate would not seat him.

Richard Bassett (*Fed.*), 1789–1793
George Read (*Fed.*), 1789–1793
John Vining (*Fed.*), 1793–1798
Henry Latimer (*Fed.*), 1795–1801
Joshua Clayton (*Fed.*), 1798–1799
William Hill Wells (*Fed.*), 1799–1804

Samuel White (*Fed.*), 1801–1809
James A. Bayard (*Fed.*), 1805–1813
Outerbridge Horsey (*Fed.*), 1810–1821
William Hill Wells (*Fed.*), 1813–1817

Members of the House of Representatives
of the United States

Note: From 1813 to 1823 Delaware was entitled to two members of the House of Representatives.

John Vining (*Fed.*), 1789–1793
John Patten (*Rep.*), 1793–1794
Henry Latimer (*Fed.*), 1794–1795
John Patten (*Rep.*), 1795–1797
James A. Bayard (*Fed.*), 1797–1803
Caesar A. Rodney (*Rep.*), 1803–1805

James M. Broom (*Fed.*), 1805–1807
Nicholas Van Dyke (*Fed.*), 1807–1811
Henry M. Ridgely (*Fed.*), 1811–1815
Thomas Cooper (*Fed.*), 1813–1817
Thomas Clayton (*Fed.*), 1815–1817

Bibliography

THE following bibliography does not list every work cited in this study or used in its preparation, but only those items that are of particular pertinence to Delaware history between 1775 and 1815.

BIBLIOGRAPHIES. Scholars will find no adequate bibliography in print to guide their research in the history of Delaware, but this lack will be remedied upon the completion and publication of just such a work by H. Clay Reed. Meanwhile, the most nearly satisfactory bibliography in print is to be found at the end of the second volume of Professor Reed's *Delaware: a History of the First State* (New York, 1947). A continuing bibliography of new publications is found in each issue of *Delaware History* (1946–), a magazine published semi-annually by the Historical Society of Delaware, Wilmington.

There are four chief public depositories of materials pertaining to the history of Delaware within this state. They are the State Archives at Dover, the Historical Society of Delaware at Wilmington, the Wilmington Institute Free Library, and the Memorial Library of the University of Delaware at Newark. Experienced staff members at these depositories can be and enjoy being of great assistance to the student and can guide him in the use of special finding aids developed in each institution for its own collections.

MANUSCRIPTS. Of the manuscripts used in the preparation of this volume, I have drawn particularly heavily upon two groups of Rodney papers at the Historical Society of Delaware, the Brown Collection and the Rodney Collection. At that Society I have also used the African School Association Papers, Almshouse Papers, Banking Papers, Gunning Bedford, Jr., Papers, Bringhurst Papers, Broom, Hendrickson, and Summerl Company Letter Book, Bush Family Papers, Church Papers, Corbit, Higgins, Spruance Papers, Memoir of John Dagworthy, Delaware General File, Delaware Slavery, Militia, and Lottery Papers, Delaware Schools Papers, Delaware State Bank Papers, John Dickinson Papers, Oliver Evans Papers, Ferris Papers, John Fisher Papers, John Fisher Photostats (originals in New-York Historical Society), Garrett Family Collection, Edward Gilpin Papers, Haslet Papers, Latrobe Papers (copies of originals in Library of Congress), Legal Documents, Lewden Papers, Allen McLane Photostats (originals in New-York Historical Society), Medical Society of Delaware Minutes, Thomas Mendinhall Papers, Morse

Abbreviations frequently used in text:

DAB—*Dictionary of American Biography,* ed., by Allen Johnson, *et al.* (21 volumes and index, New York, 1928–1944).
DSA—Delaware State Archives, Dover.
HSD—Historical Society of Delaware, Wilmington.

Autograph Collection, Jane Robeson Letters, John Vaughan Papers, and John Vaughan's Wilmington Medical Register for 1803.

At the Delaware State Archives, Dover, I found especially useful the manuscript petitions among the Legislative Papers. I also used the Continental Loan Office Accounts with Delaware, Council of Safety Minutes, Executive Papers, House of Assembly Proceedings, Papers relating to the Settlement of Delaware Revolutionary Claims with the United States, and Stockton Papers.

At the Memorial Library of the University of Delaware, Samuel H. Black's Commonplace Book, Newark Academy Board Minutes, and Petitions relating to Newark Academy were consulted.

Other manuscripts were examined as follows: at the Historical Society of Pennsylvania, Philadelphia, the Abolition Society of Delaware Minutes, Delaware Miscellaneous Papers, Miscellaneous Papers for the Three Lower Counties, Dreer Collection, Gratz Collection, Thomas McKean Papers, Jonathan Potts Papers; at the Library of Congress, the Papers of the Continental Congress, Miscellaneous Colonial and Revolutionary Documents of the State of Delaware, Read Family Papers, Rodney Papers, Van Dyke Papers; at the Presbyterian Historical Society, Philadelphia, Lewes Presbytery Records, New Castle Presbytery Records; at the New York Public Library, Rodney Corespondence; at the Library of the Veterinary School of the University of Pennsylvania, Philadelphia, Manuscripts of the Philadelphia Society for Promoting Agriculture; at the Maryland Historical Society, Baltimore, papers in the Vertical File; in the collection of Mrs. William S. Hilles, Ommelanden, James A. Bayard Papers; in the collection of Mr. Charles Gilpin Dorman, Wilmington, Thomas Rodney's Propositions for New and Useful Inventions and Improvements, Philosophical Tracts and Journals.

PRINTED OFFICIAL RECORDS. The journals, minutes, votes and proceedings of the two houses of the Delaware General Assembly have been consulted. Of them, one group has been reprinted together as the *Minutes of the Council of the Delaware State from 1776 to 1792* (Dover, 1886). It is to be noted that this is not complete and that since the time of printing at least one of the missing journals has been found. A nearly complete collection is in the Delaware State Archives.

Other official journals consulted are the "Minutes of the Delaware Council of Safety," ed. by Leon de Valinger, Jr., *Delaware History*, I (1946), 55–78; *Proceedings of the Convention of the Delaware State held at New-Castle on Tuesday the twenty-seventh of August, 1776* (Wilmington, 1927); and *The Journals of the Continental Congress, 1774–1789*, ed. by Worthington C. Ford, *et al.* (34 vols., Washington, 1904–1937). Executive proceedings appear in the *Governor's Register, State of Delaware* (Wilmington, 1926); military records and correspondence in the first three volumes of the *Delaware Archives* (Wilmington, 1911–1919).

The state constitutions appear in *Federal and State Constitutions, Colonial Charters, and Other Organic Laws*, ed. by Francis N. Thorpe, vol. I (Washington, 1909), and also in the collected *Laws of the State of Delaware*. Of this latter work, the first five volumes are pertinent to my study. Volumes

I and II were printed in New Castle in 1797, volumes III and IV in Wilmington in 1816, and volume V in Dover between 1813 and 1819.

OTHER PRINTED CONTEMPORARY MATERIAL. At the time that most of my notes were taken for this volume the Ridgely Family Papers at the Delaware State Archives were just being sorted and calendared. Consequently they are employed in this study mainly to bulwark points already made from other notes. Had they been used from the beginning, citations from them would have been much more numerous, for they are very rich in the social history of Delaware. Two volumes have thus far appeared of *A Calendar of Ridgely Family Letters, 1742–1899, in the Delaware State Archives,* edited by Leon de Valinger, Jr., and Virginia E. Shaw (Dover, 1948 and 1951), and another volume of complete letters under the title *The Ridgelys of Delaware & Their Circle, What Them Befell in Colonial & Federal Times: Letters, 1751–1890,* by Mabel L. Ridgely (Portland, Me., 1949).

The following additional collections of Delaware correspondence were consulted: Henry C. Conrad, ed., *Letters of James Asheton Bayard, 1802–1815 (Papers of the HSD,* XXXI, Wilmington, 1901); Leon de Valinger, Jr., ed., "Rodney Letters," *Delaware History,* I (1946), 99–110, and III (1948), 105–115; Elizabeth Donnan, ed., "Papers of James A. Bayard, 1796–1815," *Annual Report of the American Historical Association for the Year 1913,* II (Washington, 1915); B. G. du Pont, ed., *Life of Eleuthère Irénée du Pont from Contemporary Correspondence* (11 vols., Newark, 1923–1926); George V. Massey, II, ed., "Eleazer McComb Letters," *Delaware History,* II (1947), 41–55; Lynn Perry, ed., *Some Letters of and concerning Major William Peery* (Strasburg, Va., 1935); William Stevens Perry, ed., *Historical Collections relating to the American Colonial Church, V, Delaware* ([Hartford], 1878); William T. Read, *Life and Correspondence of George Read, a Signer of the Declaration of Independence* (Philadelphia, 1870); George H. Ryden, ed., *Letters to and from Caesar Rodney, 1756–1784* (Philadelphia, 1933). Valuable Delaware letters are to be found in Edmund C. Burnett, ed., *Letters of Members of the Continental Congress* (8 vols., Washington, 1921–1936), and in Hezekiah Niles, ed., *Principles and Acts of the Revolution in America* (New York, 1876). Letters and similar material are published in connection with two articles by Harold Hancock in *Delaware History:* "Thomas Robinson: Delaware's Most Prominent Loyalist," and "The New Castle County Loyalists," IV (1950–51), 1–36 and 315–353.

Journals, diaries, and reminiscences consulted include the *Personal Recollections of Captain Enoch Anderson (Papers of the HSD,* XVI, Wilmington, 1896); *The Journal of Francis Asbury* (3 vols., New York, 1852); Henry Boehm, *Reminiscences, Historical and Biographical, of Sixty-four Years in the Ministry* (New York, 1865); Elizabeth Booth, *Reminiscences of New Castle, Delaware* (New Castle, 1884); *The Experience and Travels of Mr. Freeborn Garrettson, Minister of the Methodist-Episcopal Church in North-America* (Philadelphia, 1791); John Hamilton, "Some Reminiscences of Wilm't'n and My Youthful Days—&c., &c.," *Delaware History,* I (1946), 85–98; Hilda Justice,, ed., *Life and Ancestry of Warner Mifflin, Friend-Philanthropist-Patriot* (Philadelphia, 1905); *Journal of the Life of Nathaniel*

Luff, M. D. of the State of Delaware (New York, 1848); *The Narrative of Patrick Lyon* . . . (Philadelphia, 1799); Allen McLane, *Eulogium to the Memory of James Tilton, M.D.* . . . (Wilmington, c. 1823); Samuel Miller, *Medical Works of Edward Miller* . . . *with a Biographical Sketch* (New York, 1814), and *Memoirs of the Rev. John Rodgers, D.D.* (New York, 1813); Elizabeth Montgomery, *Reminiscences of Wilmington, in Familiar Village Tales, Ancient and New* (Philadelphia, 1851); Archibald Hamilton Rowan, *Autobiography* (Dublin, 1840); C. H. B. Turner, ed., *Rodney's Diary and Other Delaware Records* (Philadelphia, 1911), and *Some Records of Sussex County, Delaware* (Philadelphia, 1909); *The Remains of the Rev. Charles Henry Wharton, D.D., with a Memoir of His Life by George Washington Doane, D.D.* (2 vols., Philadelphia, 1834).

Among the best-known travel accounts consulted are those of Andrew Burnaby (New York, 1904), the Marquis de Chastellux (London, 1787), Nicholas Cresswell (New York, 1924), Philip Vickers Fithian (Williamsburg, 1943), Robert Honyman (San Marino, Calif., 1939), Robert Hunter, Jr., (San Marino, 1943), Francisco de Miranda (New York, 1928), the Duke de la Rochefoucault Liancourt (3 vols., London, 1800), J. D. Schoepf (2 vols., Philadelphia, 1911), Louis Philippe, Comte de Ségur (London, 1825), Ambrose Serle (San Marino, 1940), Thomas Twining (New York, 1894), and William Winterbotham (4 vols., New York, 1796). Shorter accounts are the "Journal of a French Traveller in the Colonies, 1765," *American Historical Review*, XXVI (1920–21), 726–747, and XXVII (1921–22), 70–90; "James Hemphill's Account of a Visit to Maryland in 1802," ed. by J. A. Munroe, *Delaware History*, III (1948), 61–78; *Journal of Benjamin Mifflin*, ed. by Victor Hugo Paltsits (New York, 1935).

Tracts and other contemporary material found useful include the following: *Address from a Late Federalist of Kent County, To his Fellow-Citizens* (no place or date); *An Address to the Freeholders and Electors of the County of New Castle upon Delaware, By a Lover of his Country* (1767); R. O. Bausman and J. A. Munroe, eds., "James Tilton's Notes on the Agriculture of Delaware in 1788," *Agricultural History*, XX (1946), 176–187; Robert Coram, *Political Inquiries, to Which is Added a Plan for the General Establishment of Schools throughout the United States* (Wilmington, 1791); William Currie, *An Historical Account of Climates and Diseases throughout the United States of America* (Philadelphia, 1792), and items on Delaware in other works by Currie; *A Directory and Register for the Year 1814* . . . *of the Borough of Wilmington and Brandywine* (Wilmington, c. 1814); Morgan Edwards, "History of the Baptists in Delaware," *Pennsylvania Magazine of History and Biography*, IX (1885), 45–61, 197–213; Oliver Evans, *The Young Mill-Wright & Miller's Guide* (Philadelphia, 1795); *Features of Federalism: or a Brief History of the Principles and Views of the Federalists from the Revolution to the Present Time, by Publicola* (Wilmington, 1803); Freeborn Garrettson, *A Dialogue between Do-Justice and Professing-Christian* . . . (Wilmington, c. 1805); Joshua Gilpin, *A Memoir on the Rise, Progress, and Present State of the Chesapeake and Delaware Canal* (Wilmington, 1821); Jesse Lee, *A Short History of the Methodists* . . . (Baltimore, 1810); E. Miriam Lewis, ed., "The Minutes of the Wilmington Academy, 1777–1802," *Delaware History*, III (1949), 181–226; Thomas

C. Miller, ed., "St. Peter's Church, Wilmington, Del., Notes Taken from Its Registers, Oct. 20th, 1885," *American Catholic Historical Researches,* XIII (1896), 65–66; *Minutes of the Methodist Conferences 1773 to 1794 under the Superintendence of John Wesley, Bishops Asbury and Coke* (1794); "A Morning's Walk in the State of Delaware," *Analectic Magazine,* X (1817), 374–381; John A. Munroe, "William Plumer's Biographical Sketches of James A. Bayard, Caesar A. Rodney, and Samuel White," *Delaware History,* IV (1951), 354–377; *Observations on Infidelity* . . . (Wilmington, 1809); J. H. Powell, "Speech of John Dickinson Opposing the Declaration of Independence," *Pennsylvania Magazine of History and Biography,* LXV (1941), 458–481; H. Clay Reed, ed., *Readings in Delaware History, Economic Development* (mimeographed [Newark], 1939); Charles L. Reese, Jr., ed., "A Brief Sketch of the Military Operations on the Delaware during the War of 1812," *Delaware History,* III (1948), 79–96; [Caesar A. Rodney], *The Oracle of Liberty, and Mode of Establishing a Free Government* (Philadelphia, 1791); John Spurrier, *The Practical Farmer* . . . (Wilmington, 1793); [James Tilton], *The Biographical History of Dionysius, Tyrant of Delaware, addressed to the People of the United States of America, by Timoleon* (Philadelphia, 1788); James Tilton, *Economical Observations on Military Hospitals* . . . (Wilmington, 1813); Barkley Townsend, *A Declaration of the Holy War: Shewing the Fiery Trial, the Commencement of the Millenium, and the Destruction of the Wicked* (c. 1801); John Vaughan, *A Concise History of the Autumnal Fever Which Prevailed in the Borough of Wilmington in the Year 1802* (Wilmington, 1803); "Wilmington, Delaware, and Its Vicinity," *Niles' Weekly Register,* IX (1815), 92–97. Much contemporary material relating to Delaware is to be found in the *Memoirs of the Philadelphia Society for Promoting Agriculture* (6 vols., Philadelphia, 1808–1939).

LOCAL HISTORIES AND BIOGRAPHIES. The two best-known state histories are J. Thomas Scharf, *et al.,* *History of Delaware, 1609–1888* (2 vols., Philadelphia, 1888), and Henry C. Conrad, *History of the State of Delaware from the Earliest Settlements to the Year 1907* (3 vols., Wilmington, 1908). The Scharf cooperative work is a marvelous thing, full of letters, reminiscences, and other primary material that make it a trove of Delawareana. Unfortunately it is also highly inaccurate. Conrad's work follows Scharf closely but is more attractively arranged. H. Clay Reed, ed., *Delaware: a History of the First State* (2 vols. and a third biographical volume not bearing Reed's name, New York, 1947), is the most recent state history, incorporating the latest scholarly research, but uneven, like most cooperative works. From it I have drawn partly upon the contributions of the Rev. John W. Christie on the Presbyterians, the Rev. Eugene J. Kraemer on the Catholics, Augustus H. Able, III, on literature, Elizabeth Howell Goggin on public welfare, and W. Edwin Bird on medicine. Other state histories of varying value are Wilson L. Bevan and E. Melvin Williams, *History of Delaware, Past and Present* (4 vols., New York, 1929); *Biographical and Genealogical History of Delaware* (2 vols., Lancaster, 1899); Benjamin Ferris, *A History of the Original Settlements on the Delaware* . . . *and a History of Wilmington* . . . (Wilmington, 1846); *Historical and Biographical Encyclopoedia of Delaware* (Wilmington, 1882); Walter A. Powell, *A History of Delaware*

(Boston, c. 1928). Mention should be made of the excellent volume by the Federal Writers' Project, *Delaware: a Guide to the First State,* of which a new and revised edition is to appear in 1954.

In addition to the biographies already noted in other connections, a student should know of Greville and Dorothy Bathe, *Oliver Evans: a Chronicle of Early American Engineering* (Philadelphia, 1935); Roberdeau Buchanan, *Life of the Hon. Thomas McKean* (Lancaster, 1890); William B. Hamilton, *Thomas Rodney* (Durham, 1953), also printed in his *Anglo-American Law on the Frontier: Thomas Rodney and his Territorial Cases* (Durham, 1953); Dorothy Hawkins, "James Adams, the First Printer of Delaware," *Papers of the Bibliographical Society of America,* XXVIII (1934), pt. 1; John A. Munroe, "Senator Nicholas Van Dyke, of New Castle," *Delaware History,* IV (1951), 207–226; James H. Peeling, The Public Life of Thomas McKean, 1734–1817 (Ph.D. thesis, University of Chicago, 1929); John H. Powell, John Dickinson, Penman of the American Revolution (Ph.D. thesis, State University of Iowa, 1938); Charles J. Stillé, *Life and Times of John Dickinson, 1732–1808,* (Philadelphia, 1891). Many biographical sketches are in the *Papers of the Historical Society of Delaware* (Wilmington, 1879–1940).

Other useful studies include Morton Borden, "The Election of 1800: Charge and Countercharge," *Delaware History,* V (1952), 42–62; Harvey C. Bounds, *A Postal History of Delaware* (Newark, 1938); *A Brief History of the University of Delaware* (Newark, 1940); Robert G. Caldwell, *The Penitentiary Movement in Delaware, 1776 to 1829* (Wilmington, c. 1947); Henry S. Canby, *The Brandywine* (New York, c. 1941), and *Family History* (Cambridge, 1945); Kenneth Carroll, "Joseph Nichols and the Nicholites of Caroline County, Maryland," *Maryland Historical Magazine,* XLV (1950), 47–61, and "More about the Nicholites," XLVI (1951), 278–289; Edward W. Cooch, *The Battle of Cooch's Bridge* (Newark, 1940); Richard B. Cook, *The Early and Later Delaware Baptists* (Philadelphia, c. 1880); Ernest C. Hallman, *The Garden of Methodism* (c. 1948); Harold B. Hancock, *The Delaware Loyalists* (Wilmington, 1940); Dorothy L. Hawkins, A Checklist of Delaware Imprints up to and including 1800 (M.A. thesis, Columbia University, 1928); Anna T. Lincoln, *Wilmington, Delaware: Three Centuries under Four Flags* (Rutland, Vt., 1937); James W. Livingood, *The Philadelphia-Baltimore Trade Rivalry, 1780–1860* (Harrisburg, 1947); Dudley Lunt, *The Bounds of Delaware* (Wilmington, c. 1947); John A. Munroe, "Nonresident Representation in the Continental Congress," *William and Mary Quarterly,* 3rd ser., IX (1952), 166–190; Munroe, "The Philadelawareans: A Study in the Relations between Philadelphia and Delaware in the Late Eighteenth Century," *Pennsylvania Magazine of History and Biography,* LXIX (1945), 128–149; Munroe, The Relations between the Continental Congress and the Delaware Legislature, 1776–1789 (M.A. thesis, University of Delaware, 1941); Lyman P. Powell, *The History of Education in Delaware* (Washington, 1893); H. Clay Reed, "The Delaware Constitution of 1776," *Delaware Notes,* VI (1930), 7–42; Nelson W. Rightmyer, *The Anglican Church in Delaware* (Philadelphia, c. 1947); Rightmyer, "Swedish-English Relations in Northern Delaware," *Church History,* XV (June, 1946); Richard S. Rodney, *Colonial Finances in Delaware* (Wilmington, 1928); Rodney, "The End of the Penns' Claims to Delaware, 1789–1814," *Pennsyl-*

vania Magazine of History and Biography, LXI (1937), 182–203; George H. Ryden, *Delaware—the First State in the Union* (Wilmington, 1938); Charles Shorter, Slavery in Delaware (M.A. thesis, Howard University, 1934); Helen Black Stewart, The Negro in Delaware to 1829 (M.A. thesis, University of Delaware, 1940); James M. Tunnell, Jr., "The Salt Business in Early Sussex County," *Delaware History,* IV (1950), 48–59; J. L. Vallandigham and Samuel A. Gayley, *History of the Presbytery of New Castle . . . 1717–1888* (Philadelphia, c. 1888); Christopher L. Ward, *The Delaware Continentals, 1776–1783* (Wilmington, 1941); Elizabeth Waterston, *Churches in Delaware during the Revolution, with a Brief Account of their Settlement and Growth* (Wilmington, 1925); C. A. Weslager, *Delaware's Forgotten River: The Story of the Christina* (Wilmington, 1947).

NEWSPAPERS AND MAGAZINES. Delaware newspapers were consulted as follows, all being published at Wilmington except the first: Dover *Federal Ark,* 1802; *American Watchman, and Delaware Republican,* 1809–1810; *Delaware and Eastern Shore Advertiser,* 1794–1795, 1797–1798; *Delaware Gazette,* 1786, 1789–1790, 1795–1796, 1799, 1809–1810, 1814–1815; *Delaware Statesman,* 1811–1813; *Mirror of the Times & General Advertiser,* 1799–1804; *Museum of Delaware,* 1807–1809. Out-of-state papers used were the Easton *Maryland Herald and Eastern Shore Intelligencer,* 1791–1803, and occasional Philadelphia papers.

The most useful magazine is, of course, *Delaware History* (Wilmington, 1946–   ), the semi-annual publication of the Historical Society of Delaware. *The Delaware Register and Farmers' Magazine* (Dover, 1838–1839) is also helpful, and I also checked files of the *American Museum* (Philadelphia), 1787–1790; *Columbian Magazine* (Philadelphia), 1786–1788; and *Niles' Weekly Register* (Baltimore), 1811–1815. Of modern out-of-state journals, the *Pennsylvania Magazine of History and Biography* is especially rich in Delaware references.

Index

Adams, James, 66, 171, 182, 185
Adams, John, 185
Adams, Samuel, 185
Address from a Late Federalist, 231
Agriculture: 11; in the 1770s, 25-27; post-Revolutionary, 114-119; and Negroes, 219n; and Federalism, 241 ff.
Aitkin, John, 125n
Alderson, John, 42
Alexander, Archibald, 146, 178, 202, 205, 206, 243n, 248, 254n
Alien and Sedition Laws, 208, 209
Alison, Rev. Francis, 59, 63, 64, 65
Allen, Richard, 168
Alrichs, Jacob, 217n, 227n
Alrichs, Jonas, 129
Anderson, Enoch, 33
Anderson, Joseph, 173
Andrews, Samuel, 184
Anglicans: 41; in the 1770s, 43-46; and Methodists, 56; and Federalism, 239; *see also* Episcopalians
Annapolis Convention, 104-105
Annesley, James, 148
Appoquinimink Creek, 136, 139
Apprenticeship, 62
Armed forces, 88-89
Articles of Confederation, 95-97
Asbury, Francis, 20, 32, 50, 51, 53-54, 55, 56-58, 61, 67, 167
Assateague Sound, 118
Assawoman Bay, 118-119

Bail, Capt. Robert, 135
Baker, Elijah, 50
Bancroft (Dr.), 116
Banks: 28, 134, 145-146; incorporations of, 248-250
Banning, John, 90n, 170
Banning, Sally (Mrs. H. M. Ridgely), 211
Baptists, 49-51, 169
Barnett, Sampson, 129
Barratt, Andrew, 240, 248
Barratt, Philip, 240
Barratt's Chapel, 57, 167

Bassett, Richard, 41, 54, 90n, 96, 105, 106-107, 109, 142, 146, 152, 158, 159, 161, 168, 185, 195, 198, 199, 206, 207, 210, 240, 244, 265, 268
Bauduy, Peter, 149, 150, 214n, 225, 244n
Bayard, James A., 41, 159, 170, 173, 198, 199, 206, 207n, 208, 212, 214n, 217n, 233, 234, 245, 246, 248, 250, 253, 256, 257, 258, 259, 268
Bayard, Thomas F., 263
Bear, 255
Beard, Duncan, 129
Bedford, Gunning, Jr., 100, 102n, 103n, 105, 106-107, 159, 185, 206n, 207, 216, 267
Bedford, Gunning, Sr., 102, 103n, 152, 182, 198, 205, 206, 207n, 265, 267
Bell, John, 26, 140n
Bell, Thomas, 218n
Bellach, James, 119
Bellach, John, 217n
Bennett, Caleb, 156
Bergerac, M., 174
Berry, Tom, 206
Bird, John, 213, 243n, 252
Black, William, 185
Blackbird, 224n
Black Harry, 168
Blue Hen's Chickens, 39
Bohemia River, 61
Bond and Lees, 132
Bonsal, Vincent, 184
Boon, Lydia (Mrs. Luff), 154
Booth, Mrs. Ann Clay, 188
Booth, James, 146, 202, 254n
Boundaries, 16
Boyce, Jonathan, 144n
Brandywine millers, 146n, 216n, 224n, 244, 246n, 248
Brandywine River: 92, 118, 136, 221 ff.; and mill sites, 28, 119-125, 126, 127, 130
Brandywine village, 22, 173
Brian, James, 217n, 246
Bridges, 217, 251-254

277